THE

DAILY JOURNAL,

FOR

18

PUBLISHED ANNUALLY, BY

FRANCIS & LOUTREL,

MANUFACTURING STATIONERS,

45 MAIDEN LANE,

NEW YORK.

MANUFACTURERS OF
Account Books, Manifold Writers,
Croton Inks, &c. &c.

AUGUSTA'S JOURNAL

VOL. I

*Experiences of a Young Pioneer Woman
Pre Civil War in the Kansas Territory*

A BIOGRAPHY

BY

MARJORIE LUND CRUMP
&
RALPH EUGENE CRUMP

authorHOUSE®

AuthorHouse™
1663 Liberty Drive, Suite 200
Bloomington, IN 47403
www.authorhouse.com
Phone: 1-800-839-8640

© 2008 . All rights reserved.

No part of this book may be reproduced, stored in a retrieval system, or transmitted by any means without the written permission of the author.

First published by AuthorHouse   9/15/2008

ISBN: 978-1-4343-8069-2 (sc)
ISBN: 978-1-4343-8175-0 (hc)

Library of Congress Control Number: 2008902972

Printed in the United States of America
Bloomington, Indiana

This book is printed on acid-free paper.

Contents

About This Book .... *vii*

An Historical Synopsis .... *xiii*

Acknowledgements .... *xvii*

1. *Leaving Michigan, July 1856* 1

2. *Crossing Iowa to The Missouri River, July 1856* 17

3. *From Tabor To The Kansas Territory, July to August 1856* 57

4. *Plymouth, K.T., August 1856* 81

5. *The Battle of Hickory Point, August 24th to September 15th 1856* 103
   Father Becomes a P.O.W.

6. *Colonel Cooke, Late September to October 10, 1856* 129

7. *Captain Henry's Strange Proposal, October 1856* 147

8. *A Pleasant and Social Interlude, Autumn 1856* 171
   Father is paroled by President Pierce

9. *The Prison Camp Visit, January to March 1857* 205
   We Get a Job with Mrs. Gates

10. *The Founding of Eldorado, March to July 1857* 233

11. *An Outbreak of Small Pox, Summer 1856* 247

12. *Preparing to Leave Lawrence, October 1857* 265

13. *Eldorado, November 1857 to February 1858* 279

INDEX 309

About This Book

A handwritten journal of three bound volumes was dutifully handed down through four generations in my family. The journal was begun by my maternal great-grandmother, Augusta Stewart, about 150 years ago, before the Civil War, before she was seventeen years old, but not before she knew she wanted to be a writer. Though none of it was lost, it remained dormant, unexamined by those before me. I have it now.

The journal begins in 1856 at the height of the national debate and zeal between the abolitionists and those favoring slavery.

Augusta's father, Sam Stewart, who owned a successful sawmill in Michigan, became so committed to the abolitionists' cause that he sold his business, bought a prairie schooner and took his two daughters to the new Kansas-Nebraska territory. Augusta began her journal. She continued for the next fifty years, making 2,000 entries, which contained upwards of 180,000 words chronicling her family's involvement in two great and defining American events, first:

The territorial struggle created by the Kansas-Nebraska Act of 1854, which followed the failure of the Missouri Compromise to determine Kansas' territorial status i.e., slave or free. Congress, in their indecision, invented a cynical plan called Popular Sovereignty to let the people in the territory vote whether they wanted to enter the Union, free state or slave, knowing that those already there were predominately proslavery. However this set in motion a northern response followed by a large migration of abolitionists aimed to out-vote those proslavery settlers already there and offset the votes from new Southerners coming in. The struggle between these two opposing ideologies erupted into sporadic armed conflict, increasing when the population on both sides was about equal. By 1858 enough abolitionists had flooded in to create a plurality, which snatched the Kansas Territory from the clutches of proslavery. Those abolitionists' votes produced a bit of historical irony or maybe justice, but it was certainly the unintended political consequence of the Doctrine of Popular Sovereignty.

The "bleeding" in Kansas continued on and off for seven years, becoming a prologue to our Civil War.

Upon arrival, Sam Stewart and his two daughters were quickly swept up into those events. Sam and about 100 more abolitionist militia became P.O.W.s charged with murder, but were released and pardoned by early 1857.

In the spring of 1857 a small party of abolitionists, some of them ex-P.O.W.s headed by Sam Stewart, went west to create a new predominantly free-state voting district and in the process founded Eldorado out on the west bank of the Walnut River, some 160 miles south-west from Lawrence. Sam was elected to represent the new District 17 and he was involved with the committee writing the new Constitution, banning slavery.

The second significant historical event was the westward movement of the American frontier. By 1861 Sam Stewart had been killed. Augusta, now widowed, traveled to the Gold Fields near modern day Denver, remarried in 1864 and with her new husband moved on to Virginia City, the new Montana Territory gold strike. They eventually prospered with several ventures including two small mines that remained in our family for nearly one hundred years.

These first three volumes of her journal close 1860 with Augusta, a young widow, and her sister selling their sawmill, their Sorghum mill and three claims in Eldorado. They moved back to Lawrence and bought a house on Rhode Island Street (later #672)…and two cows. Kansas was still a territory, but would

About This Book

become a free state by January 1861. The Civil War was in its very early stages.

In addition to inheriting the three original journals which is the essence of these three books, we found three books in the attic earmarked by her to references that confirmed (to her and therefore to us) many of the pre Civil War events in the Kansas Territory from 1856 to 1869. They were volumes 7, 8 and "II" all titled "Transaction of the Historical Society of the State of Kansas" that contained articles written mainly by pioneers of the Territorial period (often dominated by their abolitionist attitude and written well after the Civil War.) Augusta obviously had these transactions bound well after they were settled in Montana. The index and text of volume 8 contains references to both Augusta's (first) husband and her father, of whom she was obviously proud.

After we discovered these books and realized that so many of Augusta's pioneer experiences had also been recorded by so many of her contemporaries, we contacted the Kansas State Historical Society at Topeka and were invited down by the then Director Ramon Powers who gave us access to the Archives and "stacks." Mr. Powers could not have been more accommodating. Through him we were able to get photocopies of volumes 1 through 11 of the Transactions. Later with frequent success, we linked-up events and personalities described mostly in the earlier Transactions that confirmed or described differently Augusta and Adda's experiences during the proslavery-abolitionist struggles during the Territorial, pre Civil War period.

We found the Transaction references surprisingly scanty in dealing with the founding and early settlement of Eldorado and four or five other town sites in those western-most counties, Hunter and Butler, which was a plan Sam developed while he was a P.O.W. None of them had the details, personalities (some transient), the weather, the nationalities including Indians, etc., that appear in Augusta's Journal, which we have been faithful to use. Probably the most significant historical contributions from these journals are to the founding of Eldorado, K.T. by her father, Sam Stewart, in the summer of 1857 and its early settlers. We've been careful to index them all together with other early events in the territory (1856-1862), which Augusta details in her journal.

It seems strange now, that this journal was "unexamined" by my mother and my grandmother, who lived with us. No doubt they heard all these stories first-hand. Knowing that the journal contained some very personal, tragic episodes, my grandmother probably considered it to be her mother's private diary, which it was. I can't explain why my own mother carefully preserved the journals, yet, to my knowledge, also never read them. Well, we have and in consummate detail.

Although the journals gathered dust for all those years, I heard enough "family talk" about the pioneering adventures and tragedies of Grandma's people to fuel a consuming curiosity and after her journals were passed on to me by my brother, James L. Lund, this book is the outgrowth of that curiosity satisfied.

As Augusta approached nineteen years of age, aspects of romance as practiced in the mid nineteenth century, started to appear in her journal. Prior to her engagement to Jacob E. Chase in March of 1858, until their marriage eleven months later, she makes entry after entry questioning his intent, mulling over other proposals, always comparing her distance from the altar to her female friend's, measuring his ardor (or lack of it) against her expectations, yet all the while falling more deeply in love with him and telling us about it.

About This Book

As Ralph and I got into the journals, the first thing that struck us was the planning and deliberation in her purpose. Augusta's penmanship borders on calligraphy. She used ink exclusively (occasionally homemade) and exceedingly fine-nibbed pens, though after 150 years the ink was fading and we didn't know how long it, or the paper, would last. So to preserve her work I first began by carefully typing the journal. Augusta had obviously sought out and used bound, professional-level hard cover journals, the type that green eye-shaded bookkeepers used for their handwritten accounting ledgers. The journals were manufactured by the New York stationer Frances and Loutrel (see the frontispiece for the company's trademark on the front page of the journal.) The page size was eight by thirteen inches. The pre-acid paper and binding were of such quality to have survived for nearly 150 years! Augusta dated all of her entries, and few weeks went by without some note.

When Ralph and I decided to expand her entries into a book, we ran into several problems: Augusta's writings, which were in bare outline form, needed to be put into the existing rich historical context. Luckily from the moment Augusta, Adda and Sam left Michigan, they joined others in a series of events that have, by now, become well-recorded history.

We have used the abundance of those records to enhance and explain some of Augusta's entries, which occasionally she made later from notes taken and hidden from the Army and other proslavery authorities, who after their entry into the territory in Plymouth frequently searched their wagons and cabins and confiscated what they pleased. (On at least one occasion…October 10, 1856…the searchers were rewarded by finding a barrel of gunpowder hidden under the floor boards of the house the girls and others occupied. Luckily the Army missed three other barrels of powder, a small cannon, and some ammunition for their new Sharps rifles. This was detailed by Augusta from hidden notes; the episode is in chapter 7 of volume I.

From 1854 to 1858 abolitionists coming into the territory were officially labeled insurrectionists and invaders. Some entries read as though she intended to expand them later into articles. In fact, years later, she did do this, when she was asked to write some newspaper articles about the abolitionist period. In December of 1882 and again in May of 1901, she wrote long, detailed articles expanded from her journal entries about the territorial days of Eldorado. Each filled a full page of the Walnut Valley Times, the town's paper.

We decided that her entries, standing alone, would not make a suitable book. Daily entries about the weather, which were of more significance then than now, were excessive. Also other than dating each entry she seldom wrote a transition from one event to the next.

Since the facts about these events were obvious to her, she seldom explained them. Why, for instance, were so many of the west bound immigrants Irish? Curious, Ralph and I did some research and discovered that to escape the Famine and English oppression in their country, they flocked to North America and provided President Polk with thousands of soldiers for his War with Mexico and supplied much of the labor for the western gold strikes. Many Irish passed through Eldorado. A few stayed. Whether they were visitors or settlers several of these immigrants became colorful characters in her journal.

Our research occasionally provided additional information to expand some of her entries into a broader history of her time and place, we've added nothing of substance. We have her story. It was her observant entries that provided us with the book's skeleton, muscle, and historical continuity.

In the end, all we've added are a few cosmetic touches.

An Historical Synopsis

There have been three or four historical events or moments in North America that defined or redefined whom we were at that time. Certainly the Civil War between the English Subjects in North America and the English King, George III, that earned on the battle fields our independence in 1776 and a new and glorious sense of freedom, equality and liberty; self-determination was such an historical event, that to this very day probably distinguishing us from many others on earth, every man an individual with his own set of rights. Winning the war provided new, perhaps unlimited dimensions of personal independence without economic restrictions, social restrictions or geographic restrictions. Then only seventy-five years later, with the idea of independence and disunion as its means to achieve it still fresh in Southern minds, their Southern Declaration of Independence and its resistance from the North resulted in our Civil War.

To France reeling from chaos and terror of a failed revolution came a young (Corsican, not French) genius in the waning days of the 18th Century who, like despots before him, would and for a short interval did see a solution to France's problems by making war on its neighbors. He would "Save The Revolution," he told the Frenchmen. "Just send me your sons." No problem was too difficult for this genius. But war takes money. Sooner or later despots resort to selling off or mortgaging their assets to finance their military campaigns. Napoleon was no exception. All that North American land should fetch enough cash to finance one more war. Thomas Jefferson loved France and loved freedom and independence for the individuals. He wanted the French Revolution to succeed. He was also amenable to a deal.

Napoleon had his eye on the Hapsburgs and was aiming for Vienna, unaware that Russia would come to Austria's aid. That same year England declared war on France. Napoleon was desperate for money. In France, James Monroe offered $7.5 million for New Orleans alone. Talleyrand, one of the few aristocrats who survived the Revolution, offered on Napoleon's behest all the land stretching from the two great rivers to the Pacific for twice the price of our offer for New Orleans! That purchase, even with its doubtful borders, doubled our landmass.

With our $15 million Napoleon raised an army of 100,000 and prepared to invade England. He failed to reckon with Admiral Nelson and the British Fleet.

That tall column standing in downtown London with the one-eyed, one armed Nelson standing on top…amid the disrespectful pigeons, does not stand there for nothing, nor has that square in which he stands ever…ever…had a name change!

After the Louisiana Purchase of 1803, it took nine years to define a territory and cut Louisiana, the first state out of it. With President Monroe's acquisition of the "Floridas," Mississippi was granted statehood in 1817, followed by Alabama and ultimately Florida: three more Slave States. Missouri followed in another nine years and Arkansas in 1836. And after a costly squabble with Mexico, that many Northerners believed was instigated by President Polk to obtain one more Slave State, Texas was admitted in 1844. Four Slave States in a chronological row connecting Georgia, an original colony to these new Slave States fulfilled the South's ambition to have an uninterrupted plantation with slaves coast to coast. With or without slavery, this purchase with all of its unsurveyed land and unimaginable natural resources constituted an historical event equaled only by the American Revolution. In

An Historical Synopsis

gratitude or folly the least we could have done was to have named the Rocky Mountains after Napoleon!

The Great Economic Depression of the 1930s and our response to it carried such profound social and economic changes, as the Federal Government tried to solve the problem, is for us a major historical event.

And finally the role of the U. S. in World War II redefined us industrially and militarily and gave us a new international status.

Occasionally in history two major events intersect.

Shortly after "Kansas" received territorial status in 1854, political conditions there became a preview, a local prototype for conditions that soon prevailed throughout all the States. To pick one or two precipitating events out of a hundred strong differences of opinion is foolhardy, but certainly the formation of the Republican Party, that stood for equality for all, Emancipation of the Southern Slave and its nomination of Abraham Lincoln as its 1859 candidate * founded by abolitionists and elected President in 1860, was clearly one of those defining historical events. Southern Congressmen and Senators had asked repeatedly for assurance that Southern property rights would be respected. "Property" included the slave...all three million or more. In this matter the North was adamantly opposed. Even the Supreme Court came down on the South's side with the Dred Scott Decision. The election of Lincoln caused North Carolina in protest to declare its intention to leave the Union.

Lincoln, caring more about an indivisible Union than the slave as property, declared that secession could not be tolerated. By February five more States had left the Union then Texas, the sixth, and was agitating for California to come in as "Slave". A

---

*   He opposed slavery "in the West" and called Popular Sovereignty a fraud.

big fraction of the people rushing to California in 1848 and 1849 were from the South. More California newspapers favored slavery than opposed it.

The Secessionists saw in their movement the same virtues as the original colonies saw in their claim for independence: equality, rights to govern themselves as they saw fit, which included their independence. Jefferson Davis looked at Lincoln and saw George III.

While all this arguing about the South's right to extend slavery into the territories, the population in the Kansas Territory shifted from Pro Slavery in 1854-1856 with the Lecompton Constitution calling for slavery, to an abolitionist population with its new constitution calling for Freedom For All.. By the time Lincoln was in the White House six or seven years of hard work (in Kansas) had been done. Popular Sovereignty had been used to deny the extension of slavery. All those Abolitionists migrating to the Kansas Territory turned the original purpose of Popular Sovereignty on its head.

Did that cause the Civil War? Of course not, but the great social movement, the concept of Liberty for All that propelled 100,000 Abolitionists, including Sam Stewart and his two lovely daughters, helped elect Abe Lincoln. His physical presence in the White House in 1861 started the Secessionist ball rolling, and in the end knocked away from the Union eleven slave-holding King Pin States.

Acknowledgements

Donnali Fifield of San Francisco who has edited for Forbes Publications and recently translated "March of the Penguins" and other books from French to English, painstakingly edited all fifty-two chapters (and more) . . .(a task of one and a half years)

My brother, James L. Lund, Esq., inherited the three original volumes from our mother, Hazel. Sometime in the 1980s he passed them on to me.

Dr. Ramon Powers, Executive Director of the Kansas State Historical Society in Topeka in the early 1990s invited us to use their library and gave us access to twelve volumes of the transactions of the Kansas State Historical Society, where several references of the territorial period verified some of Augusta's journal entries, though it appears to us that Augusta has provided some of the best accounts of the first few years of Eldorado and its founding by her father and a few like-minded abolitionists in the summer of 1857.

Dr. James Simon, professor, Dept. of English, Fairfield, University edited volume 1 for punctuation, typos, etc.

1.

LEAVING MICHIGAN,
July 1856

When our relatives heard we were going to the new territory of Kansas, several of them encouraged me to keep a Journal. Actually it didn't take much encouragement. I had read journals of other travelers in newspaper accounts of their lives on the way to California or Oregon. It was exciting to realize that we would be among the first organized migrants to the territory slowly being created out of the Louisiana Purchase, the vast tract of land sold to Thomas Jefferson about fifty years ago by Napoleon to finance his wars. Of course, every schoolgirl knew of the famous Journals of Lewis and Clark, who had been authorized by President Jefferson to explore this new landmass, and I was no exception.

An earlier source of encouragement to keep a record came the year that Father asked me to write to all our relatives about my mother's death. Several of them complimented me on the quality of my letters, the style in which I informed them of her declining health, her final passing on and how Father, Adda and I were getting along without her. I kept for years the purple envelope and note from Aunt Julia, in which she said "what a nice letter" I had written. Though I was flattered by her compliment, I wondered how an obituary of a loved one could be "nice"? I became the official Stewart family correspondent and was delighted with this self-appointed position. It was then, sparked by their compliments, that I decided to be a writer. I was eight or nine years old.

I also wrote long letters to my relatives when I was away at school. A few of the schools Adda and I attended were public schools but where the community lacked them or if Father thought they were inadequate, we were enrolled in "private schools." Most of the schools obliged me to live away from home. Father has always been attentive to our schools and our teachers; his expectations of our education were quite high, I must say.

Being away from home was lonely, but I used my spare time to read. I was encouraged by one of my teachers to write letters and I did. I suppose all that writing served as a good grounding for keeping a journal.

My early life was far from what I would call orderly. Indeed I was exposed to an unusual amount of death in our family and, as a consequence, there was a great deal of moving to and fro, particularly after my mother's death when I was eight years old. Moving seems to run in the family and maybe in the "American family." My grandfather moved from Colrain, a small farming valley in the foothills of the rocky, green mountains of Northern Massachusetts for better opportunity in New York State and prospered as a builder and operator of steam and water-powered sawmills and gristmills. Later, after a long and bitter legal dispute over water rights in Onondaga County, he moved to Michigan to be with a colony of like-minded brethren. Many of his children from his second marriage (there were twelve children in that family) followed him including Grandma Gates. Sometime before his twentieth birthday, Father and one of his brothers, who became a trader with the Chippewa Indians, moved from New York State to Michigan.

Father now seems to think that fortunes are to be made faster in the new western territories and speaks about all that land out there to be surveyed, all the sawmills required to provide timbers for house building and gristmills for the grain.

In 1838, when he was nineteen years old, Father married my mother, Jane S. Taylor, the "Belle of Flint, Michigan." Mother was eighteen years old, born in 1820. One of her suitors was a Mr. Begole,[1] later governor of Michigan.

I was their first child. I was born August 8, 1839, in Genesee, Genesee County ten miles from Flint, Michigan. Although I was christened Laura Augusta, it was my mother who began calling me Augusta, perhaps because I was born in August.

In December of the following year my sister Adelaide Henrietta was born, also in Genesee. Another sister, Cornelia, was born in 1844, four years after Adda, but she lived for only two years.

Adda was a robust baby. Mother seemed to have sacrificed some of her health, beauty and vibrant spirit to Adda. And I might add, it never left Adda, who was the strongest and most resilient of us all, save perhaps my Grandfather Charles, who signed up with the Massachusetts militia before there was a U. S. Army, or a United States for that matter. In those days each Colony had its own militia. He fought as a private in the Revolutionary War, was called a "Minute Man," (like his own father, John) re-enlisted and fought Indians who had been armed and trained by the English to fight the rebelling Colonists and to kill their rivals in North America. The French had also trained Indians to fight

---

[1]Ref. Biographical Directory of The Governors of the United States 1789-1978 Vol. II, Meckler Books, Westport, CT 1978 edited by Robert Sobell and John Raimo, pg.(s)752-753 states that Josiah W. Begole came to Michigan in 1836. He married Harriet A. Miles in 1839. They had five children. In 1872 he served as a US Congressmen. He served as Governor of Michigan 1883-1884 on the Greenback/ Democratic Party Fusion tickets. He was a prominent businessman in lumber banking and manufacturer: co-owner of Begole and Fox Lumber Mill.

for their side. After the Revolution killing by Indians continued, since the Colonists were white and the Indians didn't care whether they were English or French. Grandfather sired twelve children, had a long prosperous business as a builder and died of natural causes when he was seventy-four years old. Adda, I'm convinced, inherited his health and indomitable spirit.

Adda's birth in 1840 seemed to rob my mother of her vitality because shortly after her birth, Mother took sick. To lighten her load, Father took me to live with an aunt, the wife of his brother in Truxton, New York. Adda remained with Mother in Genesee, Michigan.

Truxton, in Cortland County, had earlier had been cut out of Onondaga County. We had many relatives in this area on both sides of the family. Several of the surviving twelve children of my grandfather, Charles Stewart, lived near Truxton. He had built many of the mills and other structures in the area, particularly in Onondaga County.

A year or so after I was brought to Truxton, Mother joined us, leaving Adda with one of her sisters in Genesee. We lived for a while in Truxton, where my first recollection is of starting school there. Mother was having a small house built in Albion, New York, where she could be near one of her sisters, Aunt "Swiss," and when the house was ready, we moved there. While we were living in Albion, Aunt Swiss took sick. I shall never forget her lingering illness and death. Mother was also in ill health and unable to attend to her sister. I remember Aunt Swiss' horrible anguish and suffering to this day and always shall. Following this family tragedy Mother wished to return to Michigan. I was six or seven years old. We were reunited with Adda and Cornelia, who had been staying with another of Mother's sisters in Genesee.

Mother had a small house built in Genesee. Within a year after the four of us moved in little Cornelia took sick. First she had the ague, and then caught whooping cough. Between the two diseases, she died. I was about seven years old. A year after Cornelia died, during one of Father's visits in Genesee, he found Mother extremely sad over losing her.

As I recall, Mother was again in poor health. Father suggested taking me with him to Gibraltar on Lake Erie, where he had a general store and a sawmill. He suggested that Mother take a year or so to recuperate, then we would all get together again. Alas, this was not to be. We never met again. I remember that she didn't want me to go, and that she cried as I left, but for me, at that age, the prospect of a nice long ride and new adventures were a pleasurable distraction from the sorrows of parting.

Father and I took a carriage to Detroit. About five miles north of Flint, we visited with my Uncle Ransom Stewart for a few days. Then we took another carriage on to Flint to visit another of Father's brothers, Addison. From Flint to Pontiac we took a bouncing stage (coach) for about thirty miles and that was exciting. Our traveling companions were quite interesting. I took my first train ride from Pontiac down to Detroit, which took less than an hour. In Detroit we boarded a passenger "steamer" for Gibraltar, which is about twenty miles south of Detroit on Lake Erie. Looking east across a narrow bay fed by the Detroit River, we could see Canada.

Mother corresponded regularly with us that year. We all looked forward to our reunion, but she failed to tell us of her declining health. On July 30th 1848, Mother died in Mount Morris (just outside Flint) and was buried in the Upton Cemetery near Genesee. She was only thirty-eight years old. She was born on March 6, 1820. The year she died I was eight years old. I turned nine in August of that year.

It took years for me to get over my mother's death. It was months before I accepted the fact that we would never be together again.

At first I simply did not accept or believe she was dead, during which time I grieved, sometimes sobbing for hours. Occasionally I wondered if I had contributed to her demise by not being with her to help with the house, to run little errands that might have taxed her. With her passing I became nostalgic for the days we had together, even though some were sad days. I never discussed these matters with anybody. I began secretly itemizing in my mind ways I missed my mother: her companionship, when we went to Sunday school together, or when she "did" my hair; her cooking; her loving household; I would recall vividly her features, her movements, the color of her hair and the various styles she used with it, some of which I mimicked for years; still do. For years a little random event during the day would, in a flash, call to mind my mother and our times together.

After Mother died, Father returned to Genesee for Adda. That fall Father enrolled us both in a small private boarding school for girls within walking distance of Gibraltar. The school was owned and operated by a Miss R.E.W. He was much impressed with this very well educated and ambitious teacher; during the six years we attended her school he visited us often.

When I was nine or ten years old I saw that I was different from the other girls in Miss Widener's school. Occasionally I would look up and down the rows of desks in my classroom and wonder if any other girl was motherless. Since I knew them all (this was a boarding school), I realized I was the only one in the class without a mother. In later years I came to understand that was simply a part of grieving.

Father continued to run his store in Gibraltar, which he had owned for a number of years, but I believe his true love was operating the sawmill that he'd built there. The Gibraltar area was growing and Father prospered from that growth. He would often entertain us with stories of his boyhood spent around his father's sawmill or those his father built for other sawmill operators in Onondaga County. Grandfather was an expert on wood, sources of timber and wood products. He taught all that to Father. "Augusta," he would often tell me, "if there's one thing I know, it's how to build and run a sawmill."

Except for the month of July spent with Father in Gibraltar, we were to remain at Miss Widener's school for the next six years. During that time the school grew, as the community grew, and Miss Widener "took on" other teachers. It was a fine school but the work was relentless and hard. Miss Widener was a good but very demanding teacher, who set very high expectations. When her student met those expectations, she was generous with praise. She was applying a method of teaching that was popular then. She claimed it was ancient and called it *laudando praecipere*. Sometimes, when praise yielded even better results, *laudando perdocere*.

As the school grew, my class was assigned a new teacher, Miss Chapin. She was a good teacher, strict and demanding, but easier to get along with than Miss Widener. We all loved her. We had arithmetic every day and homework in that subject. We had reading assignments and little rewards for extra reading. We often had to do written reports and we were graded on our penmanship. Occasionally a visitor would come to our school and instruct the older students on penmanship. Miss Widener was a Latin scholar, so we had lessons in that language, which gave me an appreciation for Roman Life and Culture, as well as Latin's contribution to English. By the time we left for the new territories I could read Cicero, Marcus Aurelius, and some Caesar but so could others in my class. Later I realized that thanks to Father's attention to the matter, Adda and I were much better educated than most of the women we were to encounter.

Adda and I spent eleven months of the year at Miss Widener's school. She usually dismissed her students about the first of July. Some of her students were allowed to return as late as September 1st, but not Adda and me. Father would take us, with our trunks and books, back up to school the first or second of August, where we boarded until the following June 30th. Some Sundays during the school year, after Sunday School, which was also taught by Miss Chapin, Adda and I would walk down along the lake road to visit Father at the mill.

I recall with great pleasure those six summers when Adda and I could spend all of July with him at the mill, which was on a small, clear water cove or inlet on the north bay of Lake Erie.

One July, when I was fourteen or fifteen, Father had accepted his usual delivery of a float of logs, which would always arrive a few days after the Fourth of July. They had been lashed together and pulled down from logging camps north of Port Huron, sometimes from as far north as Saginaw Bay. Not all of the logs in the float belonged to Father, so he asked Adda and me to help locate his logs in the float. His could be identified by a small brass disk nailed into one end or the other of each log. Ten to twelve large logs, thirty feet long would be lashed together to form a single float. There were maybe ten of these floats all connected together in a procession three to four hundred feet long.

Using rubber-soled shoes and old clothes, our job was to scamper about the floats to locate logs containing Father's little brass disks with a big "S.S." stamped on one side. Whenever we found one of Father's logs, someone from the tugboat would unlash it from the float. Father said he'd made partial payment for one hundred logs, but storms and rough weather on Lake Huron and Lake St. Clair occasionally broke up the log floats. Father was only obliged to pay for logs delivered to him. Remaining logs were towed down to a mill in Monroe at the mouth of the Raisin River or down to Marblehead.

It's good that we looked. We only found eighty logs with Father's disk. Some of Father's helpers busied themselves re-lashing our logs together, tying them with long ropes to large stumps along the shore. Later, they would use mules to pull the logs up out of the water into the mill yard, where using large yardarms and pulleys, they would stack them in great piles.

During those warm July days the three of us would take delightful late-afternoon swims, diving off of the log floats into the clear water of Lake Erie Bay. In the summer of '48 Father had taught us how to swim, using the ever-present float of logs in front of our mill. We swam pretty regularly through those memorable July visits.

We were pleased that Father could visit us at the school so often. He would spend hours discussing our progress with our teacher, Miss Widener (Rebecca E. Widener). In time it became clear to me that Father's interest in the school went considerably beyond just our education. He was as taken with the charms of our teacher as we were with her stern but effective teaching abilities. On the 3rd of March of that year, 1854, before I turned fifteen years old, Father married Miss Widener and, without saying anything to Adda and me, brought her home to live. When she was fairly settled in Gibraltar, Father asked that we call her "Mother" and told me to behave toward her as I would as if she were my own mother. I can understand his motives, but I don't think he realized the gravity of his request or the difficulty of it for us. I was with Mother through some of her sickness, during Aunt Swiss' death and when my little sister died. Cornelia's death seemed to increase Mother's depression and more of the household chores fell to me.

Our dependence on each other developed into a strong, and affectionate bond between my mother and me. I'm not sure that Father understood the depth of my love for her. My heart rebelled at what I thought was his casual suggestion. I couldn't bring myself to call another by that name, the name I'd called my own dear, sweet and loving mother nor did I really care for the new housekeeping arrangement. Prior to his marriage I made out the shopping lists and planned the meals. After he married, my stepmother took over many of these household assignments. Things went along smoothly for only few weeks before they began to be disagreeable with her. One day I was mopping the kitchen floor just as she was bent over to look at something in the oven. I accidentally slopped some water near her dress. She rose and shook her dress as close as possible near my face and taunted and scolded me until I was pretty angry. She led me rather roughly by the arm towards her room, threatening to punish me unless I promised never to do that again. Of course, I promised. I hadn't intended to get water on her dress. It was a simple accident. After all, she ought to have been able to see me mopping the floor. I was not an invisible mopper.

In the fall, after my fifteenth birthday, Father and his new wife moved to Detroit. She released her other scholars and discontinued her school. After inspecting Mrs. Chase's Boarding School in Trenton, two miles or so north of Gibraltar, and interviewing the headmistress she recommended that Father enroll us there. In time our stepmother became dissatisfied with that school and Adda and I moved to Detroit. After careful interviews and inspections by our stepmother, we were both enrolled in the Capital School, a private school in Detroit. When the headmaster needed to assign Adda and me to our proper grade, he realized that we were ahead of students our age by at least two years, maybe three in Latin and English, thanks entirely to the quality of schooling in "Miss

Widener's Boarding School." When our stepmother saw the textbooks we were assigned and the quality of the homework, she had a long conference with Father, which culminated in a visit by her to the school principal. The next day without any fanfare Adda and I were both advanced two grades from our original grade assignment. Nevertheless I found the new schoolwork much less demanding than at Gibraltar.

In November of that year another sister was born, named Clara Ella. Her mother continued to act in the same way toward Adda and me, but seemed to think (as most mothers do) that of all children, hers was the best. Of the difficulties that were of daily recurrence, it is unnecessary to speak, except to say that obviously Father loved Adda and me and wanted the best for us. He also loved his new wife and new daughter, but the relationship among our stepmother, Adda and me was still strained. It lacked the warmth and good humor that we had with Father or the warmth and affection that we had with our mother. I don't think Father ever understood this or, if he did, I suppose he thought that, in time, everything would work out.

One day when I had stayed home to help with the wash and the new baby, something occurred that made my stepmother angry. She seemed rather quick to take offense, especially if the offender was me. She said that she sincerely wished that "one day I would marry a widower with two or three of the ugliest children who ever lived."

I replied, "I would take care not to marry a widower."

"You will marry the one that is allotted to you," she said.

Well, I bit my tongue. I knew I should not respond because by doing so, she would say I was "talking back" and I would hear about it when Father got home. I thought her prophecy for my marriage prospects seemed like something out of the Old Testament. Obviously she was referring to Father as the "widower."

For some reason I never thought of Father as a widower and I didn't believe that Adda and I were ugly children. To label my sister ugly would be to admit to some strange eyeball disease: distorted vision. Adda was an active girl, a headstrong girl; she was anything but ugly. Indeed, she was quite attractive, another inheritance from our mother, who in the opinion shared by many was a beauty.

The next spring (1855), when I was fifteen years, she took Clara Ella and left our house to return to Rochester, New York for good. The day she left, she simply turned on her way out the door and merely said, as though she just was off to run an errand, "Good afternoon, girls." Those were her last words.

In September, when the Capital School resumed, I was sixteen and went into the 12th grade, Adda the 11th. In October Father went down to Gibraltar and sold his store and sawmill. He had learned surveying working with Grandfather, which he decided to work at before going to the new territory. I think Father wanted to renew his "hand" at it before we left to be prepared for what he expected in the new territory. He said that all that land out there would have to be surveyed. In Detroit he found all the surveying work he could handle.

Father had been following the political events that led up to the creation of the Kansas-Nebraska Territory, about which there was great discussion where we lived. Michigan was a haven for several religious settlements, all sympathetic to abolition to one degree or another. Antislavery speakers from Chicago and New England were steady visitors. Adda and I occasionally went with Father to these meetings, if they were after school. Local newspapers were full of articles dealing with the issue, many deploring the fact that Texas, which had just been annexed after the Mexican War, had almost overnight become a Slave State. I recall people speculating that the Mexican War was simply a plan of President Polk and the Southern Democrats to acquire one more Slave State. Since the time of the Louisiana Purchase eight or nine new Slave States, all Southern of course, had been admitted to the Union, including three from the new Florida territory (Florida, Mississippi, Louisiana), and Arkansas; all of these states were cut from the new land President Jefferson had purchased from Napoleon in 1803.

In the fall of 1855 we began making preparations for moving. Adda and I remained enrolled in the Capital School until the last day of June the following year, when I graduated from the 12th grade.

Afterward, for a month and a half we packed and made plans.

Earlier that spring and summer Father continued to attend abolitionist gatherings. The most important was an assembly on June 2nd when several members of the Central Committee also called by some abolitionists the Free State Advocates came up to Detroit by train from Chicago. The party of dignitaries included one of the first governors of the Kansas-Nebraska Territory, John Reeder, who had been appointed by President Pierce. Though he was expected to carry out his proslavery policies, he had become a Free State advocate, and General Jim Lane, a major organizer of abolitionist groups interested in immigrating to the New Territory. General Lane had been a Democratic congressman from Indiana and was a powerful public speaker. He was to exert a major influence on our family in the new land. Another leader of the June 2nd assembly was Colonel Shalor Eldridge, who, it was claimed, had built an elegant hotel in Lawrence and who, with his family, and relatives, had lived in Lawrence almost since its inception and had been a member of the New England Immigrant Aid Society. The delegation also included a committee member from each northern state. The main speakers were on

Leaving Detroit, Sam misses the train
July 1856

a "swing" through the northern states to talk-up the Kansas Territory. Father said that it had potential for anyone who was adventuresome and ambitious, but mostly he felt we should move there because he thought slavery was wrong and he wanted to help make the territory a Free State. While the North was "wringing its hands" about the perils of slavery, the South had relentlessly acquired eight more states, which would require more slaves.

That spring Father purchased a large, well-built wagon, called a Studebaker. Later in Iowa City, we had it outfitted with a large white canvas cover stretched over metal hoops. These wagons became known as Prairie Schooners. Fellow travelers indulged in a bit of pride by calling their large white covers sails.

We had two horses. One was a prized French Canadian named "Puss." We planned to put horses and the wagon, fully loaded with our household effects, on the train on the day of our departure. We were "ticketed" all the way through to Iowa City, the nearest point to Tabor, Iowa, where we were supposed to join other abolitionists. Our first stop would be Chicago.

We arrived at the Detroit train depot, accompanied by some friends who came to see us off. Father had gone there earlier to make arrangements for our horses, wagon and household effects. Just minutes before our departure, as Father joined us in the Parlor Cars, I suddenly realized that I had left my new shawl draped over a bench inside the depot. With fatherly irritation I'm sure, he left the car to retrieve it. The conductor told him we had thirteen minutes before the train left. The shawl was a distance of only 200 to 300 yards away. No sooner had Father left than the train began to move. By the time Father got back to the platform, his daughters, his wagon, his horses and household effects were disappearing down the track. Father didn't have thirteen minutes; the conductor was wrong. Father had only three minutes and he'd used some of that time to chat with a friend who was a ticket seller.

But beginner's luck was in our favor. We were on the morning train, which was not the Express. When we arrived at Ypsilanti, the conductor handed me a telegraph that said that Father would catch the evening Chicago express and meet us en route about midnight at Ann Arbor, which he did. We all arrived in Chicago a day later, a little before supper. It took less than two days to cover the first leg of our trip: Detroit to Chicago, 200 miles. It would take about twenty-five days to cover the balance of our trip, by wagon 400 miles from Chicago to the Kansas Territory.

2.

CROSSING IOWA TO THE MISSOURI RIVER,

July 1856

We arrived by train in Chicago about 4 p.m. Tuesday, July 15th. Father transferred our freight and horses to the Chicago-Rock Island Rail Road, which went down to Rock Island, Illinois, on the Mississippi River, where we planned to take the ferry to Iowa.

It was hot in Chicago. We asked for directions to the Dearborn House, where we intended to stay, and learned it was within walking distance of the depot. We were assigned one large room on the second floor and we opened the windows to cool things off while we went downstairs for supper. The lobby of the hotel was rather spacious, you might say elegant.

The dining room of the Dearborn Hotel is just "off" the lobby. As we joined a small group waiting to be seated, an aroma that included tobacco smoke seemed to be coming from a crowded, bustling public room to my left. To satisfy my curiosity, I walked over for a closer examination. Peanut shells covered the polished wooden floor from customers dropping their shells wherever they cracked them open. Each table had a generous bowl kept full by a squad of young Negro boys. Beer also seemed to be very popular. Attractive young ladies, each carrying four or five steins in each hand, served their customers. And the constant spitting, another peculiarity in this town, also contributed to the smell. I had noticed it in the depot and the walk to the hotel. Some of the men in the public room spit into brass spittoons, others simply spit on the floor. Outside they spit on the sidewalk. The main cause for all this spitting was the excessive use of tobacco: both chewing tobacco and large cigars, which get both smoked and chewed.

The supper, with just the three of us, began nicely until we were introduced to another Chicago custom. The headwaiter escorted three other customers to our table and without asking permission said, "These people will join you." They were not related. They were all quite well-dressed; maybe over-dressed, and they were all very "forward." No sooner had they been seated, one of them addressed Father as "Governor," asking what "line" he was in. Father answered that we were on our way west without going into particulars. With an interesting German accent this gentleman volunteered that he was a wholesale meat dealer specializing in Chicago ham, bacon, sausage, etc. By ordering beer he let us know that the glasses used here were siedels not steins. Well, this seemed to spark in the other two enthusiastic descriptions about their businesses. When the waiter came to take our order, the meat dealer interrupted with suggestions what we should eat at this hotel, insisting that Father order spare ribs and sauerkraut and he did and in all fairness, Father said after dinner how good it was. Father thanked the gentleman, whereupon he offered Father a cigar. The wrapper, which I saved, carried an advertisement for his meat firm. By the time the meal was over they were all calling Father "Sam," and were entirely too presumptuous for me, but maybe that's life in the "Big City."

They had finished before our desserts arrived; fast eaters all three, and their eating speed was entirely due to their unusual table manners. Most of the food got to their mouth on their knives. The trick was to put a generous blob of mashed potatoes on the knife, and then with dexterous use of their fork they embedded pieces of meat or vegetables in the potatoes. I declare, half the knife blade went into their mouths. This use of silverware was not unique to them; other men in the dining room were doing the same.

One of our supper companions was in real estate. He also spoke with a foreign accent and gave us a big "run down" on Chicago, which he pronounced "chick kaga". I thought he was much more interesting than the other two, though I was afraid that the three of them would monopolize our evening, which of course they did.

He claimed that Chicago had about 60,000 people and 150 hotels: one in six of Chicago's citizens, he said, lived permanently in hotels, one in four lived in boardinghouses, and it was also customary for an employee to board with his employer. His knowledge of Chicago was as boundless as the meat merchant's, who advised us on where and what to eat, while we were here.

In the lobby, waiting for our room to cool down, Father, Adda and I got into a discussion about land. I asked Father how much we would be able to buy in Kansas. He said because there were discrepancies between federal and territorial land-purchase laws, he wasn't sure, but that he intended to file a claim on at least one quarter of a section or 160 acres, A section contained 640 acres: thirty-six sections make a township.

Father went on to say that it wasn't his main intent to buy land for farming but as future town sites. This would be different from a homestead claim. He said it was his ambition to organize a town site, raise the money for a few buildings and sell the city lots off to newcomers, four residential lots to the acre, and double that for commercial lots.

Adda asked, "When we pay for our land, how will we know we own it? Whom do we buy it from?"

Father said land out there would cost $1.25 per acre, or $200 per quarter section, purchased from a government land office.

I asked in a low voice if we had that much money. He smiled, "Yes, but don't worry about that. We will only have to pay $50, or 25 percent of the full price, with the balance to be paid over several years." Adda asked if the two of us could file claims. He smiled and said, "We'll sure try."

"We'll try to buy land on a large stream or small river. People think of the new territories as being all prairies. In fact, there are plenty of streams and rivers and along their banks are large tracts of timber." Father told us that just as soon as we made it to Kansas, he would quickly get a sawmill going, followed by a sugar or sorghum mill and a gristmill, all on our land.

We left Chicago by train early on Thursday morning, July 17th, but arrived at Rock Island, so late that night we couldn't see the Mississippi River, which was a disappointment. Our plan was to take the ferry to Davenport, Iowa, the next day.

When we got off the train, several boys and young men at the depot crowded around offering us transportation to various hotels. There was no charge for the ride if we chose the hotel the "runner" was working for. Father asked if one of them represented the Chicago Hotel. One answered yes and said he would provide the ride but we might have to share it with other passengers from the train. One or two traveling salesmen joined us in the carriage. On the way the driver offered to get up early and, using the hotel's rig, stand in line for us at the ferry landing. Adda and I thought that was clever. We figured half the people on the train were going to use the ferry tomorrow. Father said he would get our horses and wagon off the train that night, which would allow us to "move along" tomorrow. He asked the driver if there was more than one ferry. The driver said, "No."

The next morning, we woke up looking forward to seeing the Mississippi, expecting it to be a very wide river. Well, at Rock Island it is not wide; indeed, it seemed narrower than our own Detroit River, and not as clear. "Ole Miss" was very muddy. The ferry people told us that the river at Rock Island was deep, swift and treacherous, contained within a narrow limestone channel. A large rocky island is midway in the river.

Rock Island's main east-west road led directly down to the single ferry dock that had been there since 1833.

The rates were prominently displayed:

Wagon and two horses	$1.00
Man and Horse	37 1/2¢ or 3 Bits
Horses or Cattle, each	12 1/2¢ or 1 Bit
Extra Travelers older than 12	25¢ or 2 Bits
Freight per 100# Wt. (estimated per displ.)	12 1/2 ¢ etc.

To save money, the sign read, "Owners of horses or cattle could let them swim, but at owners' risk and with the owner's rope."

While we waited, we estimated our fare. The problem was judging the load in our wagon. I guessed about a ton, which would cost $2.50. Father thought it weighed more. We got into a quite a discussion on how the ferry operator would be able to figure the weight of our cargo.

Presently a man came by with a pad of paper. Without saying anything after he walked around our wagon he spoke up and asked Father if we had used the train on any "leg" of our journey. Father answered, "Yes."

"May I see your manifest? We know the railroads weigh your freight accurately. Using their weight makes our job easier and keeps us from overloading our ferry."

The manifest read, "Cargo, all in one six by twelve wagon, 2,250 pounds. Extra freight forwarded to Iowa City."

The man looked up our charge for the ferry ride from a table and wrote something on a slip of paper and handed it to Father. I pasted it in my journal and discovered later he could have charged six cents more, but he didn't.

Wagon, a driver and two horses	=	$1.00
Freight @ 22.50 C. wt. x 12 1/2¢ per C.	=	$2.75
Two Females	=	.50
		$4.25

He told Father to pay the invoice in the house (pointing toward a nearby house) and get a "ticket." We boarded the large steam-powered ferry at 10 a.m. Our first ferry crossing was quite adventuresome and took about fifteen minutes.

We had left a portion of our belongings on the train, knowing that it would be waiting for us in Iowa City, the state capital, which is fifty or so miles west of Davenport. It had been our plan all along to forward some of our freight allowing the horses to get accustomed to pulling a partial load before they had to pull it all.

We left Davenport on Friday about noon. Contrary to all advice we decided to travel alone, rather than joining one of the various outfits, which was customary. We might do that later, but Father seemed to enjoy this independence, which we would surrender if we joined a wagon train.

When we got off the ferry on the Iowa side, climbed up on our wagon and headed west, we were filled with idealism, purpose and hope. Each of us had our own version of what life would be like in the Kansas territory. Father had brought home that summer in Detroit pamphlets and tracts about the new territory. There were glowing stories of opportunity and for months, on and off, we heard Father talk about building cities and about his heroes who had done it. Eighty million acres of land all free, well, almost free, and none of it surveyed. In contrast to the comfort of the railroad cars, relying on horse and wagon from Davenport on was quite a change. Now we felt like real pioneers. From our wagon, we could almost inspect the shrubbery as we passed it. Now and then the shrubbery inspected us as it rubbed against our wagon. On the train the scenery rushed by, became distant and once seen, gone forever.

It was a good, clear day for traveling, promising to be sunny. A cobblestone road led from the ferry landing uphill into Davenport, which had some rather large buildings along the river, no doubt quarried from abundant ledges of it along both sides. On the outskirts of town the cobblestone paving ran out and our iron-rimmed wheels immediately dropped into two ruts and a third, more shallow rut in the middle for horse or oxen. Going downhill the ruts seemed to get deeper. They were deepest at the bottom. Well, we hope it doesn't rain; these ruts might become difficult to manage.

The first night in Iowa we stayed in a little hotel on the west edge of Wolcott or Stockton, I've forgotten which they were both such little places. Adda and I slept in the hotel but Father made room in the wagon for a bedroll. He said he wanted to keep an eye on "our stuff." There were over twenty other wagons in town. Four or five families traveling west were staying at our hotel, most of them going to California or Oregon. The hotel served a fried chicken supper about 6 p.m. and we struck up a conversation with our supper companions, two families traveling together from

Kentucky and Tennessee, though they all seemed to be related. The Tennessee family included two girls both a few years older than Adda and me.

It was still daylight after supper. Adda and I, and the two girls from Tennessee, decided to explore the countryside, at least within walking distance.

The two Southerners had very polite manners. As we walked, we asked them if they had slaves. They said they had a "Mammy" housekeeper with them. They had sold their other slaves to simplify their travels, they told us, but as soon as they bought a claim in the New Territory, their father would go back to Missouri, which was a Slave State, and buy all the slaves he thought they would need. One of the sisters added that they hadn't been big slaveholders, like planters further south. I said it would be too cold to raise cotton in the Territory, but the older girl replied, "We intend to have a very large farm, buy up as much land as we possibly can, and raise grain. The Darkies will do all the work, just as they do in Tennessee." Changing the topic she said, "Mama's brother, Wiley Beddoo Grady, owns a warehouse at Westport Landing, where the riverboats from St. Louis dock. Some boats can go north all the way up to Iowa or west out to Lawrence on the Kansas River. Uncle Beddoo says that Westport is a busy little town and very friendly toward Southerners. Ah suppose y'all be goin' on out to Lawrence. Uncle Beddoo says, it's a hotbed of abolitionists. It was started by a bunch of abolitionists from Boston.

"Uncle Beddoo visited us this summer and persuaded us to come out. He says there are acres and acres of free land. That's the main attraction for us, the land."

She continued to tell us about their hopes for Kansas and their connections there. She seemed anxious to impress us. I became a little envious when she said her Uncle Beddoo was a friend of Mr. Donaldson, the U.S. Marshall, and Judge LeCompte, the Chief

Justice of the Territory. She said both of those fine gentlemen thought all citizens of Kansas should be able to own slaves. And, she said, if they chose not to, that was their God-given right, just as it would be in Tennessee or Georgia or Alabama. "It's the law, honey. It's all decided, been decided for two years now, since '54."

Adda piped up, "What law? We think Popular Sovereignty will determine whether Kansas territory is to be Free Soil or Slave. That means we'll all go to the polls and vote, well all the men, that is!"

"Honey, first, Popular Sovereignty is just a replacement for the Old Missouri Compromise, an' it's our turn for a Slave State an' Kansas will be it. The votin's over. The new state constitution is written, and it's already been approved by the citizens and is in Washington. It's been approved by Congress an' I think the Senate. When President Pierce signs it, if he hasn't already, we'll be a state before Christmas; in fact, Uncle Beddoo says by Thanksgiving. Honey, it's already a Southern State, the settlers who are there are mostly Southerners and can own slaves if they want them. We've been comin' in a constant stream since '54. Why, they've just finished naming all the counties, an' they're all named after Southern men of distinction." Well, that was a surprise.

She said, with a very convincing certainty, "Y'all see, in no time at all, y'all be going to Kansas City to buy slaves to work your farm, just like us."

Adda spoke up, "We aren't farmers. Our father is a surveyor and a land developer. We will operate sawmills and gristmills, as our grandfather did in upstate New York."

"Sawmills? Honey, who's going to cut those trees and pull them down to your mills? You'll see. It will be the Darkies. There's nothin' new about this. All civilizations have used slaves. How do you suppose Greece and Rome grew so powerful?"

Adda, "You said you have a 'mammy' with you. Does she have a family?" The older girl paused. "Well, sure she has a family. We're her family."

"No, no," said Adda. "What I meant was, was she ever married? Does she have a husband? Does she have children?"

"My, my, now ain't you nosey. We don't talk much about those things, and we sure don't discuss them with strangers!"

Adda kept on, "We know how children born to slaves are separated from their families and sold like sheep or ponies at auction. We've all read Harriet Beecher Stowe's book…I have a copy with me of Mary Boykin Chestnut's stories about real slave life, the things you say you don't talk about. We know that in the South you can't be seen reading an editorial against slavery. We know that you can't attend a public assembly if it is to debate slavery. Vigilante groups will break it up. Our papers are full of this."

"Honey," the older girl said, "I notice we're all wearin' cotton this warm afternoon. Now, chances are that cotton was raised in the South an' shipped to your mills in the North. What do you think is goin' happen to the price of cotton when all those slaves are free? You think they'll stay and pick cotton? My guess is lots will come north for factory jobs. You think those workers in New York or Philadelphia or Boston will want to compete with people who don't know what it is to get paid? Well, we got real quiet now, didn't we?"

"I was only quiet," said Adda, "because I was trying to figure out a polite way to point out that we'll outnumber you at the polls. Count the number of westbound antislavery immigrants in this town, we'll beat you two to one, maybe three to one. You'll see."

The older girl said, "If the slaves are all free, do you have any idea what carnage would take place, 'specially to the women? Do you abolitionists want that to happen? So you see, it ain't jes' goin' to go away."

On the walk back we paired off as sisters, Adda and I walking together. In the twilight, we could see the fireflies in the woods and hear the crickets. It was all very peaceful here in "Ioway."

I have often thought of those two sisters with their nice manners but with firm convictions of their God-given right to own slaves.

The next day we were up at dawn and leaving the hotel before our Southern friends came down to breakfast.

Even though we had left a part of our freight on the train, the horses really labored going uphill in Eastern Iowa. We helped relieve the load by getting off at the bottom of most hills, a practice we were to follow all the way west. I declare I must have walked the entire width of Iowa.

Back in Detroit we hadn't anticipated the walking, but we really didn't mind. In contrast to traveling forty miles an hour on the "cars," whether we were riding on the wagon or walking, we were traveling at a snail's pace. I will never, ever, get accustomed to such a slow pace.

I asked Father how fast we were going.

"Five miles an hour."

I think that is optimistic. We know Iowa City is fifty miles from Davenport, so by keeping track of the time it takes us to get there we will be able to reckon our "real" speed.

We are anxious to estimate the time it will take us to cross all of Iowa, which we believe to be 250 miles, more depending on just where we cross the Missouri River.

We arrived in Iowa City about 4 p.m. on Sunday, July 20, and immediately located the depot. Our freight was waiting for us.

Iowa City was the "end of the line" for the Chicago-Rock Island Railroad.

Adda and I had kept track of the traveling time from Davenport to Iowa City, which we know is fifty miles. We traveled a half day Friday, all day Saturday and most of Sunday—we were on the road twenty-four hours or about two miles for each traveling hour and we had good weather.

At the depot it took almost an hour to load our "things," even with the help of the stationmaster who wore a black, military-looking hat. He advised that we should be very alert and discreet while in this city. He said many of the town's residents dislike the Mormons, and many are also known to be hostile to abolitionists. "So," he said "keep your destination and your opinions to yourselves. There are a few gangs in town who prey mostly on abolitionists. They will steal your livestock or anything else that isn't nailed down and will get 'away with it' because Mormons and abolitionists are fair game." Well, that was sobering news!

Iowa City teemed with outfitters of every description. The city had about 3,700 people and most of them seemed to be in "outfitting." Agents were swarming around the depot with their cards, offering goods or services and advice.[2] Of course, we knew their advice to be self-serving and I'm afraid this made us too skeptical for our own good.

Some scoffed that our horses wouldn't be able to pull our large load over the hilly Iowa terrain. Of course, this advice was offered by mule salesmen, as well as a gentleman who sold ox teams. So we were dubious, though this advice was later to be proven correct. We began looking for an outfitter dealing in canvas products (tents, etc.) with enough heavy white canvas to make a large balloon-shaped cover for the "Studebaker," the heavy wagon

---

[2] A pamphlet that we had carried with us from Michigan warned about buying wild, unbroken mules, several "tests" were suggested prior to purchase.

Father had purchased in Detroit. This addition was something we'd planned and looked forward to since leaving home. We asked the outfitter if he wasn't going to take measurements. He said, "There's three general sizes of wagons and we have those patterns. Yours is four by twelve," adding that the "bed" of the wagon was so tightly joined that it would float and support the wheels if we would have to ford deep water. We weren't aware of this feature, and we're quite pleased to hear it. Later we were to discover that our big wagon had sled runners hinged under the wagon bed, allowing the wagon to be converted to a large wintertime sled after removing the wheels and "flapping" the runners into a vertical position.

After cutting and sewing the canvas, which was done by the fitter's wife, the cover was draped over and supported by five large vertical iron hoops, that Father and one of the outfitters had bolted to the inside walls of the wagon. These hoops could have been wood. We chose iron. Our hoops were tall enough to allow us to stand up in the wagon.

The fitting consumed most of Monday afternoon. Over a dozen small brass grommets had been placed on both hems of the canvas cover to hold the sides close and tight to the outside of the wagon. A clothesline rope was strung through these eyelets to connect them to a series of hooks that were screwed into the wagon in a very straight line near the outside bottom of both sides. The wife brought the light rope for the eyelets, and she got up in the wagon and tugged here and there to make sure everything fit.

The front of our canvas cover was split in the middle, and could be closed shut or pulled to one side like curtain drapes. The two halves could also be laced together with more rope to keep out the weather or snoopy visitors. Inside the front cover were several pockets to store small items, such as tools, books, maybe a side arm.

The back cover was similar to the front. The front and rear hoops were taller than the middle hoops and both were fitted to the wagon at an angle off vertical, making the top protrude out in front and back. This cleverly provides the driver with protection from the sun and rain.

Adda struck up a conversation with the outfitter's wife. The woman said she and her husband had come out from Cincinnati but they had stopped in Iowa City to nurse their daughter, who had taken sick on the trail. Her little girl had died and was buried in Iowa City. She said that was the second child they had lost. The illness and death, she said, was just about all they could take. They had considered going back to Ohio, she told us, adding that they were really from Kentucky, but many settlers from Kentucky moved to Cincinnati before going further west. Toward the end of her story Adda and I were leaning against our wagon. The mother was standing close to us. It was a warm, sunny afternoon. The wagon was in the shade of a large maple and occasionally a few rays of sunlight would filter through the maple and fall on the face and hair of this sad and mourning mother. But she took no comfort from the occasional sunlight. "Blessed are they that mourn," but the Biblical promise of comfort, like the warmth of the sun, was of no comfort to her. And I understood. When my beloved mother died, only time was my comforter: not relatives, not poetry, not a Beatitude about my mourning, just time. Thank God he gives us all the time we need to heal our grief. Perhaps that's the promise in the Beatitude, not how we will be comforted, but that we will be: by time.

Adda asked the woman how she had learned this business. She said she had been a tailor's assistant in Cincinnati. The tailor had occasionally made canvas tents on Army contracts. Our tents, she said with some pride, were used in the Mexican War.

During the entire conversation the outfitter's wife never smiled once. I thought she was a very somber woman for one not yet thirty, but perhaps if, before thirty, I had lost two children, maybe that's the way I would be.

It was pleasant to meet travelers, like us, while helping her husband, she said, and the work occupied her mind, but her real reason for doing it, she admitted, was to save enough money to pay a Cincinnati tombstone cutter to cut from a small block of white Vermont marble a statue for her daughter's grave. She described what she wanted: a small kneeling sorrowing angel, similar to one she once had seen in Cincinnati. She said she'd already written to the stonecutter. He replied that he knew the pattern and had already begun. The outfitter's wife said she was sure they would leave Iowa City someday but not before they could place the tombstone on her little girl's grave. Her monotone, there in the shade of that big Iowa maple, and the complete lack of emotion in her voice made her story one of the most compelling and poignant stories I was to hear.

The sadness of her story was sobering. Its reality has never left me. She said they had left Kentucky with such expectations and high hopes: they considered themselves healthy and ambitious enough to work hard, but they never expected to be plagued by an illness, that would take their only remaining child.

I wondered if her story spelled an omen.

This outfitting consumed almost all of Monday but after we finished we looked like other pioneers we saw going west in their Prairie Schooners. If I do say so, we looked very handsome and substantial. And, of course, we had the utility wagon and a team, which also implied a bit of prosperity.

The fitter seemed to be curious about our two rear wheels. I thought, aha, he's about to suggest another item without which we won't make it to the Promised Land.

He took from his back pocket a carpenter's rule, one of those small, hinged wooden contraptions that unfold into a long "yardstick." Some of them extend over five or six feet long. Bending down, he measured the distance between our rear wheels. I was standing within a few feet when he straightened up. I must have had a quizzical look on my face.

"Well, you'll be all right."

"How's that?" He pointed across the street. "See that wagon? It was made by people who don't know their craft and purchased by people no smarter. It might make it to the Missouri River but I doubt it. A few hundred miles of prairie ruts will shake it to pieces because eastern wagon wrights made the axles too short, so the wheel spacing is too narrow to fit the ruts." I glanced at his object of scorn and it looked pretty good to me. He said, "Some ruts between here and the Rocky Mountains are a foot deep but rut-to-rut they all measure four feet eight and a half inches."

He then gave me quite a speech about what happens to a wagon whose wheels haven't been correctly spaced for that width, telling me about the discomfort to the rider and the danger to a loaded wagon that has one wheel in and one wheel out of the rut.

He said the California Gold Rush had created such business for wagons that people who had never built them before got into it. Some of them had never even bothered to check on the correct wheel-to-wheel distance before selling their wagons to unsuspecting buyers, who were anxious to get on the road.

He told me how a few months earlier he had done some minor outfitting for a small team of Government surveyors going west on a survey contract. The lead surveyor was an old timer, a West Pointer and a gent who had been in and out of the Army. The surveyor told me that twenty years ago President Andrew

Jackson had sent him to Europe to study military construction. He was allowed to use the Archives of the Vatican, which houses a library of texts dating to the Caesars. He knew the Romans were great road builders and had evolved a bureaucracy that regulated the design dimensions of everything Roman. The surveyor discovered, said the fitter, that the Old Roman wagon wheel spacing was equivalent to four feet eight and one half inches, which he presumed accommodated the width of two old Roman War-horses, harnessed side by side.

As the fitter was educating me about the proper width between wagon wheels, six Indians sauntered by to my right, all adults. Two Squaws were among them, bringing up the rear. Bareheaded, the squaws had long, black braids, were middle-aged and ugly. Their shoes seemed to be a cross between a moccasin and a soft boot that came up under their ample, heavy, dark skirts. The four men, looked alike to me, except that two of them had a few streaks of decorative paint on their faces. The men's hair was long and held in place with a beaded band. They were shorter and smaller than I expected. These were not James Fenimore Cooper Indians. The men wore leggings but had old commercial shirts and worn jackets. The Indians all looked at us but didn't speak nor did they move towards us or make any gesture of recognition. I raised my arm to wave. Thinking better of it, I brushed the hair from my forehead instead. They couldn't have been more than ten feet from me. It was quite exciting.

After they had passed us, I asked the fitter in a soft voice what sort of Indians they were. He didn't know but said Iowa had a local tribe called Pottawattamie, but these Indians could also be from tribes moved here from the East. These were the first Indians that I'd encountered on the trip and I was anxious to get them into my journal.

The fitter continued talking about the appropriate spacing for wagon wheels. "Your wagon is gonna make it 'cause it fits the ruts," adding with a chuckle, "old timers call 'em rits."

He said our wheels were first-rate. "See, these spokes are oak and if you look closely, the wood rims are hickory, hard hickory. These hubs are made of elm. Your forged steel tires are at least three eighths of an inch thick. So you've got good stuff here and I bet you never noticed."

Well, I was so fascinated by his favorable appraisal of our wagon that it didn't dawn on me 'til later that I knew our wheels fit the ruts and had realized it ever since Davenport. I simply hadn't thought about the significance of the dimensions.

Before we left Iowa City, a gentleman came by our wagon to ascertain if we were going to Kansas. He raised both eyebrows and clucked his tongue derisively when we told him we were traveling alone. Unlike most of the pioneers in Iowa City that July, and I counted over thirty wagons, we were still traveling alone.

He gave us a printed circular, dated July 4th, addressed to the "Friends of Free Kansas." Father never spoke about the exact route we would take across Iowa. We had heard troublesome rumors about hostility of the proslavery "elements" near Kansas Territory, that some towns in Southern Iowa were not friendly to free staters.

In Davenport we had spoken to a family from Chicago that had originally planned to travel by riverboat to the Kansas Territory. They changed their mind and decided to take the overland route instead after hearing that proslavery marauders in Western Missouri,[3] operating with the blessing of the Missouri authorities, had robbed two riverboats, stealing from Northerners, Kansas bound in order to dissuade them from going to the New

---

[3]   In the early summer of '56 two riverboats, Star of the West and the Sultan had Kansas-bound (Free Soil) passengers robbed and badly treated.
One Missouri newspaper bragged that the proslavery gang had captured the Cream of Jim Lane's Army including 78 leading abolitionists. Wm. Connelley, *Kansas and Kansans*, Vol. II, pg. 605.

Territory. Missouri and Illinois and parts of Iowa had for years been unfriendly to Mormon travelers; that was well known. It was understood and excused by all because of the peculiar ways of the Mormons. But now the Northerners were also at risk.

Father had not previously shared with us what he thought was the best route across Iowa. That uncertainty bothered me, but I kept my worries to myself, knowing that Father would figure it all out and let us know. Well, that day in Iowa City turned out to be very providential. The official circular recommended the safest generally southwest route to the Missouri, suggesting specific towns in Iowa to go through. It was a relief to know the matter was settled.

I have kept that letter[4] and now, here are some of the important parts:

To the Friends of Free Kansas:

The undersigned, IOWA STATE CENTRAL COMMITTEE, for the benefit of FREE KANSAS, beg leave to represent that the dangers and difficulties of sending Emigrants to Kansas through Missouri has been attempted to be remedied by opening through Iowa an Overland Route. At present Iowa City, the Capital of Iowa, is the most western point that can be reached by Railroad. Arrangements are being made by Gen. LANE, Gov. REEDER, Gen. Pomeroy, Gov. Roberts, and others to turn the tide of emigration in this channel, and thus avoid the difficulties heretofore experienced in attempting to pass through Missouri.

It is proposed to take the following course through Iowa:

Leaving Iowa City, proceed to Sigourney, thence to Knoxville, Winterset, Osceola, and to Quincy in Fremont County, Iowa, thence to Sidney, on the Missouri River, 80 miles east of Topeka,

---

[4] *The entire letter is available from the Kansas State Historical Society, Early Days of Kansas, by Shalor Eldridge, Vol. II, pg. 71. Marjorie L. Crump*

the Capital of Kansas. An Agent has been through the State by this route, and the citizens in each of the aforesaid towns have appointed active committees.

The inhabitants of this line will do all in their power to assist Emigrants. Iowa City to Sidney on the Missouri River is 300 miles.

    W. PENN CLARK, Chairman
    G.W. HOBART, Secretary
    H.D. DOWNEY, Treasurer

W. PENN CLARK, E.W. HOBART, L. ALLEN, JESSE BOWEN, M.L. MORRIS, G.D. WOODIN, J.N.JEROME
 J. TEESDALE, *Kansas Central Committee of Iowa*
    Iowa City, July 4, 1856."

The gentleman who gave us the letter called it "Lane's Trail." Of course, we were to learn later the importance of Jim Lane. He also said that there was a shortcut or cut-off, he called it, "between Knoxville and Osceola that bypassed Indianola." He said the Northern Route was called Plumb's Route, named after Preston B. Plumb, the founder of Emporia in the new territory.

He told us that we would have two options for crossing the Missouri River. One would be slightly southwest of Sidney, a landing called Eastport; the other was at Civil Bend, three miles or so southwest of Tabor. He told us that we would all congregate at Tabor, where we would be assigned to companies. Our river crossing site would be decided out there.

The gentleman explained to us that this overland route had been scouted by members of Iowa's State Central Committee under the authority of the Governor of Iowa, and that seventy to one hundred wagons had taken it so far without incident.

Then he said something that was more startling than frightening. He told us that the land routes across Missouri were now made perilous,[5] and that migration by river was totally blocked to Northern Immigrants across the State of Missouri to the Kansas Territory. He added that General Persifer Smith, the newly appointed Chief of the U. S. Army of the West, could not be counted on by Northerners for general protection or safe conduct in any part of Kansas Territory. We found that hard to believe.

This man also told us that General Smith was currently concerned that a force of 250 abolitionists under General Jim Lane was somewhere in Iowa preparing to "invade" Kansas Territory by crossing into Nebraska at Council Bluffs and Omaha and that he had dispatched a Capt. T.J. Wood to prevent the "ingress of Lane's party."

Indeed, it was this type of military action that had caused these secure routes to be established for Northerners, with river crossings where the ferries were known to be owned by abolitionists and where Free-State people could post well-armed guards on both sides to scare off any proslavery ruffians intent on mischief.

Later I asked Father if he thought we might be among that party of 250 characterized by this General Smith as an "invading" force. Father said he supposed so.

After the gentleman departed, Father added in a low voice that he already had a copy of the circular the man had given us. I asked him when he got it since it was dated July 4th and we had left Detroit on July 14th. Father smiled, didn't answer, but

---

[5] See Shalor Eldridge's *Early Days of Kansas Vol. II, pg. 69* Kansas State Historical Society for an elaboration of Augusta's "peril."

touched his index finger to his temple and gave me a smile and a big, reassuring wink.

At supper, we discussed the letter in greater detail. Father took a map of Iowa from a thick packet of papers. In the lower right-hand corner, the map was stamped "Kansas Central Committee."

Someone had circled on the map all the cities mentioned in the letter, and ten or twelve other cities between them. Near the Missouri River both Sidney and Tabor were circled, as possible departure points for the river ferry crossing, so Father had known all along which route we would use to cross Iowa!

Father spread the map out on the table and we studied it. He said we would leave Iowa City about noon the day after tomorrow, July 22nd, and make Chestnut by nightfall. Father said the maps in the pamphlets, he had, drew an irregular north-south line near Quincy as the "frontier". Pamphlets, he said, warned potential shopkeepers that getting too far west beyond the "frontier" would invite bankruptcy. The pamphlet described a fifty-year history of bankruptcies studied by an Eastern scholar, who identified the "frontier", as a west-moving vertical "line," where the population was two to six inhabitants per square mile, and claimed that he could predict the onset of bankruptcy if a commercial establishment was near or beyond the frontier. Father said this map locates the current frontier line a little west of Quincy, so we should not expect to find stores or hotels beyond Quincy and be prepared to camp out.

Tapping his packet of papers, Father said we would probably join a wagon train in Sidney or Tabor, both abolitionists' strongholds. He expected abolitionist scouts to meet us there and give us safe escort across the Southern Nebraska Territory down to settlements in the Kansas Territory.

We left Iowa City, as planned, on Tuesday, July 22, 1856 about noon.

The road west out of Iowa City began with a mile, maybe a mile and a half, and a long gentle uphill slope, which Father said surveyors call a "gradient." The mule salesmen and the ox-team salesmen, back in the city, predicted our horses wouldn't make it forty miles. We knew their speculation was self-serving but we were also afraid it might be true. Father said he wasn't a "teamster" and wouldn't know how to detect when our horses became exhausted. We'll just have to wait and see.

Father thinks he can buy grain all the way across Iowa, to Quincy or maybe Sidney. But beyond that it might be as much as $4 a bushel for oats or corn, with freight accounting for much of that cost. We know that our horses will lack stamina if they only eat grass, whereas oxen can get their nourishment from grazing. So, we watched our two horses very carefully for any sign of fatigue, particularly as they pulled our load uphill.

Halfway up the grade we overtook a young couple pulling a strange, partially loaded two-wheeled handcart. It was a lovely, sunny day. Father and I were walking and we struck up a conversation with them while Adda drove our wagon a little ahead of us. They said they were camped west of town. They were both sweating. She was wearing a very attractive blue-and-yellow sunbonnet; so large it obscured her rather pale features. Father suggested we tie their wagon to the back of ours, which we did "on the run," and in the process we continued the usual set of inquiries: "Where you heading," etc.

"Oh, Kansas Territory."

"But why there?" etc.

But we soon exhausted our mutual curiosity and they fell silent and began walking a few feet behind us. I should add that they had very limited English and an accent we couldn't identify, though we were too reticent to ask its origin. But they did say they were Mormons and I tried to frame a polite question about whether they intended to pull this flimsy two-wheeled contraption all the way to Utah, though I think they called it Deserta or Deseretta or Zion. He laughed, "Vell, some vill pull and some vill push." I'm afraid his humor was lost on me.

In about an hour we had negotiated the hill. Off to our left, south of the trail, we noticed a large camp with hundreds of handcarts more or less identical to the one the couple had tied to our wagon.

As we came within sight of the camp, Adda, who was learning to drive our rig, slowed to a stop.

They untied their cart and made little gestures of thanks. Before they pulled away, I asked, "If you are all going to Utah, why are so many people working those fields? Are you working for local farmers or is the farm part of your camp?" They said something to the effect that yes, they were all going west, but I didn't understand their few words explaining the farming activity.

Adda asked, "How many of you are there?"

The woman answered, "More than a thousand."

"Are you German?"

"Nein."

Well, I wondered how many other languages use "Nein" for no.

Her answer did confirm a remark I'd heard on Monday back in Iowa City. Someone had said rather disparagingly that about 1,300 Mormons were camped west of town.

So, it will remain one more mystery in my little book of mysteries. How long will it take us to get to the Missouri? What cities or villages will we encounter? Where will we settle in the New Territory? And, if these Mormons are planning to go to Utah, why are they bothering to tend what appeared to be acres and acres of farmland here in Iowa?

Forty or so miles west of Iowa City Father decided that the hills were tiring out our horses. We begrudgingly admitted that the Iowa City outfitters had been right. While Adda and I stayed with a family at their boarding house, Father returned and bought a pair of oxen together with the yoke and other paraphernalia for $70.

One mid afternoon, as we approached Knoxville, which was about one hundred miles west of Iowa City, Father said he wanted a blacksmith to look at one of our wagon wheels. The large iron rim almost 5 feet in diameter was working loose and it needed a blacksmith to "tighten it up."

Just as we arrived on the outskirts of this little settlement, we were surprised to hear music behind us. Adda and I jumped down off the wagon and walked back up the trail several hundred yards. An outfit of twenty-five or so horse-drawn schooners was approaching the town and bringing with them clouds of dust. Several youngsters were cavorting in front of the lead wagon.

But what was so pleasant and unusual was this outfit had a band marching out on the prairie along side the wagons. We could see the brass instruments glisten in the afternoon sun. As the wagons approached us we could see banners and flags flying. The travelers were obviously in good spirits. When the second wagon went by, Adda yelled to the young driver, where they were from. He yelled back, "Chicago, hoo-ray, Chicago." The people in the wagons behind him laughed and said they were from Milwaukee, Wisconsin, that the musicians were all Germans from Milwaukee. Well, they certainly livened-up our dusty afternoon.

When the band went by, Father, tapping time to the music, suggested I skip ahead into the village and secure a room before the musicians bought up all the accommodations. I did but his concern was groundless. The German band continued to kick up dust but camped on the west edge of town.

That night the band put on a concert and all of Knoxville turned out, and for good reason.

It wasn't only the music that drew the crowd. General Jim Lane was in town and gave a rousing speech. I had never heard such an animated, powerful speaker. His words seemed to flow hot and relentless, like I would imagine lava flowing from Vesuvius. I must say that the General gave a very enthusiastic speech.[6] He is obviously a natural leader and in the introduction we learned he had been a U. S. Congressman from Indiana.

People we saw this afternoon from Chicago and the Wisconsin Germans all turned out to hear the general. He spoke on a raised platform in the town green. When Father saw him, he pulled Adda and me along through the crowd to where the General was standing, talking to two or three Knoxville officials. Father walked right up and said, "General, I'm Sam Stewart, the Surveyor. You and I met on June 2nd this summer when you, Mr. Eldridge and Governor Reeder came to Detroit with the Free Kansas Committee. You were the main speaker and you were very persuasive. These are my daughters, Augusta and Adelaide."

Father and General Lane exchanged a few remarks and the other two gentlemen introduced themselves. And as luck would have it, one of them was the town blacksmith.

He said he was an ironworker from Holland. There was a colony of Dutchmen in Knoxville. The next morning he tightened the rim on the wheel so well we've had no problem with it since then, which was the last day of July.

In Knoxville, we bought a small utility wagon and lightened the big wagon, which our oxen pulled. We had kept our two horses, especially our prize "Big Canadian" father's favorite harnessed

---

[6] I've added this postscript in 1858. I've heard that General Lane that summer, traveling up and down his "trail" in Iowa, spoke seventy-two times!

to the utility wagon and we all took turns driving, which was a diversion from the tedium of the trip.

We were fortunate to be going west in July. Farm produce was abundant with fresh vegetables of every description: fresh fruit, apricots in Sigourney, peaches in Osceola, Iowa cantaloupes and a white Iowa sweet corn that we didn't have in Michigan. And the abundant July grass was a godsend for our two oxen.

When we left Winterset after breakfast, the family had a gift for us, a wicker basket so heavy we both had to carry it and insisted that we accept the contents as her family's wish for our success and good health in Kansas. It was a large basket of Golden Cantaloupes. She said it was a new strain of melon called, "Heart-of-Gold." We ate two melons a day, usually at noontime, until they were all gone, except: we kept the seeds. What melons we were to raise from them in Kansas!

Since leaving Iowa City we've gone through Sigourney, Oskaloosa, Knoxville, and Winterset. We must have found the only house in Winterset friendly to abolition. We were told that most of the settlers in that town thought we should mind our own business. I believe we are about two-thirds of our way across Iowa. Late in the afternoon on this last day of July we had the prospect of a long, gently downward sloping hill. Somewhere not far ahead of us laid Indianola. In the distant valley, perhaps a mile or two ahead, we could see a line of dark trees meandering along a north-south line. Father remarked that no doubt there was a small river or creek down there.

The gentle slope must have relieved the oxen. They responded by expelling great quantities of air, audibly wheezing and by making quick, jerky rotations of their heads in the yoke.

In steeper sections the road had occasionally traversed the hill at an angle to its fall line, no doubt made that way to accommodate eastbound teams climbing the hill.

Father remarked that our team seemed grateful for the favorable gravity, saying that its force is one of Nature's many mysteries. He said in all his studies and discussions he'd never met a man who understood gravity, nor did he, he added. As a boy in New York State, he knew an old sailor who had sailed on every sea, and in his middle years had developed a hobby that consisted of inquiring at the various ports if gravity was constant there. He reasoned that since air and sea temperature were not constant, gravity shouldn't be either. But very few people understood his question. Father said the sailor's problem was that he lacked an instrument to measure gravity, though Father thought some old Italian had. Perhaps it was Galileo, who believed he could calculate it by measuring the return swing of a pendulum. Father said the old scientist got into trouble with the Catholic Church, and was jailed (he died in jail), and that ended his studies of gravity.

By now we were halfway down the hill. The sun was lower in the west and it seemed to be getting cloudy in the north.

Father seemed to enjoy examining with us several of nature's other mysteries. He wondered whether magnetic forces had anything to do with the attraction between men and women, and with a chuckle said, "Now that's an experiment we can all do and you girls, in your time, will experience it." He was quiet for a spell. The wagon creaked irregularly as it accommodated the variation in the ruts and I thought about the wheelwright in Iowa City who pronounced the width between our wheels to be within the ancient specification. I decided not to discuss it, since it was far more interesting to listen to Father.

Looking straight ahead, seeming to address the western sun, Father said, "I've never ceased to be amazed at the strong attraction I felt for your mother, stronger than gravity. And it was mutual." Looking at me he said, "My God! What a unique beauty she was! I'll never forget her. It's as though she will be waiting for us up in Quincy. Yes, we had our differences. She was occasionally unwell, especially when she was expecting you children and she thought I lacked sensitivity to her burdens …and I suppose she was right. But we loved each other. She was my first sweetheart and, Augusta, you are the product of that attraction." Of course I knew this, but having Father say so seemed to give it a blessing I'd not known before.

Father lapsed into a long silence, and I wondered if he was thinking of his first love…and I wondered if he ever thought how I, in my own way, missed the mother I loved with such tenderness.

We were approaching the bottom of the hill. The smell of the air changed: an aroma linked to lightning, a fragrance carried on a breeze we all learn as children that announces rain is coming before it comes. The northern sky turned gray, then dark. Our animals became restless. A little warm breeze came up and with it a hard summer shower, which settled what little trail dust there was. Jagged steaks of lightning appeared all round us. The thunder disturbed the animals. The thin brown film of dust that had accumulated on the cover of our wagon quickly washed off.

And as suddenly as it came up, the squall passed, having cleansed our wagon and the grass by the trail. Suddenly straight ahead of us, between us and the recently returned afternoon sun, appeared a glorious rainbow; it filled the horizon stretching as far north and south as we could see.

There was a long silence as we all admired the summer scene ahead.

Father broke the silence, "Girls, that rainbow is a good omen for us. In the Book of Genesis God and Noah have a conversation after the Great Flood. When Noah came out of the ark, having been cooped up with all those animals for forty days, it must have been a great relief for him to get a whiff of fresh air.

"It had stopped raining. The sun was out but results of the flood were death and destruction all about. As Noah contemplated this scene, it must have struck him like a hammer blow that only he, his family and his animals had been spared.

"There was a great rainbow in the sky. God spoke to Noah and said that the rainbow was His sign, His covenant, that peace and orderliness would be restored to the Earth. God promised Noah that he would never again unleash his wrath on the people. His Covenant with Noah was the magnificent rainbow."

Father recited some lines from Genesis: "I will remember my Covenant, which is between me and you and every living creature of all flesh and the waters shall no more become a flood to destroy all flesh."

I was impressed that Father could recall these lines.

I had remembered the Noah story from Sunday School but the significance of the rainbow as a covenant, if it was even discussed, was lost on me until now. Father's retelling of the story, under such appropriate conditions as we headed west into this glorious arch with such high hopes just beyond it, made a great impression on me.

Adda broke the spell of Father's parable. "Well, that was a pretty piddling rainfall for such a glorious rainbow. And if the rainbow was God's promise to Noah that he was over his wrath and that Noah's ancestors would enjoy peace, why did He later visit the seven plagues on the Egyptians and the Black Plague that killed off one third of the Europeans? And did God exempt the Negro Slave from that covenant?"

Hmm, I thought, my little sister is getting to be a philosopher.

Having decided to take the northern cutoff called Plumb's Route; we arrived at Indianola two days after leaving Knoxville and found a small four-room "hotel" for the evening. At supper, a man approached us and inquired if we were westward bound. When we answered, "yes," he casually asked if we were going to California or Colorado. "Neither," we replied, "We are going to Kansas Territory." By looking around the room, he assumed a conspiratorial air. Without bothering to ask if he was interrupting our family supper, he pulled a chair up to our table, he said he was an Iowa member of the Kansas Central Committee, and took out a circular from his pocket. He told us we should study it.

Father quickly perused it. He thanked the gentleman and said that he had received a similar bulletin in Detroit before our departure but that he noticed that this circular contained the names of all of the members of the Central Committee and that it was obvious that some very important people in the North were concerned about the safety of the immigrants. Father told the gentleman that he had met General Lane, Colonel Eldridge and others whose names were on the letter at a rally in Detroit, where upon the man excused himself. He walked across the small dining room to a table that had become occupied after he had joined us. I noticed he again took a circular from his pocket and handed it to the people at that table also.

After dinner, when we were back in our room, I asked Father who were these important northern politicians who had signed the letter.

Father gave me the circular, suggesting I paste it in my journal. As I scanned the names, I became very proud to be part of this immigration. Father seems to have been interested in shielding Adda and me from all the complexities of our trip. This letter explained a different, less personal aspect of our sojourn. I asked Father how long he had been aware of this Committee. He said that on June 2nd he had been invited to hear some Free State Advocates come up to Detroit from Chicago by train. He said the three principals were Governor Reeder, General Jim Lane and Colonel Shalor Winchel Eldridge.

General Lane and his party had stopped in Detroit on their way to a Free State convention in Buffalo, which was to be held on the 9th of July, just a few days before we left Detroit. Father said delegates from thirteen Northern States attended the Buffalo meeting, which was called a National Convention of the Friends of Freedom in Kansas.

Father said a Detroit newspaper claimed that the Chicago gathering was the largest group yet assembled on behalf of keeping Kansas a Free State. General Lane had come from Lawrence, which, ten days earlier, had been destroyed, people killed, hotels burned, including the Governor's house. The clipping, Father said, called Lane a spellbinder, particularly when it came to whipping up sympathy over the treatment of the abolitionists in Lawrence.

Later I read out loud to Father and Adda some of the names that were on the Central Committee circular the Iowa man had given us, and, I must say, these men seem to occupy seats of power. Some of them: Thadeus Hyatt of New York City, president of the Committee; Dr. Samuel Cabot of Boston; W.H. Hoppin, Governor of Rhode Island; Dr. S.G. Howe, General Financial Agent; Congressman Abraham Lincoln of Springfield, Illinois; and Congressman William Russell of New Haven, Connecticut. Five additional gentlemen from Chicago were named and we noticed that the business headquarters of the Committee was in the Marine Bank Building, corner of La Salle and Lake Streets, not far from where we stayed at the Dearborn House.

As planned we traveled alone until reaching Quincy, where we fell in with two families, the Strongs and the Van Curens. Quincy is about sixty miles east of the Missouri River. This party was also bound for Kansas and they wanted us to bear them company, so we accommodated our pace to theirs. There were now ten in our party, not counting three drivers, men the Strongs had hired to drive their three extra wagons; these were freight wagons, not schooners. Altogether, the Strongs and the Van Curens had six wagons, pulled by oxen. Mr. Strong was a grocer from Wisconsin and the Van Curens were Indiana farmers. They called themselves "Hoosiers."

Before joining the Strongs and the Van Curens we had no reason to camp out. Across Iowa up to Quincy we could always arrange for a night's lodging and an evening meal at the little towns that miraculously seemed to appear about sundown. But in Western Iowa the towns were scarce and not always arranged to our traveling convenience, so our three families took to camping out. We had arrived at the frontier as defined by the eastern scholar; less than six people per square mile.

Camping out was quite romantic and we enjoyed it exceedingly. The Van Curens had some hens and tame pigeons, which they released at night from their cages. With the horses and cattle turned loose on the prairie, our little group presented quite a home picture.

Each of our three families had to cook supper on camp stoves, using campfires. Our stove allowed us also to do a little baking. Mrs. Strong's stove, larger than ours, was called a Dutch Oven. Each time we camped, Mrs. Strong would bake a fruit cobbler from the supplies of fresh fruit we got along the way. It was quite social for us all to join the Strongs for dessert. The compliments of the men folk encouraged her to make bigger and better cobblers. It was all so pleasant that I thought I should like to live in just such a manner all the rest of my days.

On Friday, August 1, 1856 we arrived at the Nishnabotney Ferry near Tabor, Iowa.

A few miles east of Tabor, flowing south, is the Nishnabotney River, a rather small river but not one that we could safely ford.

The trail led right up to the river, near which was a small but well-built frame house. Nailed to a tree, directly in front of the house, was a sign proclaiming that this was the Huntsaker Bros. ferry, but the licensee was not Huntsaker. The ferry was either owned or being operated by a Mr. Archibald H. Argyle. At least he was the "licensee." The sign said the operator had paid a license fee of $5 annually to a local magistrate. Transportation rates were also posted.

While we waited for Mr. Argyle[7] to appear, we amused ourselves by figuring what it would cost to use the ferry.

Here were the posted rates:

A single man	5¢
A man and horse (that's us)	10¢
A two-horse wagon empty	25¢
Loaded (that's also us)	30¢
A four-horse wagon empty	40¢
Loaded	50¢
Loose cattle, pigs, sheep, etc. (each) (not us)	10¢

Adda calculated 55¢. I calculated 75¢. Father would not reveal his estimate.

Our knocks on the door of the ferry "house" produced no response. After about two hours, a barefoot youngster, ten to twelve years old, appeared. We asked him where the ferry operator was. He said he was over on the Missouri at Civil Bend, just beyond Tabor, working the ferry there for a "huge gang" of abolitionists.

---

[7] This ferry is also mentioned in more detail in Nathan H. Parker's Iowa Handbook for 1856 (with a map used by abolitionists and Underground Railroad), published by J & P Jewett & Co., Boston *Marjorie L. Crump*

"How do you know that?" asked Adda.

"I'm Angus Argyle. My Dad owns this ferry. Are you all abolitionists?"

"Why?"

"'cause we only ferry abolitionists."

"Yes, yes, we are abolitionists," replied Adda. "This is a pretty narrow river and we don't see your ferryboat on either side."

"You've got to go upriver a little bit. The ferry is up there today. That's where your people are. Mr. Belcher is running the ferry today."

"We've been out here in the sun for two hours. Why didn't you write a note and nail it to your sign, so travelers wouldn't waste their time?"

Angus looked squarely at Adda. "'cause I can't write. I come down to tell you in person where the ferry is." With that, Angus turned and began walking north along the trail. We got the oxen started but failed to keep up with our young guide.

The other landing was about a quarter mile upriver. Sure enough, there was the ferry and a Mr. Belcher was running it. Timber had obscured the view between the two ferry sites.

Mr. Belcher charged one dollar and said he would only accept silver or gold and would be happy to take Mexican money, "Four bits to the half dollar. No paper!"

He said he had "ten kinds of paper money, even some from Iowa and none of it any good."

Father attempted to josh with Mr. Belcher by saying, "I calculate we could cross on Argyle's ferry for less than 75 cents." With a big-toothed guffaw Mr. Belcher said, "Shoot, when my ferry ain't runnin', I only charge 50 cents." Then he added, "If you think my rate is high, wait 'til those Yankees git aholt of you over on the Missouri." Pointing to me, he added, "They'll probably want one of them purty girls."

But Mr. Belcher turned out to be a first-rate pilot and handled the ferry expertly. After our rig got loaded, Angus rode the ferry with us. Since he said he couldn't write, I asked him if he knew his ABCs. "Sure," he said, and recited them. I suspected he was a little like his father and was "joshing" us.

A few miles east of Tabor we overtook a train of twenty-five wagons from Illinois and Massachusetts. They were watering their stock at a creek that flowed into the Nishnabotny. We decided to stop with them and water our stock. Their story was just terrible. They had gotten all the way to Waverly, Missouri, which is south of Westport, a settlement in the Kansas Territory on the west bank of the Missouri. They had traveled from Cairo, Illinois, using riverboats down the Mississippi to St. Louis. From St. Louis some of them traveled on *Sultan,* the river steamer, which crossed the State of Missouri on the Missouri River. Before they could debark at Westport, they were confronted and robbed of forty rifles, side arms, money and other possessions by group of armed proslavery Missouri Militiamen. Some in the Westport crowd even yelled for them to be hung. But other passengers were treated quite cordially at Westport; of course, they were Southerners.

The Illinois and Massachusetts party was rudely put on eastbound riverboats and shipped back to St. Louis where they changed boats and were sent north on the Mississippi back to Davenport, where they followed the same overland route we took. All of that must have added 500 miles to their journey. While they were in Missouri, they encountered several ruffians who accused them of being Mormons, or "Stinking Abolitionists," and they said it made no difference whether they were Mormons or Yankees: they would all be chased out.

Upon reaching Iowa City, the immigrants were out of supplies and money. We didn't want to ask how they managed to pay for their supplies. We did hear later, though, that the Central

Committee was so upset about the treatment of this group that John Brown and his party will escort them from Tabor across Nebraska and into Kansas.

Sam Stewart,
Father of Laura Augusta Stewart and Adelaide Henrietta Stewart

In 1857/58 he represented District 17, Butler County in Territorial Legislature...was on the Committee to write The Free State Constitution.

CROSSING IOWA TO THE MISSOURI RIVER

We Join the Strongs and the Van Curens in Western Iowa

3.

From Tabor To The Kansas Territory,

July to August 1856

We came to Tabor, near the Missouri River, on the first of August, late in the day. We had been on the trail from Iowa City fifteen days and had covered about 300 miles, so we've averaged twenty miles per day. That's a lot slower than Father's Davenport estimate of five miles per hour. But it means we've done better than commercial freighters. I remembered the Iowa City outfitters had said: freight haulers needed to do fifteen miles per day, "rain or shine, to make it pay." Some days we did better than others. Rainy days made the trail ruts pretty muddy, which cut our speed in half. The real secret was, by traveling alone, we could regulate our travel time to suit ourselves. Our average day was ten hours, some longer.

Someone said Tabor was a town settlement of fewer than two dozen families, though ten times that number live in its township, which is named, Ross. Most of the locals are from Western Reserve in Ohio, are pro Kansas and antislavery, which is more than can be said for other settlements in Southern Iowa.

There were people in Tabor of various church denominations acting as outfitters, but they charged little or nothing, depending on the settlers' ability to pay.

These church folk were distributing all sorts of supplies: food, blankets, practical advice and spiritual encouragement and with such Christian goodwill and generosity. One particularly jolly fellow asked us over and over if we had enough Beecher's Bibles, which was our first introduction to the new military rifle with that nickname. It was to become legendary. He said every wagon needed at least one. If we had other people on the wagon who could shoot a rifle, he said, he would be happy to supply each of them "a rifle for every rifleman." Adda asked him if that included women. "You betcha, little sister!" We hadn't heard that phrase often. All afternoon Adda's response to any question was "You betcha." She became a bit tiresome.

Our outfit consisting of six wagons belonging to the Strongs and Van Curens plus our big schooner and the utility wagon was formally assigned to the larger train from Illinois and Massachusetts that we'd met a few hours earlier. Each able-bodied man of this group had been issued one of these new Sharps rifles made in Connecticut.[8]

---

[8] The Sharps rifle, sometimes called the "Kansas Bible or "Beecher's Bibles," because they were occasionally shipped to the Kansas Territory in wooden crates, marked "Bibles." Invented by Christian Sharps, he manufactured them in Hartford, CT near the famous Colt Factory on the Connecticut River. Mr. Sharps was later to move his plant to Bridgeport, CT. He served a gun making apprenticeship under the famous gunsmith, John Hall, who was probably the inventor of the first breech-loading rifle. He was chief gunsmith at the Harper's Ferry armory-factory (the one John Brown intended to blow-up.) Mr. Sharps was awarded a U. S. patent on his breech loading rifle issued in 1848 and a patent in 1852 for a cartridge containing an improved percussion cap. By 1865 he had built almost 100,000 rifles. After Kansas became a State, the Sharps were for several years the most popular buffalo gun, then known as "Old Reliable." After moving to Bridgeport, he fell on hard times, went bankrupt and his business was resurrected by none other than Phineas T. Barnum! The Post Civil War Sharps was for a period the U. S. Army's favorite, including General Custer. Some historians say his gun was the origin for the term, "Sharp" shooter. Others disagree. His "rolling block or falling block design dominated U. S. and European gun design for 50 years. Ref. "100 Great Guns" by Merrill Lindsay, *Antique Firearms*, F. Wilkerson.

We were told this rifle was a major improvement in arms. We intended to use ours against Indians should the need arise. In the next few weeks Adda and I were to learn much more about this new invention. It had been tested by our troops a few years earlier in the Mexican War.

A major improvement is the finger-sized cartridge that contains the correct powder charge, the right-sized ball, and a percussion cap all properly arranged in a tightly wrapped waxy paper cylinder about the size of my middle finger. Each settler was given several tins of these factory-made cartridges.

Another unusual feature; the rifle's breech is opened by activating a lever which allows the cartridge to be inserted into the barrel at the breech; i.e., opposite the muzzle. The fast lever action and the one-piece ammunition allows this gun to shoot ten times faster than muzzleloaders.

Tabor, in Southwestern Iowa, was known as "The Free State Rendezvous." There were all sorts of tracts being distributed by various sponsoring groups. Some pamphlets offered spiritual counsel. Some dealt with the slavery. Others had specific advice giving information on the best routes to avoid Indians and proslavery settlements or detailing where land was available in the New Territory. Some Quakers from the Shawnee settlement along the Kansas River seemed anxious for us to know that five million acres of the Eastern Territory, in irregular tracts along the Missouri River west of Kansas City, had already been deeded to Indian tribes. One of their pamphlets listed the names of almost twenty tribes that held separate claim to these vast tracts that the Indians had received in treaties over the past sixty to seventy years from the Federal Government in exchange for their leaving Kentucky, or Ohio, or New York State, or Michigan, etc. Some tribes had been moved more than once, some several times. This information, particularly the pamphlets describing the five million acres all unavailable to us, was disappointing, as it limited our choices and would push us further west than we had originally thought we would be. The Quakers assured us that west of those reservations there was plenty of land, all the way into the Rockies. One of their pamphlets said that there was eighty million acres of land available in the New Territory, so I guess five million acres is only a small part of the whole.

A well-dressed gentleman we met in Tabor gave Father his business card, saying he represented a bank, owned by Messieurs Corcoran, Riggs and Paine, who, he said, were establishing themselves in Lawrence as Mortgage Bankers for Land and Timber purchases. When we told him about all the land claimed by the Indians, he scoffed at this news. At least half of that land, he informed us, had been re-treated by Mr. Manypenny the Territorial Commissioner of Indian Affairs.

He went on to say that the New England Immigrant Aid Society, which had settled Lawrence, had raised $5 million to invest in the New Territory, much of it in land. One of the Society's plans was to buy as much land as possible to keep it out of the hands of the Missouri proslavery speculators who had already bought up large tracts of the Territory. His bank, he told Father, provided capital for Mr. William Russell of the freight firm of Russell, Modelle and Majors, a proslavery outfit that had major Army contracts handling freight by wagon from Fort Leavenworth to the other Army forts farther west.

In Tabor the stories we heard about Lawrence drove home the dangers of living there. We heard our first news of battles that had taken place in the New Territory, including gruesome details about proslavery groups attempting to wipe out Lawrence about a year ago. Until our arrival in Tabor, we had been led to believe that Lawrence was a thriving metropolis settled mainly by Free Soil advocates from Massachusetts, the famous Massachusetts

Immigrant Aid Society. One pamphlet in Tabor invited us to an impromptu lecture every hour (on the hour!) sponsored by that famous Aid Society.

Late the next day in Tabor, who should locate our wagon camped on the "town square," but the missing Nishnabotney ferryboat operator, Mr. A. H. Argyle, claiming he was also an officer of Ross Township, Fremont county. He apologized for not being at his "post" but he had heard that Father was a surveyor and wanted to speak with him. Mr. Argyle quickly got down to business. It seems that Tabor's Town Council had passed a resolution to make Tabor's main street eighty feet wide for a half mile through town, and they needed a surveyor to lay it out. He suggested that he could make it worth Father's time to remain in town and do the necessary surveying.

Mr. Argyle said the population of Ross Township included about 150 families, mostly Congregationalists from Oberlin, Ohio, but only twenty-five or so of those families lived in or near Tabor. He said the township had about 348 children enrolled in ten schoolhouses. I thought, "Ah ha! One of those who isn't enrolled is your son, Angus, who said he couldn't read." Mr. Argyle added that there are twenty-four full-time teachers. One school, he said, needs a teacher. She had gotten married and the newlyweds had gone off to seek gold in California. I asked what they were paying the teacher who left. He said about $100 per annum, but teachers only worked for seven and a half months. He must have over estimated my age. He asked if I'd ever taught school.

It was getting late in the day. I could see that Father was intrigued by Mr. Argyle's proposition and what's more, Mr. Argyle could see it also. I was afraid that he might persuade Father to stay a few weeks to layout the street.

Father suggested that the four of us find a place for supper and continue the conversation. Mr. Argyle said he knew just the place. Our supper in his friend's home began with a prayer offered by Mr. Argyle. It was most cordial of him to seek the Almighty's blessing and protection for us. He called us, "Pilgrims to the Promised Land."

"Either of you ladies play a walking instrument? We're trying to recruit a band of musicians." Adda piped up and said she had taken clarinet lessons and could read music. I do believe Mr. Argyle intends to recruit our whole family. We've known this gent for maybe an hour and he has offered Father a surveying job, me a teacher's job, and without so much as a "recital" he wants my sister in his military band.

Well, I simply don't have room or time or the memory to record the whole conversation that evening, except that Father said to Mr. Argyle, in parting, that he would need to "sleep on it." Mr. Argyle would not give up. He put his arm around Father's neck and said, "Stewart, we aim to build a college here. It will be patterned after Oberlin in Ohio. Ever lay out a college? Stay here with us. I'll get Augusta the schoolteacher's job and when the college gets up and running your girls could enroll in the first class. Now that, Stewart, is a full pillow to sleep on."

As he was leaving, Mr. Argyle wished us good night, then paused, "By the way, if you do move on, the ferry at Eastport, will be very crowded. There is another ferry about half a mile south, operated by a Mr. Sam Nichols and a group of his slaves. I'd advise that you suffer a day at Eastport rather than be rebuffed and insulted by Mr. Nichols. Occasionally Nichols entertains a Company of Missouri Rough Necks to harass Northerners dumb enough to go down there. Only a few days ago we expected a dustup at his site. One of your leaders, a Mr. Hinton, a proper Englishman, I believe, grew impatient with the long line at the

Eastport Ferry. He had been told not to use the ferry at Civil Bend, because it would be crowded with other trains, so he took three men and rode down to pay Mr. Nichols a commercial visit. Mr. Nichols declared that he would not transport abolitionists. Mr. Hinton said he understood a man of such high scruples and suggested two solutions: one, that he would pay double the upriver ferry rate and, two, that Mr. Nichols and his loyal associates need not work up a July sweat. Mr. Hinton said he had two gentlemen in his party, who were Eastern mechanics perfectly capable of running a steam ferry. With the help of any of Nichols' crew that cared to volunteer, he and his men could operate the ferry on their own. In the absence of any Missouri Roughnecks to reinforce Mr. Nichols' loyalty to his cause, our English friend sent word for his company to come down to the Nichols' site. They all crossed the Missouri without further ado! Mr. Hinton told some of us later that the double rate plus the fact that all his 'passengers' were well-armed and determined, all proved to be—well, persuasive."

Mr. Argyle took his leave.

We spent the night with the Tabor family that had fed us supper. The next day we were told by a Kansas Committeeman that our train was due to move out and head south the following morning. We were supposed to spend the next night of August 4th in Sidney, which is only a half-day's drive from Tabor, and close to the river ferries.

As we approached "our" ferry, our outfit had swelled to about fifty wagons. A very large train had already preceded us out of Tabor. A gentleman joined Father as he walked alongside the wagon. He said he was from General Jim Lane's headquarters. He told us that there were trains stretching in front of us and trailing behind us, and our party included no fewer than 500 people. He said there were a few wagons that had traveled alone to Tabor, like our small group, but most had come in well-organized companies and that from here on it would be too dangerous to travel alone. He said in the train there were two companies from Wisconsin, a company each from Indiana and Ohio, three companies from Iowa (one from Iowa City, one from Davenport), and two from Illinois (one larger than the other) one of those two was probably the musical outfit that had paraded into Knoxville and produced the music for General Lane's speech. He said the largest company was from Massachusetts. A Mr. Stowell was its conductor.[9]

"In a few days," said the gentleman, "we would join this outfit and settle temporarily in Plymouth. A Colonel Shalor Eldridge would also become of our leaders. In parting, this messenger said that a few days ago (July 28th and 29th) Mr. Thadeus Hyatt of New York, the president of the Free Kansas Committee had been in Tabor for a meeting with Dr. S. G. Howe from Boston, also a member of the Committee and a member of the Massachusetts Immigrant Aid Society. They had met with two leaders of the Illinois group that had gone all the way to Kansas, only to be robbed there and, had to return by riverboat (as I have explained before.) Those leaders were A. D. Searl and E. B. Whitman.[10]

As a result of that meeting and the treatment of the Illinois Party, Dr. Howe and Mr. Hyatt now believe they must increase considerably the size, training and arms of the escorting parties as they join immigrant trains in eastern Iowa and escort them into Kansas.

One of the results of this meeting in Tabor, Father said, was the heightened awareness among us Northerners of just how well-

---

[9] These companies are confirmed: See page 85 - Shalor Eldridge, *Early Day of Kansas* by Kansas State Historical Society, Vol. 3.

[10] E. B. Whitman was listed in Augusta's Summary Journal as president of the company that founded the Fall River town called *Eureka*, A. D. Searl was its treasurer and Sam Stewart was trustee. E. B. Whitman is also listed as a member of the *Eldorado* town "company."

organized the South is and how determined the Southerners were to repel us wherever they can. Of course, all Northern parties this summer will be sternly warned east of the Mississippi not to attempt crossing the State of Missouri by land or by riverboat. The river is blockaded to Free Staters. All this will crowd the three or four ferries from Council Bluffs down to Sidney, near the Missouri line.

Eastport, the ferry landing on the Iowa side was maybe three miles southwest of Sidney. Nebraska City in Nebraska Territory was two or three miles due west over the bluffs beyond the river. Half the people of Nebraska City, we hear, are proslavery and we are advised to "watch our tongues while we are there." From Nebraska City we'll be obliged to go south, more or less parallel to the river to get into Kansas Territory.

August 5. We are at the Eastport ferry rendezvous on the bluffs majestically over-looking the Missouri River due west of Gaston[11], which earlier today we passed through without stopping. It is a very small settlement, though there were some outfitters available for last minute stuff. The Strongs and their three freight wagons will not spend the night with us. They have been assigned to leave ahead of us before twilight on the late ferry, crossing the river with a "military" guide who had joined our train in Gaston.

Someplace between Nebraska City and the new settlement (in the Kansas Territory) the Strongs are to meet up with General Jim Lane. He will assign some armed guides to return with Mr. Strong to our southbound party in Nebraska and guide our train, which has now grown to seventy or so wagons, into the New Territory.

---

[11] History of Freemont County says that Gaston became Percival after the Civil War.

Their job is to avoid any armed proslavery elements from Missouri who will try to turn us back. They tend to be small mounted groups of ten to twelve men. Our force must be...and will be...larger and better armed. We must also be alert for the U. S. Army patrols stationed near the border. If they decide that we are too heavily armed, they can declare us to be "Invaders," though it isn't clear how the Army will deal with us. In the process of avoiding the well-marked trails used by the Army, we could get lost. The armed scouts from General Lane's camp that will meet us will apparently know how to avoid the Missourians, the U. S. Army and hostile Indians. Well, that sounds like a tall order!

This afternoon, a gentleman from General Lane's camp rode up and asked some men in our outfit to arrange a meeting. Adda and I went with Father. He is very well informed and obviously well trained. He appears older than Father, stands erect, commands and gets attention. He wears a short coat or jacket, apparently of Mexican War vintage. I mustn't record now everything I hear, but some items of a military nature are very interesting. This gentleman (whose name, I probably shouldn't disclose) served with General Lane as an officer in the Mexican War. He has been escorting people from Tabor to Lawrence and other abolitionist settlements for two years. He delivered his speech as though he had done it often.

He spoke for several minutes in a very military and official manner. Then he launched into an interesting discussion about the various dangers that might confront us in the next few days. It seems that when we get into the New Territory we will be assigned to temporary camps, each of them large enough to defend itself against the Missourians. Our men will all be given military training.

When asked by our group about the dangers posed by the Indians in the area, he simply scoffed. He said we would pass through one or two of their camps and might spend a couple of nights on their reservations, but otherwise there would be little contact. He pointed out that there would be more of us than them in any one camp and the Indians would be well aware of that.

Prior to the Mexican War, he had occasionally fought Indians when he was with the U. S. Army, he said. It was his experience that the history of the American Indian showed him to be generally disorganized. The Indians were well organized within their own tribe, he explained, but there was so much hostility between the tribes, that they seldom, if ever, came together and organized themselves against the White Man. He said that if the really fierce tribes, like the Sioux (here in Western Iowa), the Comanches, and some tribe in Michigan whose name I didn't get, and the Iroquois and the Apaches, put away their differences and formed a unified army, New England would now be fortified in walled cities, like the cities in Europe. As guerrilla fighters, he said, their riding and fighting skills exceeded ours because those skills were more ingrained in their culture, and until the Sharps rifle came along, Indian muskets were as good as ours.

"Remember, during our War for Independence the English taught them to shoot the French with English muskets. The French taught them to shoot the English. The Indians often fought with either the English or the French but always against us. Had they raised an army from several tribes, they could have beaten us, but their culture is tribal. They stick to their tribes, and nurse old hatreds. One of the rules of the U. S. Army is to keep the tribes separate. That's easy. They prefer to be isolated.

"No," he said, "the Indians will not be a major problem for you, but you will have to watch out for the proslavery militia, who are supporting the Southern immigrants, who are coming into the New Territory at about half our rate. The militias will be aided by the Missouri border ruffians. And, as an army veteran, I'm ashamed to tell you that you cannot expect help from any of the Army forts in this area, particularly Fort Leavenworth or Fort Riley: They are proslavery and would prefer to see the likes of us, move on."

As he spoke, he used an interesting military jargon. He roused the crowd, "We will persevere in the New Territory because we will out organize the Southerners. We will bring in more settlers, like you folk, and each settlement will be well armed and well organized. We will raise more money for supplies from the North. In time, we will prevail, because we are finally benefiting from wider popular support in the North. It's all a matter of organization, planning and leadership." These remarks drew a huge applause, whistles and encouraging yells.

Our group included a few wagons of Germans from Illinois and Wisconsin. A large bearded gent in our crowd (I think from Wisconsin—he spoke with a heavy accent) said, "Ya, if you fellas are so smart, how come you let the Missourians almost wipe out Lawrence this spring?" There was a sobering stillness. I thought his question impertinent and rude, but it provoked an honest answer. The old soldier's response was slow and deliberate. "The leaders of Lawrence were taken by surprise by the attack. Their citizens were unprepared and poorly organized. They didn't have an armed militia to mount an adequate defense to repel the Missourians, and they naively counted on the U. S. troops from Fort Leavenworth to protect them. Lawrence taught us a lesson. We now have a militia of over 3,000 trained soldiers stationed in several camps around the city. General Lane has things under control mostly by arming the soldiers with Sharps rifles and some cannons. It won't happen again." This gentleman then rode off down towards the river.

The Iowa side of the Missouri was on very high ground well above the river, which afforded us a grand view of it. They call it a "bluff" and it runs for miles in an undulating north-south direction, fifty to one hundred feet above the wide river plain. Areas east of our trail are heavily wooded. As we are headed south along the East Bluffs of the river we must be very close to the Missouri line; and that is sobering.

The grass on the wide plain down on the river level can almost conceal a rider on horseback who ventures into it. From a distance it creates the illusion that the rider is floating in a sea of yellow grass. We could see the ferry making its slow progress across the river, and we could see the string of white-topped wagons stretching ahead of us, and behind us, clotting here and there in groups of five or six wagons—a single file of them angled down the grade to the flat plain just above the river. I believe our party of wagons now stretches out over a mile in length.

We had to stop for an hour or so while the members of our train began loading onto the ferry. A young man came by with a roll of tickets and in a friendly manner said we needed to pay him for the passage. Each ticket, he said, had a number, that determined the order in which we boarded." The fellow took Father to one side and said, out of earshot of the other wagons, that if we had any "trouble with the fare," the Massachusetts Aid Society would "take care of it." Father declined his generous offer. I suppose he made that same offer privately to each wagon.

When we got down to the ferry landing, there were several teams ahead of us. The ferryboat was much smaller than the one we had used to cross the Mississippi at Rock Island.

Waiting "our turn" to cross the Missouri would be a good time to unravel the big mystery of the Missouri River Crossing. When we had nothing else to do while crossing Iowa, we would speculate just where we would cross the Missouri, entertaining the folly that the choice would be ours to make; little did we know how rapidly we would be organized into "a company." And we didn't know then that immigrant traffic would be so heavy that at least four ferries were operating in the vicinity of Sidney, three catering to abolitionists.

After Tabor, we began to feel much more regimented. We saw more escorts---all very efficient and business like all very organized. We are now part of a company of fifty to seventy-five wagons, though it is hard to tell on the trail, spread out in single file where one company ends and the other begins.

So it's been fifteen days since leaving Iowa City and twenty-three days since we left Detroit. Before we were given the "official" map and the rather stern instructions in Iowa City, we had assumed that we would cross the Missouri at Council Bluffs, but the map and instructions were silent as to exactly where we should cross.

Nobody ever really explained that the ferries on the Iowa side were located such that when we crossed the river, we would not land in Kansas Territory since most of those settlements are proslavery, offering temporary housing to the Missouri Roughnecks who cross over the river to raid and harass the abolitionist settlements further west. No matter which of the three abolitionist ferries we would have been assigned to, we must debark on the Nebraska side, well north of the Kansas Territory line. So the mystery of the Missouri River Crossing is solved!

We spent our last night in Iowa, camping out on the high bluffs and watching a magnificent sunset out over the western plain.

At 10 a.m. the next day, August 6th, it was finally our turn to load up the ferry with our two oxen and the big wagon. The two horses and Father's smaller wagon were assigned to take the next ferry.

There was a great deal of cargo shifting from one wagon to another, as well as matching wagons with horse or ox team to get the most value from each crossing. This stevedoring was done by a gang of men who worked for the ferry company. We wondered who paid them. There was a rumor that they were Quakers. Another rumor was that they were part of the Massachusetts Immigrant Aid Society and that the Eastport ferry was owned by them, but these matters were never confirmed.

Mr. and Mrs. Strong and their three freight wagons all had crossed the river on Tuesday evening before dark ahead of us, together with a few other wagons of our outfit. At Nebraska City, Mr. Strong was to leave his freight wagons in the care of Mrs. Strong and his hired drivers. He and an armed guide would swiftly ride south to make contact with General Jim Lane's Company, rumored to be in or near Plymouth, just inside Kansas Territory. We understood this was about thirty-five or forty miles south as the crow flies from Nebraska City. It was Mr. Strong's assignment to obtain a mounted escort of men, return to our party to accompany us from Archer, south of Nebraska City across the southeastern part of Nebraska Territory and down into Kansas. These escorts would know the safest routes into the New Territory, and it was rumored that they would be heavily armed, and they would expect us to be as well.

We had enjoyed such pleasant times with the Strongs, particularly when we camped for the night. On the trail Adda and I would often jump up on their wagon and ride with Mrs. Strong as she ran the team. Mr. Strong then would walk "a spell". She had an endless supply of stories about her girlhood in New York City, then of her life after moving to Wisconsin. She said while Mr. Strong was getting his grocery store up and running, she planned to operate a boardinghouse after it was built. When that happened, she wanted Adda and me to come work for her.

We crossed the Missouri and continued due west through the Nebraska Territory, aiming to arrive in Nebraska City about noon. From there we would turn south.

Coming up from the river bottom onto the prairie, we were, more by default than assignment, the lead wagon of perhaps twenty to twenty-five wagons. Some had preceded us earlier that morning, but had needed to stop to make repairs, or to rearrange their possessions. It was a bright sunny day. A few scattered clouds were ahead of us. The Nebraska prairie stretched out ahead, absolutely empty, not all flat but not as deeply rolling as the Iowa prairie with its round hills and round valley bottoms. The rutted trail ahead of us pointed due west until it disappeared out where the plains met the blue sky. We knew there was plenty of game, wild turkey by the flock, deer, antelope and huge herds of buffalo. But on this sunny August morning, just two days this side of my seventeenth birthday, we saw nothing but blue sky and quiet prairies. Out here we can see to the horizon on all four points of the compass. I think I will find it easy to get used to this Nebraska blue and vast openness. The dominant color in Iowa and Illinois and Michigan, for that matter, was green, the color of the trees and crops. Until we reached the frontier over in Quincy, much of the land was in cultivation. Out here, as we continue our westward trek, the plains are yellow brown, but the sky is blue, a lighter, different blue than the sky back in Michigan.

Three hours after leaving the ferry, we arrived at a small settlement consisting of a single cabin on a new town site named after Worcester, a town in western Massachusetts. They pronounced "Wooster."

Just beyond this was Nebraska City. We learned that there was a very large camp, possibly with as many as 600 people, a little south of here. These were parties mainly from Wisconsin, Illinois, and Iowa and were mostly farmers intent on settling at once. They had twenty-five tents and twenty-three covered wagons. It was obviously a camp of "Free Staters." But we were shocked to hear that they were unarmed, or at least inadequately armed, to mount a defense against the proslavery militias rumored to be in this area. We wondered how they had managed to pass through Tabor, with all those groups distributing Sharps rifles and ammunition, and remain unarmed. Well, maybe they didn't go through Tabor. Maybe they crossed the river at Civil Bend.

The leaders of this camp were fearful of being attacked by proslavery elements, so they chose a Mr. A .C. Soley of the Worcester, Massachusetts company to travel down to the U. S. Army fort at Leavenworth on the Missouri River to confer with the fort's commandant, General Persifer Smith, to request that his troops provide the group safe conduct to the Kansas Territory. Mr. Soley's mission was a failure. The General not only rejected his request but also went so far as to say that Kansas was intended to be a slaveholding State and that if he had the say-so, "he would hang every d ... d abolitionist." Under threat of physical harm, Mr. Soley was ordered out of Fort Leavenworth.

Soley then went on to Topeka and Lawrence to appeal to the Free-State people, but failed to obtain the help that he wanted from that quarter. In Topeka, however, three Kansas citizens familiar with the countryside were assigned to guide the party across Nebraska and down into Kansas in such a way as to avoid both the proslavery militia and any patrols sent there by General Smith to prevent them from "invading" the territory. The guides cleverly led the settlers through the tall prairie grass and woods and on August 7th the group crossed over into Kansas Territory. They avoided General Smith's troops, which our spies confirmed had been posted along the Brownsville Road.

We camped out that night at Nebraska City but without one of Mrs. Strong's fruit cobblers. The next morning, some miles beyond Nebraska City, our outfit, which was stretched out in single file, made a wide arching turn or "wheel" south. We had been following westbound ruts out of Nebraska City until we had come to this wide dip or swale in the prairie. The first wagons had already dropped out of sight, but we were so far behind them that we hadn't seen this south-wheeling maneuver.

Once the wagons dropped into the shallow valley, they did not reappear on the other side. Our wagons followed them into the valley. The swales in the prairie afforded us protection. We traveled through these creek beds and depressions for several hours. To hide us from the Army patrols and the Missouri ruffians, the guides led us along this route.

By noon we arrived in Archer (also Nebraska Territory), south of Nebraska City. It was Friday, August 8, 1856, my seventeenth birthday. Archer is twelve miles northeast of Plymouth, which is our temporary destination.

In Archer we met-up with Mr. Strong and four young guides to escort us into the Territory. They were Mr. Westerfield, Alonzo Crawford, Charles Oliver and William Leman.[12] These men were conspicuously armed with those new Connecticut rifles and had been schooled in using them.

The guides and all of us took dinner at the only hotel in Archer. Mr. John C. Miller was the proprietor. Alonzo Crawford became very friendly with Adda, and vice versa. In the afternoon we continued south, keeping out of sight and off the high prairie. We camped that night on the banks of the Big Nemaha

---

[12] All of these men were in Lane's Army of the North. Later, in August and September, when General Lane increased the Free Soil militia by inducting Immigrants who arrived in the summer of 1856, these four all volunteered. At least two of them were captured in the Battle of Hickory Point and were held with Sam Stewart in the prison camp, mainly to jail abolitionists. Ref. newspaper article, Richard Hinton, Boston Traveler, September 10, 1856.

within a quarter mile of an Indian Camp (the Sacs and Foxes tribes). Compared to all the eastern rivers that we've crossed, the big Nemaha wouldn't even qualify for "The Little Nemaha." It could easily be waded. During the night, the Indians had a noisy celebration and war dance. The men of our outfit were assigned four-hour watches through the night. They were as alert for Indians, as for bands of "border ruffians." We could hear the drums and the shouting from the Indians' camp well into the night. It was exciting to know we were almost within sight of them. It was also a bit fearsome. I remembered the speech by one of the Quakers back in Tabor about how all the land bordering the Missouri already being occupied by the Indians. Now that speech carried the stark reality that we might indeed be camping on their land. I was happy to break camp in the morning and move on. We never actually saw those Indians.

Although our trail south is not rutted, it is cleverly marked and our guides seem to know the markers, which are either little pyramids or round piles of flat stones. Occasionally a stick protrudes up out of the pile.

Now and then one of the guides will dismount, repair the marker or build a new one if he thinks it's necessary. These markers are called "Lane's Chimneys." I notice that the guides continue to keep our trail in a southbound direction, leading us through valleys that dip below the general level of the prairie whenever they can find such routes.

The guides warned us this morning to expect at anytime now to be intercepted and searched by detachments of the U. S. Army who may label us invaders if we are armed excessively (by their definition.) This news increased our apprehension.

August 9, 1856. We arrived in Plymouth, Kansas Territory, just before noon on Saturday, twenty-seven days since leaving Detroit. There was a great celebration and jubilation by all. As our wagons rolled in, we were met by a welcoming party of important people. Here were speeches, prayers of thanksgiving and singing. The welcoming committee said that the first of our party had arrived the day before yesterday. The members of the Committee expressed relief that we arrived safely and had not been apprehended by one of the U. S. Army patrols along the Brownsville Road. We had simply avoided all roads and stayed concealed on the untrailed prairie several miles north and west of where our scouts said the Army was patrolling. Our four scouts came in for a great deal of praise, compliments and good-natured backslapping.

Nevertheless the officials remain concerned about our safety. We are told there is an armed delegation camped nearby headed by John Brown. He's not familiar to us, though we've heard his name mentioned almost daily since Tabor.

Plymouth is a new "town," which had been laid out by General Jim Lane's party in June, a little over a month or so ahead of our arrival. Others credit the founding of Plymouth to Martin Stowell,[13] who was the official leader of our long, drawn out train.

We are told Plymouth is in Brown County. Well, it is certainly not a city. It seems to be more of an Army Camp than a town, and, I must say, it's rather disappointing. Not a finished building fit for occupancy, not even a log cabin. Just a high flat "table" on the prairie. We are within walking distance of the Nemaha River

---

[13] I learned later that Mr. Stowell, had been involved in a controversy involving a fugitive slave in Massachusetts. He later left Plymouth and moved to Nebraska Territory (Archer, I believe) and used his house and business as a station for the Underground Railroad.
Added later: According to Father, Plymouth is in township 1, range 15. Pony Creek is just north of us in a draw running generally east-west and feeds the Nemaha five or six miles northeast of us: It runs into the Missouri right at the Territorial Line. Plymouth is on a plain between two branches of Pony Creek… *Augusta's note*

as it flows easterly. Directly north of us is a small creek, called Pony Creek, which flows into the Nemaha a little north of here. There are springs along Pony Creek and the Nemaha, running out of the sandstone banks, usually about halfway up from the river level. I suppose we will carry our water from those springs.

After our arrival, others continued to pull in until there were seventy to seventy-five wagons to make up this settlement. Between Sidney and Plymouth, we gained about twenty wagons, two or three at Nebraska City four at Archer. Four or five, which had been camped down in a valley close to the border, were also assigned to our outfit.

Not all of the trains coming down from Archer stayed in Plymouth. There are four other settlements nearby. We seem to be both west and north of the others. Lexington is about ten miles southeast of us, in Worcester County. A company of twenty-eight, also from Massachusetts, founded that town site.

In a few weeks, Lexington would be bigger than Plymouth. It was Jim Lane's design to have a settlement of fifty to one hundred settlers friendly to abolitionists every fifteen miles (a normal day's run with a wagon) from the border to Topeka.

Hiawatha is south of us, east of Lexington, maybe five miles. Walnut Creek is another of these new settlements. The southernmost settlement is Holton, some thirty miles generally south and east, not far from the Missouri.

I understand that in this northern group, of which we are a party, there are 500 to 600 of us, and we have been divided into these five settlements. Those who don't stay here will be sent to Topeka.

There is some general excitement in our camp. There is a rumor that the famous abolitionist John Brown, is among us. We have been hearing about John Brown on and off all the way from Iowa City, especially the tactics he used in Pottawattamie.

I heard one of the Massachusetts people say that "Old Osawatomie Brown" had come out from Connecticut with five or six sons, and some husbands of his daughters. He had twenty children from his two marriages (the first wife died) to settle in the New Territory and start a new life. They had made some land claims in Pottawattamie County quite a way south of us. But his real claim to fame is as a fire-breathing abolitionist. He is also a surveyor and has had businesses as a wool merchant.

John Brown claims he can trace his ancestry back to the *May Flower* and that he was raised in the strict Puritan tradition.

One rumor had it that he and some of his followers killed five proslavery settlers further south of here in retaliation for ongoing atrocities committed by proslavery ruffians in the county where the Browns have a town site. There are several Browns down there. Father said they have their own town site and county.

Colonel Hinton arrived in Plymouth. He claims he led his company of fifty-three wagons, twenty-five men on horseback and 500 settlers, mostly on foot, across the Missouri by ferry two days ahead of us. We had already heard about him from Mr. Argyle, the ferry operator at Nishnabotney.

Almost immediately after arriving five, six or more wagons of his company left for Topeka. Many of his people seem to be poor; their wagons are in bad shape. They seem to be running around borrowing things, and I don't believe there are really 500 of them. They say Colonel Hinton is "under" Martin Stowell. Someone said he talks funny. But I understand he was born in England, so that could explain his strange accent. The wagons in his company started out on their trek in June from Buffalo. They all traveled by steamer from Buffalo to Detroit, but from Detroit on they followed our exact route. Someone in their party said that their train was three-quarters of a mile long. Mr. Hinton moves fast. Father said that within two days of their arrival Hinton and fifty-seven people in his party, many from Moline, Illinois, made a city association with Martin Stowell and formed the City of Lexington, ten miles away. I heard a rumor that Mr. Hinton is secretly a journalist and is doing all this just to be able to sell his stories to several Eastern and London newspapers.[14]

After Mr. Hinton left Plymouth, Father related a story about Mr. Hinton's party as it came through Iowa. Mr. Hinton and a few of his party called on Governor Grimes at the building serving as Iowa's Capitol. Mr. Hinton told the Governor that his party lacked firearms and would like to borrow as many rifles from the Iowa Armory as the Governor could lend them.

The Governor said he was sympathetic to their cause but lacked the authority to lend Armory property. As he spoke, he toyed with the keys to the Arsenal, which was part of the Capitol.

Toward the end of the conversation the Governor said he would shortly have to excuse himself for a meeting. As he got up to leave, he made a conspicuous gesture of leaving the Arsenal keys on his desk. He bade a cordial good luck and good-bye to Mr. Hinton and his outfit.

After the Governor left, Mr. Hinton picked up the keys, located the Armory and posted men from his party as guards outside the building, telling them, if asked, that to explain they had "permission" to take out the weapons. Mr. Hinton's men helped themselves to 1,500 rifles and ammunition. These were all well-hidden in five or six of their fifty-three wagons. He allowed most of his party to remain ignorant of these facts and to continue to believe they were unarmed.

---

[14] Richard Hinton wrote for *the Boston Traveler, the New York Times, the Anti-Slavery Standard, the Worcester Spy,* and many more publications. He also wrote biographies of John Brown and Abraham Lincoln. During the Civil War, as "Colonel" Hinton, he formed a regiment of "First Kansas Colored" soldiers and fought on the Union side. Ref. Kansas State Historical Society, Vol. 7, pg. 490.

Shortly after arriving in Plymouth, Mr. Hinton dispatched the wagons with the rifles to General Lane's headquarters, which was believed to be near Topeka, though Lane was seldom there.

The citizens of Plymouth and four other small settlements, stretching from the Nebraska line down toward Topeka on the Kansas River, are now known as Lane's Army of the North, which is rumored to be anywhere from 475 to 660 strong. Our "army" is divided into several companies. We have been told that one of the leaders of our company (Plymouth) is a Colonel Shalor Eldridge, whom we met back in Tabor as he and his people were handing out new rifles. It is rumored that Colonel Eldridge owns the Free State Hotel in Lawrence, which was destroyed this past May by Sheriff Jones, a proslavery hooligan from Missouri. Just before we met him in Tabor, Colonel Eldridge and a Bob Morrow, who is also from Lawrence, were able to obtain 200 rifles from Governor Grimes of Iowa. They must be persuasive. Colonel Eldridge's train brought the rifles to Kansas, but that is also supposed to be a secret.

4.

PLYMOUTH, K.T.,

August 1856

For the past two weeks, ever since our arrival in Plymouth on August 9th, we have camped in our wagons while Father and Mr. Van Curen build a house. Father seems much more experienced in the building business than Mr. Van Curen, and Father has all the tools.

"General" Jim Lane has assigned seventy-five men to establish and defend Plymouth. In addition to the men, our settlement includes about twenty women and fifteen to twenty children.

Since June, when Plymouth was founded, there has been a flurry of building. A road that skirts the creek was laid out. Several men are building houses, and General Lane has left instructions for a fort to be built on the high ground. Every few days, heavy logs are pulled in by horses and the carpenters and builders among us wrestle those logs into place. Building the fort is a slow process and needs constant nagging.

Father says, what this County needs right now is a good saw mill, since there's plenty of hardwood and softwood nearby. In a conversation with two or three carpenters from the Massachusetts group, Father learned that their "corporation," the New England Immigrant Aid Society, has money for saw mills, flour mills and brick factories, just as soon as we can achieve some sense of stability and safety. These men claim that the Massachusetts corporation has raised five million dollars to be invested by them in various Kansas enterprises. Many of these Massachusetts people have commercial stakes in Lawrence and are bitter that Federal troops were not made available to stop the destruction of that town last spring. I think their resentment stems from knowing that the troops were nearby, at Fort Leavenworth, but were intentionally delayed in being ordered out to protect Lawrence from the proslavery militias. I've heard several discussions as to the participation of a U.S. Senator (David R. Atchison) in this destruction. The feeling around Plymouth is, if the South in general and Missouri in particular can send proslavery militia into Kansas to harass and destroy our settlements, all aimed at driving us north to Nebraska or to get us on the Oregon Trail headed west out of here, we must resist. We have to organize ourselves, seek help from any Northern source available, and use it. We are beginning to understand how the work of the various organizations of the North that favor abolition, particularly the New England Immigrant Aid Society, are helping our efforts to settle the territory. And are starting to appreciate the role of Reverend Beecher, and his antislavery speeches, in raising support for our cause. Everybody who can read, it seems, has read his sister's book, *Uncle Tom's Cabin.*

On Sunday, August 22nd, we all went up to the fort, what there is of it, to hear a distinguished-looking elderly gentleman, "Father Moore,"[15] preach the first sermon we've heard in Kansas.

---

[15] In 1901 I learned much more about this circuit-riding preacher. In 1853 President Pierce appointed him Minister to England, but he declined, requesting an Indian agency in Kansas. Reverend Moore had served two terms in U. S. Congress and was New York's Port Authority Surveyor (1835-1845).

PLYMOUTH, K.T.

Laura Augusta Stewart

In 1854 President Pierce considered appointing him the first Governor of Kansas Territory, but Reverend Moore again declined, recommending instead Andrew H. Reeder. Reeder later appointed Reverend Moore to be Registrar of the Territory Land Office in Lecompton. I read these facts in an article in the *Denver Post*, June 23, 1901, by Ely Moore (son of Reverend/"Colonel" Ely Moore) about a convention of "Old Timers" from Lawrence, Kansas, known as the Lecompton Party, that took place in Denver.

Adelaide Henrietta Stewart (on the left), "Adda"

PLYMOUTH, K.T.

Jacob Eastman Chase
Jacob and Augusta marry on January 13, 1859
Eldorado's First Wedding

He took as a theme for his sermon a passage from Deuteronomy 8:2, "Thou shalt remember the way in which the Lord, Thy God, led thee." It was an open-air service, as there is no roof on the fort, just partially completed log walls, maybe three or four feet high. Reverend Moore attracted a congregation of thirty-five to fifty. Some stood outside. The weather certainly cooperated with the Almighty and Father Moore.

Reverend Moore finished his sermon with a prayer. Then he paused, his voice broke, and he asked the Almighty to protect his two sons who were that very Sunday captives in what he called a prisoners' war camp. That was the first we'd heard of the existence of Lecompton prison, run by a proslavery warden by the name of Jones. Then in a deep sonorous voice he spoke directly to the Almighty about us in Plymouth. He asked the Lord to grant these pious pilgrims everlasting salvation for their bravery and tenacity for a righteous cause and said God should bless us all for our willingness to expose ourselves to constant danger in a strange land, pursuing HIS noble cause.

There was a long pause. Then he said to the congregation, "Let us pray," and he lead us in the Lord's Prayer. And as we asked to be delivered from evil, our chorus of pleas sailed out over the prairie and I wondered if God was listening, if God favored the abolitionists' cause. After the prayer, we sang several old, familiar hymns and I was surprised at the vigor of his singing voice. We knew all the hymns. "Abide With Me" is one of my favorites.

Just after the service came word from the settlers in Lawrence, about thirty-five miles south of us, asking the Plymouth Company to come to their assistance. They expected another attack from the proslavery party, which was rumored to include a growing group of proslavery border ruffians from Missouri called Kickapoo Rangers. Father is already a member of the Stowell Company,

Plymouth's militia, he volunteered to go, and he begun making preparations.

During the time that we have been in Plymouth, reports have come in almost daily that proslavery men were going to attack our settlement, all of which proved idle, as they have never come—at least to Plymouth. After each of these alarms, the cannon is brought from its hiding place and mounted in the fort, pointing east, but it is light enough that two or three men can mount it in any direction they choose.

At ten o'clock, we had all retired for the night; a Mr. Dunning rode in from Lexington (about ten miles east of us) with the news that we were to be attacked at two in the morning by 200 proslavery militiamen. General Lane also heard of this and returned to Plymouth late tonight to give orders.

There was a great deal of commotion as we set about doing what he told us. We moved all the wagons, now about thirty in number, to a high point on the bank of Pony Creek, placing them side by side in a kind of connected, circular breastwork.

General Lane posted guards on the east side of the creek and asked for any of the settlers who owned horses to volunteer as "pickets" to ride a few miles east of Plymouth and to conceal themselves in some woods there to warn us if the enemy came. He obtained more volunteers than he asked for.

In preparation for the attack, ten men were assigned to improve the fort to make it more defensible. They tore up the floor, which consisted of just rough planks. They dug the floor several feet deeper, piling the dirt outside, halfway up along the walls of the fort. Then they dug three trenches around the fort. When the enemy appears, they certainly will receive a warm reception. The men have also brought the little cannon inside the fort on two large wheels, though it can be lifted off and placed among the logs, pointed in whichever direction the enemy comes. This cannon and several barrels of powder, some small cannon balls and other "shot" just seem to have materialized since we arrived here two weeks ago. Every able-bodied man, Father included, has a Sharps rifle and has been trained to use it.

But our precautions were in vain. The alarm from the pickets never arrived. The proslavery people must have discovered just how numerous and how well armed and organized we are. The idea of keeping us all together in a compound is beginning to make sense, and is becoming less offensive to our notion of independence. Adda said that one of the Indiana men of our company told her he had served with General Lane in the Mexican War,[16] and Lane knows what he's doing.

This constant threat of violence from the pro slavery element is disturbing, but I suppose we should not be surprised by it. If a group of citizens can hold sway over two to three million human beings, using them as slaves, we shouldn't be surprised they would use force against us. We are so opposed to their practice that we've come to this new land, not just to listen to sermons and cluck our tongues, but to do something about it.

This morning the same old veteran who gave us that long educational lecture a few weeks ago, while our train waited for the Missouri River ferry, rode in today with two lieutenants. They gave military training to about forty-five men of the Plymouth Company, Father among them. The Company was marched in formation out on the prairie and did maneuvers according to shouted commands. The drill included some target practice: Our men had to shoot from concealed positions—and had to move constantly after each shot.

---

[16] General Lane volunteered July 1, 1846, serving until July 20, 1848, as a brigadier general. Source *Mr. Polk's Army*: The American Military Experience in the Mexican War by Richard B. Winders (College Station: Texas A&M University Press, 1997), p. 10. —*M.L.C*

When the target practice was over, Adda and I, along with some of the men's wives and older children, walked out to meet the men coming back from their drill. Alonzo Crawford, one of the armed guides who had escorted us into Plymouth and a member of the "Town Company," was walking back with Father and the old soldier.

We were south of the camp some distance and had spotted some wild turkeys south and west of us. When we met the company, Adda said, "Alonzo, let's shoot some turkeys for supper. If you can hit yours, you're invited to supper!" When we met Father, she asked to borrow his Sharps rifle and four cartridges.

The main party returned to camp; the three of us walked off in the direction of the turkeys. It was a beautiful late summer day, cloudless, with blue skies, a unique class of blue as only the prairie can provide.

In ten or fifteen minutes, we stopped and sat down in yellow prairie grass tall enough to conceal us. We were looking slightly downhill. Occasionally we could see a turkey's head. Soon a small flock meandered into view just above a fringe of grass ahead of us. Alonzo softly said, "Now we'll all be very quiet. When they come within about one hundred yards, we'll both shoot. When I say, 'Shoot', I'll pick a bird on the left. Adda, you take one of the right. Adda and I had both shot the Sharps with Father, so we were familiar with the gun's operation.

In a few minutes Alonzo whispered, "Ready, Adda?"
"Yes"
"Shoot."

The shots were so simultaneous it sounded like one "report." Two or three of the turkeys rose up and flew low and west a short distance downhill. The others lowered their heads and disappeared in the prairie grass.

"Adda, you get your bird?"

"You betcha! How about you?"

"We'll see," said Alonzo, as we ran down to where the dead birds would be if the shots were accurate. Adda ran off slightly to her right. In a minute there was a shout. Alonzo held up his bird by the feet and walked towards me.

Without saying a word, my little sister bent over and picked up a dead turkey just as the two of us approached her. Alonzo examined Adda's turkey, laughed—and slapped Adda on the back. "I don't believe it! You took his head off with that shot! ...and that was at least one hundred yards. For a 'lefty' I don't see how you did it." (Adda is left-handed.)

Well, that night, with the Old Veteran taking supper with us, the Van Curens, and the Strongs, Alonzo made sure that Adda's rifle prowess was the main topic of conversation. Except that, now, Adda's turkey was decapitated at 200 yards! She proudly returned three unused cartridges to Father.

It was late afternoon of August 23rd. Father and Mr. Van Curen, after two weeks of work, have nearly completed building our house. Though unfinished, it is ready enough for us to live in. Today both of our families moved in. Well, at least we have a roof over our heads, which is more than I can say for most of our neighbors.

Captain Paten of Walnut Creek (a new settlement six miles from here) rode into our camp to say that 200 proslavery men camped at Iowa Point over by the Missouri River are coming to attack Plymouth in the next few hours. Maybe that's the same 200 who didn't show up at the last alarm. We made all of our defense arrangements again. General Lane is still with us. I think he never combs his hair or takes a bath, yet he's been an officer in the U.S. Army and a U.S. senator from Indiana.

Captain Paten has given us something else to think about: Some in Plymouth suspect that Plymouth is actually on Indian

Trust Land, probably belonging to the Sacs and Fox tribe, who moved here from Missouri. But Captain Paten, who knows some of the Missourians, says that part of their desire to do us harm is because some of them had previously made claims to the land here.[17]

The Stowell Company, the "Town Company," was asked (or were ordered from Lawrence, I'm not sure) to march over there and to form up with other companies on the outskirts of Iowa Point, not necessarily to do battle but to present a show of force. They were to join with other Northern companies, such that they would number 200 to 250 men. The proslavery forces would, as they had in the past, realize that the Free Soil Companies were much larger than they had anticipated, which would cause them to retire rather than fight. This military strategy seemed to be the work of General Jim Lane and was aimed at putting a stop to these incessant threats.

In the weeks we have been here, we have learned from travelers passing through Plymouth about the skirmishes in the Territory before we got here. Moving into a new town takes some getting used to, and Plymouth had a lot to get used to. The amount of north-south traffic came as a surprise.

The travelers coming down from Nebraska usually talked about whether their trains had been harassed on the way, while the visitors from the South, who came through town night and day, were always more serious, anxious to get out of the Territory. They occasionally carried cargo that we felt we needn't know about, and rather frequently bore news of terrible atrocities committed earlier this year by proslavery settlers south of us along the Kansas River. Both the North and the South had by now accumulated

---

[17] Verified in *Fifty Million Acres - Conflict over Land Policy* by P. W. Gates: Press. —*M.L.C.*

armed, makeshift squads totaling upwards of 1,000 men on each side.

Companies on both sides are usually led by soldiers with Mexican War experience. General Lane's men are all armed with the Sharps rifle, much superior to the muzzleloader. Bitter skirmishes were weekly occurrences. A year ago, the Free State people voted to make Topeka the capital of the Territory.

The proslavery establishment had picked Lecompton. The Federal Government and the Army usually favored the Southern point of view. In fact, the Federal Government appropriated fifty thousand dollars to pay for the construction of the capitol building at Lecompton. This irritated the Free State leaders, who stuck with Topeka as their choice for their capital. In October they framed a constitution (banning slavery, of course). They continued to hold meetings in Topeka. The proslavery establishment continued to be offended.

In early March, about four months before our arrival, the Free State delegates, convening in Topeka, nominated Jim Lane and James Reeder as U. S. Senators for the Territory. John Brown, Jr., the oldest of John Brown's sons, attended that session. Charles Robinson had previously been elected by abolitionists as the Territory's Governor. All other governors were or would be presidential appointees. President Pierce warned the abolitionists that this political activity would all be viewed as treasonous, "an insurrection." Jim Lane, claiming broad contacts in Washington, D.C., was assigned to carry the draft of the Free State Constitution to Washington and to lobby for Free Soil rights under the Doctrine of Popular Sovereignty. He did but was inadequately persuasive. The Free State immigrants continued to pour into the New Territory. This spring Lawrence and vicinity was receiving an unprecedented number of immigrants from all over the North, not just New England.

On April 21st, Judge Cato opened a District court in the Pottawattamie area, Franklin County, twenty or thirty miles south of Lawrence and swore-in a proslavery grand jury. Local Free State citizens were excluded.

Judge Cato said he would levy taxes on Pottawattamie property, citing his authority as the "Bogus Laws." The local Free Staters led by five or six of John Brown's sons and relatives who all had claims in the area, including a town site, said forcefully that if their settlement couldn't be represented in the local government, they'd pay no taxes. Judge Cato declared these laws would be enforced even if it meant driving tax evaders from their claims. That was an intolerable threat to the sons of John Brown.

In May, the South responded to the population growth in Lawrence by recruiting a battalion of 400 soldiers, mostly from South Carolina, under the command of Colonel Jefferson Buford. They arrived May 2nd. Alabama had appropriated twenty-five thousand dollars for their immigrant cause: Colonel Buford matched it.

On May 9th, Judge Lecompte, Chief Territorial Judge, charged a grand jury to indict all members of the Topeka government for high treason. That included Lane, Governor Robinson, John Brown, Jr., and others. The indictment also applied to the editors of Lawrence's newspaper, the *Herald of Freedom*. Its editorials fueled abolitionist zeal in the North and animosity in the South.

Two days later, Federal Marshal Donaldson called for "all lawabiding citizens of the Territory" to meet in Lecompton, grouping together so that they could disband, by force if necessary, the Free State Legislature at Topeka. In response, companies of armed proslavery men assembled in Lecompton.

On the 4th of July, when we were still crossing Iowa, Colonel Sumner, who was in charge of the Army of the West, headquartered at Leavenworth led a company of 200 mounted dragoons with

200 more horseman in reserve, to Topeka and disrupted the Free State Convention. Five hundred were in attendance. This began the open use of federal troops to aggravate and block Free State political activity, proving to everybody that Popular Sovereignty, as previously proclaimed by Congress for the new territories, might be a sham. Free State Leaders, both in the Territory and back in the States, were offended and planned ways to take action. When Jefferson Davis, Secretary of War, heard that Colonel Sumner[18] in his speech to the Topeka convention had apologized for doing his duty, the colonel was immediately replaced with General Persifer Smith, who was rabid in his proslavery sentiments. Smith, a Democrat from Louisiana, was made a general by President Polk in the early days of the Mexican War, when Smith organized a regiment of mounted rifles and volunteered them. President Polk wanted his army to dominate the field of battle and planned to achieve this by placing regiments of mounted soldiers quickly at the forefront of his army. He was no doubt a student of Napoleon, who used mounted horsemen for this purpose, followed by foot soldiers—riflemen to finish the job and to hold the site against counter attack. In a controversial bill to Congress, the President proposed to raise ten regiments of mounted soldiers, and he wanted them (ideally) to be civilian volunteers from the various states. General Smith was one of the first to raise such a regiment, and he served with such distinction in the Mexican War, he earned the right to use the title "brevet" as part of his rank i.e., brevet brigadier general

Throughout the month of May, the threat to Lawrence worsened. On May 21st, a messenger came down to the Brown Clan in Pottawattamie with news that Colonel Buford's 400 men, along with other hostile Southern groups, were milling around

---

[18]   At that time the only Northern U.S. Army officer in Kansas.

Lawrence intending to destroy it. Free State leaders in Lawrence had a small militia but felt it would be inadequate for the town's defense. Governor Robinson, under indictment, had fled, so they had appealed to the new governor, Wilson Shannon, and to Colonel Sumner at Fort Leavenworth for protection.

The previous autumn, on his way to Kansas, John Brown had, like many of us immigrants, solicited arms and supplies en route. In Akron, Ohio, he was given several old but very serviceable sabers (artillery broad swords.) Somewhere on the road he acquired a grindstone. He was also given a very large supply of Bowie knives, and he ordered more! In August or September, after we arrived in Plymouth, the Old Captain, one of our nicknames for John Brown, was in our area helping with fortification and took a few meals with us in Plymouth. He was quiet and reserved. I think he was not well. He preferred to sleep away from our settlement. Before he left, he issued one Bowie knife each to Mrs. Van Curen, my sister, and me, which out of politeness, we accepted but we really didn't know what we were supposed to do with them. Although we had heard of his abolitionist zeal, we had no idea then what a leader of men he was and/or how famous he was to become both to the North and the South. Brown had previously distributed the Ohio broadswords to his company of Pottawattamie Rifles. Of course, they also had Sharps rifles. Deciding that they would be greatly outnumbered if they marched on Lawrence, they waited south of it for news of reinforcements.

Brown later was on the horns of a dilemma. If he rode up to help defend Lawrence, who would protect the Brown families in Pottawattamie against the local proslavery militia?

The next day, the 22nd, another messenger confirmed that the Lawrence Free State men had determined that it would be futile to mount a military defense, and would rely on the U.S. Cavalry from Fort Leavenworth for protection. A second messenger arrived, who told John Brown that before the U. S. Army got to Lawrence, the pro slavery militia had sacked the town.

A third messenger came that day to Pottawattamie, saying that the U.S. troops had arrived and had taken charge of Lawrence, now in shambles, but were continuing to allow proslavery patrols to remain on the roads around Lawrence.

All of this news greatly angered John Brown and was extremely frustrating to him and his company. He and his sons felt they must do something. Lawrence must be revenged.

On the night of May 23rd, one day after Lawrence was burned John Brown declared he would "sweep" Pottawattamie Creek clear of all proslavery elements. Before the night was over, Brown and a small party of ten or so men, using their broadswords honed to razor sharpness, savagely killed five or six proslavery settlers, all of them known to be rabid anti abolitionists, loudmouths who themselves had threatened or used force on the Free Staters in Franklin County and the Browns in Pottawattamie.

Brown received news on May 24th that Governor Robinson had been captured (near Kansas City, I'm told.) Brown reasoned that the proslavery party would use the Santa Fe Trail to return Robinson to Lecompton, the official capital. Brown and his men waited near the trail, prepared to attempt rescue. They waited in vain. The party took a different route. Robinson was jailed in the prison at Lecompton a few days later. During at least one of these (several) incarcerations, Sarah, the Governor's faithful, Yankee abolitionist wife, chose to be with her husband, even in jail. Of course, this quickly made the eastern newspapers.

The fierceness of John Brown's retaliations, using swords to mutilate his victims,[19] struck fear into the hearts of the local

---

[19] Affidavits of the victims' relatives and relatives and testimony that made it to Congress and the White House attest to the ferocity of his attacks.— M.L.C.

proslavery citizens. The absolute certainty of Brown's revenge gave him the image of being invincible. He had uncanny success in avoiding capture and concealing his whereabouts, even though there was a price on his head. U.S. Army Scouts, pursuing a rumor that Brown was in Topeka, would learn that he and a son were in Boston giving rousing, money-raising speeches against slavery to sympathetic audiences, people like Emerson and Thoreau. Two weeks later, he would be seen back in the Territory. He had assumed mythic proportions—on both sides.

There were, however, many Free State people who thought the Browns were too violent in executing their anti slavery beliefs.

In June, in retaliation for the "Massacre" at Pottawattamie, H. Clay Pate, a proslavery Captain of the Missouri Militia and a U.S. Marshal no less, was assigned to take a company of his best men and capture Brown.

This is the same "Captain" Pate, simply a self-appointed Border Ruffian from Missouri, who a few weeks earlier had captured John Brown, Jr., and Jason, another of Brown's sons. Those two took no part in the Pottawattamie killings but were, with other men who did take part, turned over to U.S. troops, whose leader was Captain Woods. The Browns were marched, chained together, back to Osawatomie. All of the men were kept prisoner at Fort Leavenworth.

While this march was under way, the Brown's crops and homes in Brownsville were burned and looted by proslavery forces and their livestock stolen.

Captain Pate remained in the area looking for the Old Captain.

John Brown got wind of Pate's plans. As Pate and his company came into a valley in Franklin County, Brown's Pottawattamie Rifles were in place. There was a skirmish. Brown's soldiers had Pate's party surrounded. Four of Pate's Missourians were killed.

Pate and his militia attempted to flee, but Brown had so cleverly deployed his men that the militia's exit was blocked. Some of Pate's men did escape; some were wounded. Fearing that Brown had at least one hundred men, Pate and the balance of his company surrendered. When the dust settled, it was revealed that the whole of Brown's group consisted of only nine "soldiers." Fifty of Pate's company, including Pate himself, surrendered to nine men! That debacle for Pate only added to Brown's stature.

That wasn't the end of Pate's humiliation: U.S. troops rode in and rescued him just moments after he had surrendered to Brown. For some strange reason the Federal troops did not arrest John Brown. He disappeared, resurfacing later to organize a local station in the Underground Railroad. By June and July John Brown's victory over Captain Pate was in all the Eastern newspapers. Northern papers praised his courage and heroism. Southern papers condemned his brutality. But John Brown was now a national figure, an abolitionist hero, nine feet tall.

This incident was not the first encounter between these two political and military antagonists. In May, John Brown had rescued Reverend Moore, who had also been captured by Captain Pate. We learned this from Reverend Moore himself last Sunday, after the sermon he gave at the fort. The rescue had added one more embarrassment to Captain Pate's reputation and one more star on John Brown's epaulets

These continuing skirmishes in the Territory confirmed what the Northern leaders suspected. Discounting the Indians, the Northern immigrants had two enemies in Kansas: hostile groups of well-armed proslavery civilians and the U.S. Government. Administratively, until 1858, the Territory was proslavery. The Northerners found a very hostile environment—proslavery courts, proslavery postmasters, land offices discriminating against Free Soil Land claims, Jim Lane and his lieutenants, including

John Brown, could handle the proslavery militia, but to oppose the Federal Government and the U.S. Army was daunting, and probably foolhardy. When the troops closed down the Free State Convention in Topeka, the North lost that contest. When U.S. troops failed to defend Lawrence, the North lost that contest, too. And the North lost also whenever a proslavery judge refused to indict a proslavery citizen who had committed a criminal act. These were bitter pills to swallow. But some bitter pills make the patient get better. All of these factors were causing the North to invent new strategies such as using wagon trains and land routes to get around the Missouri River blockade, and to increase immigration and its financial support.

Throughout the summer, the skirmishes had accelerated in the Territory's eastern area. By August Jim Lane had four or five volunteer companies in the field, including Father's Plymouth Company. The proslavery militias had not only blocked the Missouri, they had also blocked the Kansas River, preventing supplies getting to Lawrence and Topeka by that river. Governor Robinson and other Free State Leaders had been subpoenaed and jailed at Lecompton. Old John Brown was soliciting help and agitating for an armed rescue of those prisoners and of his sons, Jason and John Brown, Jr., who were jailed at Leavenworth.

General Jim Lane was organizing his Free State men to retaliate against the border ruffians by systematically and swiftly raiding clots of proslavery militia in Franklin, Fort Sanders, Fort Titus and New Georgia; those were tactics he and his lieutenants had learned in the Mexican War. John Brown resurfaced in some of these battles with a new company, called the Kansas Regulars. The tide was finally turning in favor of us Free Staters.

Meanwhile 450 Southerners under Senator Atchison were forming to attack Osawatomie, Brown's abolitionist settlement, and other communities nearby. John Brown and his company were in Franklin County but were greatly outnumbered by Atchison's forces. The Southerners burned down Osawatomie. John Brown saw it all, but realized he was powerless to stop it, which greatly disturbed him.

"General" Jim Lane and John Brown.
Both were great organizers against the proslavery
establishment and were influential in bringing
the territory into the States, free of slavery.

5.

THE BATTLE OF HICKORY POINT,
August 24th to September 15th 1856

FATHER BECOMES A P.O.W

Since our arrival two weeks ago, rumors of Plymouth being attacked have increased. We have responded with a flurry of planning. The Town Company has been in training under the command of a recent arrival and protégé of General Jim Lane, Colonel Harvey. He is twenty-nine years old and was an officer of some distinction in the Mexican War. (Of course, it is common knowledge that General Lane led two regiments in the Mexican War.) Colonel Harvey is from an Illinois family of staunch abolitionists and has a wife and one child there. So, those of us who know his background hold this gentleman in high regard. Colonel Harvey was a leader of sixty or so Illinois settlers that came into the Territory about the same time our party came in.

Shalor Eldridge, whom we call Colonel Eldridge, is a man of some importance in our settlement. I often see him in conference with General Lane and Colonel Harvey, and with John Brown when he is here.

The early evening of August 24th was warm, bordering on stifling. Father said he wanted to have a little family chat, away from the Van Curens. It was still twilight as we walked over toward Pony Creek. Just as we found a grassy plot above the stream, several doves, or perhaps they were quail, took flight noisily.

We hardly had sat down when Adda asked, "Father, why did you volunteer? Others, younger than you, have not." It was evident by his long pause that the question took him by surprise. I thought it was somewhat forward of my sister to ask such a personal question. I suppose she was concerned about the two of us while he was off fighting.

Finally he responded, "I think it's my duty. On the way out here I certainly didn't imagine I'd ever be involved in fighting. But, now that we are here, I realize how well organized and established the local Southerners are. Of course they've had a two-year jump on us. These constant threats, the fighting down near Lawrence, are all measures of how deeply they resent us. They are using the same tactics they use to control their slaves to exert control over us by driving us out. It's interesting; I don't think this territorial fighting is over slavery. It's about our being here. A lesson we've all learned from Lawrence is that the threats are real and they won't go away. We simply must get organized to defend ourselves; General Lane and old John Brown have convinced us that we can't just wait around for them to attack us. We must get into the field and fight. That's why I volunteered."

This explanation was followed by an apology for bringing us out into such dangerous conditions. I spoke up, "Well, you certainly had no idea what things would be like out here." He seemed relieved by my sympathy, then he gave us some advice and precautions. "Don't take any sundown walks alone out on the prairie, and be particularly careful about what you write. It could fall into the wrong hands and be used against us." I suppose this was Father's polite way of warning me about my journal entries. In the long run, our cause would prevail, he said, but before it did, we would experience more danger. "The U.S. Army should be as helpful to us as to the proslavers, but we know they're not and I suspect their spies are everywhere. I want you two girls to be alert. I won't discourage your journal writing, but keep your written accounts in notes, then spend as much time concealing them as in the writing. Later you can retrieve them and include them in your journals. And keep your opinions to yourselves. I just learned that there is a reward for both John Brown and General Lane. If we know their whereabouts and are questioned, we could be charged with concealment."

By the time we'd finished talking, it was dark. The moon was up but low in the eastern sky. As we walked back, we could see campfires and hear some singing in our settlement.

August 25th. Today we have had more rumors of imminent attack. Father's Company is setting off to show the proslavery group that we outnumber them considerably. Our volunteers are going to Iowa Point, but Father says to keep it secret.

Father told us last night that his Plymouth Company will leave today, but he might go separately with our wagon. Our men have had a smattering of training, consisting mostly of drilling out on the prairie with their Sharps rifles. This training includes extensive target practice. A week or so ago Father displayed three or four targets with little holes in the center. He said he made the shots at one hundred and 200 yards and seemed quite pleased with himself.

Orders have come again today from General Lane's secret headquarters for the Plymouth Town Company to assemble but to travel toward Lawrence.

Father is the only one among the volunteers to own a horse team and wagon. Some had sold their horses or traded them for oxen. Of course, several of the other settlers who do own horses have chosen not to volunteer. Father has been assigned, with one or two others, to go ahead of the Plymouth troops to carry as much extra supplies food, bedding and shovels, etc. as our wagon can manage. And I suppose he has extra rifles and ammunition. All our men have Sharps rifles by now.

By watching Father and others work this rifle, I can see how the new cartridge and the gun's mechanism allows the Sharps rifle to fire and be reloaded ten times while a muzzle loader is firing and reloading once. This rifle's new, one-piece ammunition; the powder, the ball-shaped bullet, and the primer, or "cap," are all arranged in one little "waxy" cylinder, about the size of my middle finger. The rotation of a long lever hanging from the gun's underside quickly opens the breech, allowing the one-piece cartridge to be inserted. The same lever closes the breech, a hammer is then cocked, and the gun is ready to fire. Father says these guns are manufactured in Connecticut, purchased and distributed by abolitionists. None of the Southern soldiers have these rifles, and that fact makes them cautious about engaging a group of Northerners of equal size, armed with the Sharps. Because the Sharps uses up ammunition ten times faster than the muzzle loaders, the U.S. Army which tested the gun in the Mexican War, has chosen to use the older but more economical muzzle loaders.

Another benefit of the Sharps rifle is that it is shorter, lighter and in generally more accurate, though I understand that some muzzleloaders are equally accurate. It all depends on which factory makes the barrels.

Late this afternoon, just sixteen days after we arrived in the New Territory and only forty-two days after we left Detroit, Father, along with two others, left our settlement with our team and wagon heading in a southeasterly direction out of Plymouth.

If Father had orders to meet other troops, he didn't share that information with us. And we were not at all comforted to see them go off alone, knowing that if they were intercepted by Southerners out there on the prairie, they could expect little mercy. (We discovered later that Father had simply waited a little south of here for the rest of the men from Plymouth to get there where they joined up with the larger Lexington Company.)

Father left considerably ahead of the Plymouth Company, which was on foot. His final good-byes to Adda and me were rather casual, saying he'd be back in a few days and that we should be "good girls" while he was gone. It was understood that we would stay in our house, which we shared with the Van Curens, and we would also be watched over by our friends, the Strongs. With the Plymouth Company gone, there were only about eighteen men left.

Although Adda and I are proud that Father is willing to fight against the proslavery militia, and we know he is good with the rifle, we also know that Father is really not a soldier. After all, he is thirty-eight years old and a father of two almost grown daughters. He has never served in the Army, unlike our Grandfather Charles, Father's father, who had five years of military experience. Grandpa fought the British during the Revolution and the Indians after it. I have a letter from him to a newspaper in Onondaga County, New York, describing his military experience when he was a very young man:

A hundred years before the United States was the United States, there was the Massachusetts Colony. I was a citizen of Massachusetts. I was also supposed to be a loyal subject of King George III. Times were very confused and I was just a youngster but in my group we all thought that George III was crazy. In my group we called him a lunatic. Massachusetts had a charter, but they didn't have a constitution. They were afraid to draft one for fear it would offend the King and when they did draft one and put it to a vote of Massachusetts's citizens, town by town, more towns rejected it than passed it. But by then (1778) we were at war with the Red Coats and it was not going well. The British had conquered Maine. Some of my own [Massachusetts] people out in the West along the river voted to secede from Massachusetts to remain loyal to the Crown.

That's when I joined James Wesson's ninth Regiment and served under three different captains for three years until we won the War. Then I re-enlisted with John Halbert, the Indian Fighter, to fight Indians for two years. When I mustered out, I married his daughter, Mary. People we knew in Massachusetts and New England, mostly those with businesses trading with England, wanted no part of a rebellion. They wanted to remain loyal to King George. The wealthy ones closed up their houses and sailed to England. Others fled to parts of Canada. Thousands of men from New England simply joined the British Army by joining groups already stationed in New England. This was both a testament to their loyalty and a statement of protest to the rebellion. New York provided more troops for George III than they did for George Washington and they should be ashamed!

I suppose Grandpa was being interviewed about his Revolutionary War experiences years after the war.

Father had considered joining the military during the Mexican War, but when the authorities discovered he was a Whig and not a Democrat, they told him the Army had all the soldiers it needed. Father and most of the other Town Company men are simply amateurs. May God protect them.

This entry was made much later than August 25, 1856, and not in Plymouth but from notes my sister and I wrote and hid while there. Considerably after August 25th, which was the day Father left us to join General Lane's militia, I discovered that on this date Governor Woodson, headquartered in Lecompton (the Territorial Capital) and the Federal appointee as the Territory's acting Governor, published a proclamation[20] that the Territory was in a state of open insurrection and rebellion.

The newspaper article that reported this said it had come to the Governor's attention that the Territory was "infested with large bodies of armed men, many of whom have just arrived from the States, supplied with munitions and implements of war."

I wonder, as I put this in the Journal, if the good Governor had in mind the proslavery people *or us.*

Several weeks after Father and the Plymouth Company left for Iowa Point, two of them returned. One of them, a Mr. Boyce, a very young man, said he was wounded, although he seemed well enough to stand around giving us a long-winded explanation of what happened to him. All of us, including Mrs. Boyce, were excited and impatience for news. These two men were the first of Plymouth Company to return.

Mr. Boyce said the two of them had been scouts under Colonel Harvey. Yes, he told Adda and me, he knew Father. He said our company had been involved in four or five battles, he said, usually on our own but sometimes with General Lane's other companies. He speculated that General Lane's various companies had fought as many as ten battles: "Won 'em all." And he began to regale us about the various battles. Obviously he was a big talker.

Adda interrupted him to ask where our Plymouth Company was fighting now. "They aren't fighting," he said, "they have been captured and put in a war camp someplace on the Kaw River."

"Captured? Captured by whom? All of them? You were in that company. How did you escape?"

---

[20] The text of Woodson's complete proclamation is available in Kansas State Historical Society Transactions Volume 3, page 325. M.L.C.

He answered her that they fought a battle at Hickory Point that had lasted only part of two days. "Our company had gotten there the second day, which was Sunday the 14th. The two of us hadn't been caught because, after the battle, Colonel Harvey ordered us to go on a scouting mission. We were to locate an enemy camp rumored to be near Osawkee, to determineite size, and see if had cannons or other arms and report back. About nightfall we came to a wrecked shanty owned by a Free Soil family. They said a small company of South Carolinians, who were camped in a creek bed a little west of them, were continually stealing their chickens and tried to steal their horses. The missus gave us buttermilk and baked corn pones for supper. That night we snuck up on their camp.

"There were twenty-five or thirty Southerner Pukes, but there were no horses and no cannons that we could see. These men were real hell-raisers—even after midnight they were arguing and yelling and drinking. We weren't sure this was the camp that Colonel Harvey had in mind. About 2 a.m. we crawled away and headed back to report to Colonel Harvey. By dawn, when we had gotten back to the place where we thought we had left our company, we couldn't find them. We realized that either they were gone or we were lost. I don't think we were lost because we found signs of the camp. There were ashes from fresh fires, a few tent stakes left in the ground, and other signs that led us to believe that they had been there but had left.

"We couldn't stay out on the open prairie. We knew the U.S. Army patrols might get us. Between dawn and midday we saw and managed to avoid three mounted patrols. We didn't even know for sure where we were, since Colonel Harvey had the maps, and he was gone. We walked a little east looking for cover."

The Battle of Hickory Point

Adda piped up, "Mr. Boyce, could you spare us these little side adventures and just tell us if you ever got back with any of General Lane's companies . . . and are they safe?"

Mrs. Boyce glowered at her!

"I'm getting to that," said Mr. Boyce. "Toward sundown we were hiding in a little gully when a small U.S. mounted patrol surprised us and took us captive. We were questioned rather roughly by a lieutenant. I guess he assumed from our Northern accents that we were from Lawrence. We told him we were just settlers looking for claims. He said we looked to him like a couple of Jim Lane's Jay Hawkers. That was the first time I'd heard men from our side called Jay Hawkers. We just kept quiet. Then he asked us if we were sure we hadn't been involved in the fighting at Hickory Point the day before. We said we had never heard of it. The lieutenant said that two of Lane's companies had shot up Hickory Point and had been captured Sunday night and were being marched to a war camp down on the Kaw River. He said those boys were in serious trouble because they had killed some people at Hickory Point."

Adda interrupted him again. "You keep saying 'captured.' If we were winning all the battles, who captured the Plymouth Company?"

"The U.S. Army! That's who! Now may I continue?"

"Well, if the Army patrol released you two, why wouldn't the Army release all the others?"

"I only know what that patrol told us two days ago that our Plymouth men are in a prison camp."

He continued with his personal adventure.

"They were rough on us and very suspicious, but they released us. They refused us food and told us we'd better get out of the Territory, telling us to follow Stranger Creek north, to look for claims in Nebraska Territory. That's how we found out where we were. They have our names, but they don't know we're from Plymouth."

"Just a minute. Do you know who's running that prisoners camp, Mr. Boyce?"

"Of course, not. We were never there."

Adda asked, "Mr. Boyce, where's your rifle?" Mr. Boyce didn't answer, and Mrs. Boyce shot Adda a nasty look and pulled her husband away. "Come, dear, let me attend to your shoulder." I don't think there was anything wrong with his shoulder.

Adda and I wondered if Mr. Boyce knew what he was talking about. We quietly speculated that these two might have deserted. Why wouldn't the Army release Father and the rest of the Company just like it had released Mr. Boyce and Mr. "What's his name?" When they were caught, why didn't they put Mr. Boyce and the other scout in the war camp? I guess we were resentful that these two were free and Father was in prison.

On September 15th, a little after breakfast, a small party rode into Plymouth from the south, perhaps Lawrence. We found out Governor Robinson was in this party. He said that he had come up here to meet with leaders of a large, southbound wagon train due in Plymouth today. One of John Brown's sons was also with this party. He was recognized by one of our citizens, but Brown asked to be called by an assumed name. Governor Robinson reported that another very large and threatening contingent of militia was gathering in the outskirts of Lawrence. The southbound train due in Plymouth was intended to reinforce General Lane's Army, and to help replace the companies that had been captured. Although the Governor had earlier been arrested, incarcerated, then released from the war camp in Lecompton, word was that he remained "on indictment."

While the Governor and his small party waited for the southbound train to arrive, they inspected the progress of our fort,

THE BATTLE OF HICKORY POINT

which is now six or seven feet high, but still has no roof. The logs are very large and their placement has been hard to manage. After all there's only about fifteen or so able-bodied men remaining in Plymouth.

As the Governor's party was inspecting the fort, a U.S. marshal rode into Plymouth, escorted by a small mounted U.S. Army scouting party. The marshal walked over to the fort, waved a piece of paper under Governor Robinson's nose, and arrested him and two of his companions, including Mr. Brown. The Army patrol, together with the Governor's party, quickly rode off south to Lecompton (we later learned). All of this didn't take fifteen minutes. Very few of us actually saw it. I saw them inspect the fort, but I didn't see the arrest or see them ride off.

Shortly afterwards two unidentified horsemen rode in from the north. They didn't dismount, didn't ask questions, but looked around carefully, then returned in the direction they had come from very mysteriously. Then in less than fifteen minutes the lead wagons of what turned out to be a very large train, consisting altogether of twenty-eight wagons and 300 people, mostly men, began pulling into Plymouth. An Englishman, Mr. James Redpath,[21] was in charge of this group. We soon learned that they had left Nebraska City three days ago. Although they were anxious to get down to Topeka, then on to Lawrence, they had to wait here and take on arms. We heard that General Lane was in this outfit. Adda and I decided to find the General and ask him directly about the Hickory Point battle, Father's safety, living conditions in the prison, and where it was. It was a fine fall day and we scurried among the men, looking for General Lane. We

---

[21] The following year, 1857, I heard more about this gentleman. James Redpath, a printer and publisher and later the founder of the *Crusader of Freedom*, joined a group of Congregationalists and formed a church in Wabaunsee, K.T., referred to as "Beecher's Bible and Rifle Church"

were still looking when Amy Pyle, Jesse Pyle's little girl found us and said Mrs. Van Curen needed us badly. When we got back to our house, it was full of hungry and jovial new arrivals.

About mid afternoon, ten men, driving three awaited freight wagons, each pulled by two horses, arrived apparently on schedule. Mr. Redpath quickly sent out mounted sentries and half of his people were posted as armed guards on all four points of the compass to watch for Army patrols.

Things got very tense and businesslike. Plymouth became very alert. At our house, Mrs. Van Curen, Adda and I and continued feeding as many of the "Redpath boys" as could get in. Some of them remarked that they really didn't know what they would do if the U.S. Army showed up in force and inspected the supply train.

The supply train was led by three very young men: Samuel Tappan, Alfred Pierce and Preston Plumb, who was the leader. He was also the youngest. Mr. Samuel Tappan, who was from Massachusetts, had joined Mr. Plumb in Iowa City, where he was waiting for a cannon that he had "acquired" in Chicago and had it forwarded by train, along with other supplies. The men called Mr. Tappan Brigadier (a commission conferred by General Lane). I learned later from Mr. Shea that Mr. Tappan had expected to meet Governor Robinson here and was disappointed to learn that though the Governor had been here earlier, he had been arrested again. The third leader, Mr. Alfred Pierce from New York State, was twenty-one years old. He also joined the other two in Iowa City. The supplies had been paid for by the National Kansas Central Committee, the same committee that supplied our route map in Iowa earlier this summer. An Iowa committee provided these boys with six horses and three wagons. This was Mr. Plumb's second trip to Kansas.

The Battle of Hickory Point

Although everybody was willing to pitch in to transfer this cargo[22] to Mr. Redpath's wagons, the job certainly didn't require all 300 of his men. Those who weren't occupied continued to line up at our place to eat. Occasionally we feed small trains coming through, but we weren't prepared to feed such a large one. We were afraid they'd quickly deplete our larder, but that wasn't the case. They were very spontaneous and generous in bringing in their own provisions, and left us with a couple of fat Iowa hams, a dozen slabs of bacon and several kegs containing flour, cornmeal and oatmeal. They simply wanted to be social. Of course, Mrs. Van Curen was overjoyed to have the extra supplies. It was from feeding these young men for several hours that we learned the details about the afternoon supply train and the Redpath Company.

Just as soon as the southbound wagons were packed, a bugle blew and the Redpath party quickly assembled. The boys, who we were feeding, jumped up, grabbed food off the table and rushed out. Mr. Plumb's boys remained. There was some emotion in Plymouth at seeing these boys leave.

As the lead wagons pulled out, southbound, Mr. Plumb came into our cabin, smiled at me, and was humorously conspicuous about showing us he was barefooted. He did this in such a sociable way that his being barefoot was not uncouth but rather amusing. He told Adda that he and Alfred Pierce had walked across all of Iowa barefoot. In Nebraska City a friendly outfitter had given

---

[22] While the cargo was being transferred the men engaged in considerable celebration, with much backslapping and congratulations, complimenting Mr. Plumb and his associates. Later that night Preston Plumb told us what his cargo was: 250 Sharps rifles (crated ten to a box), smaller wooden boxes containing 20,000 cartridges for the rifles, 250 Navy Colt Repeaters with ammunition, one cannon that shot a twelve pound ball, and two dozen kegs of powder. They had enough powder to assign four kegs to us here in Plymouth. Needless to say, we hid these notes.

him a pair of boots. Because they had high heels and "pointy" toes those boots hurt his feet.

His party of ten stayed in Plymouth that night and we had some fine "politicking." He's all fired up about electing Fremont for President: "We need a new political party to deal with the problem of slavery. The Whig Party, which has been our only organized opposition to the Democrats, is dead—an' is looking for an undertaker." My, he exudes such confidence. Only a man with tremendous poise could walk barefoot into a house full of women and provoke no disdain or giggles. Mr. Plumb thinks the new Republican Party will take a firm stand to oppose slavery and will send Mr. Fremont to the White House. Mr. Plumb maintains that for abolition to have political force, it needs to be adopted by a national party. The Whigs lost a golden opportunity, he believes, by not endorsing it.

I don't think Mr. Plumb is more than two years older than myself, and he's very handsome and very well informed.

After supper, Mrs. Van Curen served a nice tea, which is unusual for her, but I suspect that like the other visitors (mostly women) at our house tonight she too is smitten by Preston Plumb. In one of his (many) "speeches" he said, "Ladies, I am here to tell you that the summer of 1856 has been a very disappointing season for the proslavery element. Our freight wagons are now linked together across the country, stretching from the New England states down through all the capital cities of the Midwest. By closing the River to us, they did us a big favor. Don't believe the Whigs when they say that the, south can be held in the Union if Kansas comes in Slave. That's just nonsense." It was after midnight when we went to bed.

The next morning after breakfast, on the 16th, Mr. Plumb and his party left us and headed south. We were really sorry to see these fellows leave. They had brought some stimulating discussions.

The Battle of Hickory Point

The two wagon trains meeting in Plymouth without intervention from U.S. Army patrols was the most satisfying event since our arrival a few weeks ago.

A few days after the Redpath and Plumb outfits met here, very early one morning, two young men came into Plymouth from the south, inquiring of Mr. Stewart's daughters. They were Frank O. Robinson and Jacob Eastman Chase. We learned quickly that they had come out together to Kansas Territory from Massachusetts in the Stowell Company,[23] which founded the settlement of Lexington. On the trail last summer we had met a few Massachusetts people, but not these two gentlemen. After they introduced themselves, they gave us news about Father. Their Lexington Company, they said, had joined up with the Plymouth Company south of Lexington, August 25th and quickly became engaged in several small short battles all south of here.

On the evening of September 14th, after their skirmish at Hickory Point, four of General Lane's companies were camped out on the prairie with each company separated some distance from the other. Most of the Plymouth Company and two squads of the Lexington Company were captured by troops of the U.S. Army during the night. Since both of them were only eighteen, they had been released from the prison camp, they said, shortly after their capture. Adda and I secretly wondered whether they had escaped. Father had asked these boys on their way through Plymouth to give us a report on Lecompton. Father was safe and well, as were, for that matter, almost all of the other captured Plymouth men, except for three who had leg injuries and one who had been shot through the lungs. Although most of the volunteers

---

[23] Jacob Chase is listed together with Charles Samuel Stewart as being member of the Stowell party, both arriving in the territory on August 7th 1856, according to the records of Kansas State Historical Society, Vol. 8, page 314. Shalor Eldridge's book *Early Days in Kansas*, page 84.

were unharmed, they were miserably uncomfortable at the prison camp and worried about spending the winter there. "Needless to say," added Mr. Chase, the guards are rabid proslavery people. The warden of the prison is Sheriff Johns, the same Sheriff Jones who was responsible for destroying Lawrence last May."

"Mr. Boyce told us that the Plymouth Company was involved in four or five other battles before Hickory Point," Adda said.

"Yes," said Frank Robinson, "they had a battle at Fort Titus, which is between Lecompton and Lawrence, and I believe your father's company also attacked Fort Saunders, which is due south of Lecompton." The Missourians, he explained, had built this group of fortifications to protect and supply the border ruffians who were raiding Free Soil claims and settlements in the eastern section of the Territory. "At Lecompton, we learned that General Lane and his colonels had battle plans for our four companies to attack and destroy all these forts, but while we were on the march doing that, our companies got into some battles we hadn't planned for."

"When we first got here we had threats all the time from Iowa Point, which is east of here, near the river," said Adda. "Do you suppose the Missourians have one of those forts there?" Mr. Chase said he didn't know, but he added that we all knew it was part of the plan to work our way up to Iowa Point to fight them to eliminate the constant threat to Lexington, Plymouth and our other settlements up here near the northern border."

"Well, it must have worked because for the past weeks we haven't received any more threats," said Adda.

Mr. Chase told us about other battles General Lane's companies had recently won. In early August one of Lane's companies attacked a fort at New Georgia. That same week another company captured a proslavery fort at Osawatomie. Then in mid-August they destroyed a fortification at Franklin, a little south of Lawrence."

"While we were at Lecompton," he said, "we learned that Senator Atchison, with a force of 3,000 called the Army of Law and Order, was preparing to attack Lawrence again. Though General Lane had his companies spread out mostly in Jefferson and Douglas Counties, he and John Brown kept several companies stationed closely around Lawrence. Most of our companies operated independently, attacking the Southerners wherever they could. The Missourians had to defend themselves in ten to fifteen separate places and were getting beaten so badly that I think they abandoned the idea of hitting Lawrence again.

"During the first two weeks of this month there was simply no stopping us. Even though the U.S. Army did capture a hundred of us, the Lexington and Plymouth companies are only a small part of General Lane's forces. He must have upwards of 2,000 men remaining, including those around Lawrence—still active, full of ammunition and full of fight."

I asked the boys if they thought this would be the end of the fighting between the Southerners and us. Yes, they thought so for two reasons: Lane was very well-organized with company commanders seasoned in the Mexican war, with new recruits coming in weekly plus John Brown's company, which had the strength of ten.

The second reason is more important. Governor Geary, President Pierce's new appointment, is also making it clear that the Army would now be used to enforce order on the Southerners too and that he would now use the federal troops to keep the two sides from fighting.

Mr. Chase told us that a couple of days before the Plymouth company got to Hickory Point, Father's company had engaged a group of border ruffians from South Carolina at a little settlement north of the Kansas River ten miles east of Oskaloosa and maybe twenty miles north of Lawrence. The night before, Colonel Harvey had received reports from several Free Soil people that some ruffians from South Carolina were committing outrages in that area. "By 3 o'clock in the morning his scouts had located them, and the Plymouth Company surrounded them. The ruffians were so taken by surprise that they surrendered. The Plymouth Company seized sixty rifles, two wagons and several horses in that fracas."

He told us, "On that same day General Lane had taken three of his other companies, headed for Iowa Point but changed course when he heard that another Missouri raiding party had burned buildings owned by three Free Soil families in Grasshopper Falls, north of Topeka. On the way there, General Lane confronted another proslaver group in Osawakie. During that skirmish he learned of the concentration of another raiding party south of him at Hickory Point.[24]

"Hickory Point," he said, "is in Jefferson County about twenty miles north of Lawrence, on the road from Fort Leavenworth.

"In the meantime Governor Geary arrived that very day in the Territory. That was quite a reception for him." Mr. Chase told us that the governor, who is only thirty-seven, has already lived a very full life. He is a civil engineer and also has training in law. Some of our officers knew that he was made Commandant of Mexico City after its capture.

"He had then gone to San Francisco and become its first mayor. President Pierce had appointed him to replace Governor

---

[24] There is another Hickory Point ten miles south of Lawrence on the Old Santa Fe Trail, near Prairie City near where John Brown's family had its claim—M.L.C.

The Battle of Hickory Point

Shannon. Governor Geary had arrived in the Territory on September 11th.

"On his way to Lecompton he received reports that there were as many as ten to twelve parties on both sides engaged in battles near Topeka and Lawrence. So the Governor issued a proclamation ordering all armed bands to disperse. With all the confusion of the various battles and continually moving their troops I don't see how General Lane or Colonel Harvey could have heard about the Governor's proclamation while they were in the field.

"General Lane," he said, "arrived at Hickory Point, a heavily fortified proslavery settlement on September 13th. Captain H. A. Lowe, who owned Hickory Point, had thirty men defending it. They were reinforced by another thirty or so South Carolinians under a Captain John Robertson. Hickory Point consisted of three log houses, a store, a hotel and a blacksmith's shop. Some Free State residents had already been driven off their places.

"At the end of the first day's fighting General Lane could see our troops were just exchanging lead with them and hadn't been able to dislodge them from the buildings, so he sent word to Lawrence, twenty miles away, for reinforcements, and included a request for Old Sacramento. This was a brass cannon that earlier had been buried to conceal it, then resurrected and nicknamed by the troops, 'Old Sacramento'. We had arrived about 10 a.m. Sunday morning, the second day of the battle. Colonel Harvey was put in charge of the Plymouth and Lexington Companies, with orders to continue attacking Hickory Point. Just as we got there the reinforcements from Lawrence, including 'Old Sacramento,' which was under the command of Thomas Bickerton[25] arrived. General Lane left Colonel Harvey in command of these two com-

---

25   Thomas Bickerton from Portland, Maine, was a captain of artillery in Lane's army. He was also captured (September 14th) with most of the Plymouth and Lexington companies. —M.L.C.

panies, which consisted of 250 or so of us and departed with two other companies for Iowa Point.

"We continued to fight at Hickory Point the rest of that day. Colonel Harvey ordered some of us to surround the three log buildings, holding others in reserve. Frank and I and your father were among those he assigned to attack the South Carolinians. Captain Bickerton placed the cannon about 200 yards from the front of the blacksmith's shop but didn't fire immediately. Captain Robertson and about fifteen to twenty of his men were inside the blacksmith shop and some of Captain Lowe's men were in the hotel. Many of the other proslavery men had fled the day.

"Our Lexington Company was firing from a cornfield about a hundred or so yards from the three buildings, facing one side of the blacksmith shop. Colonel Harvey also had a small company of maybe twenty-five Mounted Rifles, who were firing at the buildings from various locations.

"Colonel Harvey ordered us to fire into our side of the blacksmith shop and it was a good test of our marksmanship. We all had Sharps and plenty of ammunition. There were holes between the logs of the blacksmith shop big enough to put your fist through. Of course the South Carolinians used those holes to fire at us. We were out in the open, but they were protected and seemed so well organized that when they'd let loose a volley, we knew that a dozen or more of them had to be shooting at us at the same time, and with at least two different kinds of rifles. One of their bullets produced a whine as it went over our heads. A Mexican War veteran said these were bullets from high-velocity muzzleloaders. The other bullet produced a low-pitched buzz, like a fast-moving bumblebee. These bullets were larger, about fifty calibers, heavier than the whiners and more deadly. Both sounds were frightening. I will never forget how they sounded.

It is simply amazing that none of us were killed. But we did have some wounded," he added.

"At about 10 o'clock, one of our sergeants went over to Captain Bickerton, who was in charge of the cannon, and asked him when he intended to use it. We were wasting our time firing rifles into these log walls. The South Carolinians hadn't budged. Bickerton told him he had plenty of powder but only a few 'balls' with him and he 'needed to make every shot count'."

The next hour, said Mr. Chase, was consumed by exchanging rifle shots: largely ineffective on both sides. "Captain Bickerton finally started to work 'Old Sacramento' and we sent up a mighty cheer. After seven, maybe eight, cannon balls, all direct hits, we sent a scout behind the blacksmith shop, beyond a little stream back there, to observe how our cannon was doing and to attempt to recover a few cannon balls, if he could. When he returned, he said the cannon balls were going into the front wall of the shop and out the back, some of them lodging in the 'crick bank'.

"Colonel Harvey called for a surrender but got no response. So he asked for some volunteers to push a wagon, we had captured, loaded with loose hay, up against the blacksmith's shop, and to set fire to the hay. The Southerners began to fire under the wagon, which prevented our men from getting the wagon close enough to set fire to the building. Three of our men were hit in the feet and legs. One shot went through the hay and through the chest of one of our boys, the most serious wound of the battle.

"Before our boys abandoned the wagon, they were able to set fire to the hay, which really began burning. The Southerners sent up a cheer of their own. They saw the burning hay-wagon trick hadn't worked. Most of the smoke blew back on the Plymouth Company, and this allowed some of the Southerners in the blacksmith shop to escape out the back of the building.

"Late in the afternoon the men who were left inside sent out a white flag. The proslavery men asked for 'terms.' The seventeen who were in the blacksmith shop surrendered, and so did Captain Lowe's men in the hotel. I think Colonel Harvey was as relieved to negotiate a truce as they were. There was a mutual agreement to withdraw, and everyone who wasn't a resident of Hickory Point agreed to disperse. The battle had taken all day, but it was finally over. We rejoined our reserves, going a little south of Hickory Point until we found a spot to set up camp for the evening. For safety, our companies were spread out on the prairie at a considerable distance from each other.

"The scout who had gone to report on how Old Sacramento was doing was sent back to recover as many of the cannon balls as he could. We had so few of them that Captain Bickerton wanted to make sure he had more for the next battle." Turning to Frank Robinson, Mr. Chase said, "Frank had an opportunity to go inside the blacksmith shop before we left and was surprised at the damage the cannon had done."

"Yes," said Mr. Robinson, "the Southerners were able to survive because they dug a hole in the dirt floor. They had pulled up the floor planks and thrown the dirt out the back window, and had been crouched below the path of the cannon balls."

"If you won the battle, how is it that you were caught?" asked Adda.

"We didn't know that a company of U.S. Army Dragoons, under the command of a Captain Wood, was marching towards us," replied Mr. Chase. "A little after dark, just after we had finished our supper, their troops surrounded our company."

Adda asked, "Hadn't you posted guards?"

"Yes, but they were so inexperienced they didn't even demand passwords or, if they did, the U.S. troops had learned them. Anyway, we were easily surrounded. One of our boys on guard

The Battle of Hickory Point

duty that night later told me he mistook the U.S. troops for visitors from one of our other camps, coming over to sing with us. We'd been having some fine singing before bedtime.

"Captain Wood assigned a squad of U.S. Army Regulars to guard the captured while he continued reconnoitering in the vicinity of Hickory Point. At about midnight, Captain Wood's party came up on another of our night camps. His scouts convinced him that this was also a Free State company. A few of the men were up and singing around some campfires but most were asleep in the open or in tents. Captain Wood's troops surrounded the camp and captured them all without firing a shot. These were part of General Lane's reserves. They had not been involved in the Hickory Point skirmish, but Captain Wood had orders to round up every member of General Lane's Army he could find. Mr. Chase said that all of our men were captured in this quiet and easy fashion.

"The next morning," said Mr. Chase, "we were all marched down to Lecompton and put in prison."

"Was Father part of that group?" asked Adda

"Yes, and twenty-five or thirty more from Plymouth. Frank and I were in the Lexington Company but they got us, too. The only ones they missed from your town company were Colonel Harvey and one or two of his aides. They were off meeting with General Lane."

Adda piped up, "Well, they also missed Mr. Boyce and his friend. They are here in Plymouth now."

"Captain Wood returned to Lecompton with 101 prisoners, 'Old Sacramento', seven wagons (including your father's) and a large quantity of arms and ammunition. It was the largest number of prisoners ever brought into Lecompton. We were all detained in this make shift prison camp, and arraigned until time for a trial. While they were in the prison," he said, "they learned that one of the rifle shots from our side had wounded Captain Robertson in the leg, which had to be amputated, and the first cannon ball from Old Sacramento had killed a Southerner by the name of Charles Granville Newhall."

Adda said, with a chuckle, "I guess they didn't get that hole dug fast enough to save him, eh?"

"Your father and the hundred other men are all charged with his murder."

Of course, Adda and I were greatly relieved to hear that Father was alive, but we were naturally worried about the indictment and about his well-being, how he would survive the winter on short rations and without winter clothes.

"How did you escape?" asked Adda.

"After we were in prison a few days," said Frank Robinson, "they singled out several of the youngest prisoners for a 'hearing.' We were released and told in no uncertain terms to resign from General Lane's Army."

He told us that he thought our companies had been betrayed by a Southerner, named Grayson. "After we were captured, I heard one of the U.S. soldiers talking about Grayson, saying he had been a spy for them. He was shot and killed by mistake by the U.S. Army guards the night we were captured. Grayson had tried to pass by them to get back to his Southern company, they attempted to stop him, and, when he shot at one of the guards, thinking he was a Free State soldier, they returned the fire and killed Grayson. I heard one of our soldiers say he knew exactly where the Plymouth and Lexington companies had been camped. How else, could the Army have found us Yankees out there on the prairie in the dark?"

During breakfast, Adda asked who was in charge of the prison camp. Mr. Chase said a Warden Jones runs the camp but the guard

The Battle of Hickory Point

is two companies of mounted U.S. dragoons under a lieutenant Colonel Cooke.

After breakfast Mr. Robinson and Mr. Chase left abruptly, saying they didn't wish to remain in Kansas Territory. We had hoped that these boys would stay and fill us in on more details about Father, but they seemed anxious to leave. They told us they thought they could find carpentry work around Archer in Nebraska Territory. After they left, Adda and I went out among the tents and wagons of Plymouth, sharing the news we had just received, telling the women folk that their men were alive and safe, but in prison at Lecompton.

While we were out among the wagons, we had a sobering talk with Mr. and Mrs. Strong. With all the fighting going on, and with most of our able-bodied men incarcerated, some of them for five years, they are thinking seriously about leaving the Territory and moving up to Archer. We've heard of other families from here and Lexington leaving for this reason and the harsh living conditions.

On the way back to our cabin Adda and I discussed this situation. The Strongs were really our best friends and we weren't sure what was to become of us, particularly if the Van Curens decide to leave. We didn't tell Mrs. Van Curen about the conversation we had with the Strongs, since she is so easily "put out."

6.

COLONEL COOKE,
Late September to October 10, 1856

At the beginning, let me say here and now that the Battle of Hickory Point, like all wars I'm sure, was a disaster for both sides. The proslavery forces suffered a stunning defeat, and those of them who were over here from Missouri to harass us had to leave Kansas (even though temporarily.) Jim Lane's militia, including the Plymouth Company, won a piddling but Pyrrhic victory, which I will explain.

In a military sense, compared to a European war, a two-day battle wasn't much of an engagement, but it established in the minds of the proslavery forces that the tide had finally turned. Our troops were now bigger and better armed than theirs. We were no longer on the defensive but now had the ability to take the offensive. As John Brown had swept Pottawattamie "clean," General Lane and his companies, beginning about the first of September, were sweeping the whole territory clean by relieving that chain of small forts mostly in Douglas, Franklin and Jefferson counties of their arms and other threats to Free State settlements. I believe that Hickory Point demonstrated that recent northern immigrants could not only protect themselves, and that from now on we would not tolerate these continual acts of violence to our settlements.

Now for the Pyrrhic victory. Winning the battle turned out to be a disaster for Father, for the Plymouth Company and for the one hundred or so of our volunteers who were captured the night of September 14th—after the battle, mind you—and marched by the U.S. Army down to the recently contrived prison camp at their capital, Lecompton.

Prior to the visit and hasty departure by Mr. Robinson and Mr. Chase, we had been receiving rather frequent and alarming bits of news about the prisoners from northbound travelers. Often their stories were contradictory. One report was that Judge Cato tried all 101 on the charge of murder.

A dispatch from the Governor to the Department of State, Washington details the case and trial of the Territory of Kansas vs. Thomas Bickerton et al before S. G. Cato, Associate Justice, beginning September 14, 1856, relied on testimony exclusively from proslavery witnesses and the arresting (military) officers. The decision rendered on September 23rd: a charge of Murder in the First Degree for eighty-nine of the 101 prisoners taken at Hickory Point the night of September 14th (including Sam Stewart, Alphesus Gates, Alonzo Crawford, Francis Swift and other associates of Sam Stewart, including some founders of Eldorado).

Jacob Chase and Frank Robinson were not tried. The prisoners were committed to the P.O.W. camp at Lecompton, K.T. awaiting sentence.[26]

We heard once that some of the leaders had been sentenced to five years of hard labor at the military the prison at Fort

---

[26]   Ref. Kansas State Historical Society vol. IV pgs 573 -> 584.

Leavenworth.[27] One rumor had balls and chains on the legs![28] The only good news was that several had escaped.

News of their imprisonment, trial and convictions made all the Northern newspapers, releasing a flood of indignant letters, petitioning for their freedom. Many of these appeals got to Washington through direct government channels, but mostly the impact on the Capitol was being felt through the hundreds of editorials in the Northern and New England press. This in turn proved to be an embarrassment for President Pierce's administration. November elections were coming up.

An embarrassed administration issued orders from Washington to release all political prisoners from Lecompton. A committee would be appointed by Governor Geary to sort out the prisoners, for parole, case by case.

Adda and I wonder what is to become of us. Our house, in which we are staying with the Van Curens, has been garrisoned and expanded from the house originally built by Father, Mr. Van Curen and others has become a boarding house operated by Mrs. Van Curen. Adda and I are assigned daily household chores of cooking, bed making, laundry, serving three meals a day to boarders and a constant stream of visitors. Mrs. Van Curen charges for the meals but we get none of the money. When Adda

---

[27] This rumor is not far from fact. Twenty of the 101 were separately sentenced to the penitentiary for five years; among them were Samuel Stewart, Frank Swift, Jeremiah Jordan, A. C. Soley. Annuals of Kansas by D. W. Wilder (new edition) pg. 137.

[28] Sheriff Jones, who was in charge of the prison camp, wanted to clamp chains on the prisoners to prevent them from escaping. Jones wrote a purchase order for one hundred iron balls, six inches in diameter, forged to leg chains and leg irons. When Gov. Geary saw the order, he refused to approve it. Sheriff Jones was to become his mortal enemy. *Kansas & Kansans*

complained, she was told that as females we own none of this house...that we are working for our board and room.

Mr. Van Curen had not joined the Plymouth Company's expedition to Iowa Point. Taking part in the fighting was voluntary, but helping to build the fort was not. It should be done by all the remaining seventeen or eighteen men, since it was supposed to protect us all in the absence of the men off fighting. Mr. Van Curen said he thought he should stay and work on the Fort, but he hasn't gone over there since the volunteers left.

The last week of September the Strongs left. He was afraid if he opened his grocery here, it might get raided, as businesses and houses have been destroyed east of here, particularly around Fort Leavenworth. They will move to Archer and promised to stay in-touch with us. That will be easy since our closest post office is in Archer.

One day near the end of September, Mr. Van Curen and a newcomer, a Mr. Towne, said they were going south to try to locate the U.S. Army Company that had Father's wagon and our team of horses, which was taken when he was captured. Mr. Van Curen told us that he would see if he could get them returned to us. The trip would include a buffalo hunt.

They were able to see Governor Geary, who had met Father and Mr. Dietsler and other prisoners during a hearing and an inspection of the camp. The Governor ordered our wagon and horses turned over to these gentlemen.

Mr. Towne told us afterwards that the Governor wrote Adda and me a letter and asked Mr. Van Curen to deliver it. Included in it was some money for us. It was no doubt money that Father had in his possession when he was taken prison. Mr. Van Curen never delivered the letter from the Governor to us.

When Mr. Van Curen recovered the property, he had two wagons and two teams to deal with. As luck would have it, he met a Mr. Richards who had decided to leave the Territory, on foot. They struck a bargain. If Mr. Richards would deliver our horses and the Van Curen wagon to us in Plymouth, it would beat walking—and Mr. Van Curen could get on with his hunt. Some distance south of Plymouth, however, Mr. Richards "overtook" a runaway Negro and offered him a ride. During the night when Mr. Richards and his passenger got within three miles of us; he accidentally ran into an Army patrol camp and was taken prisoner.

The troops searched the wagon, found the darkie and took charge of the whole lot. This was Wednesday. The next day the slave managed to escape anyway. Mr. Richards remained in custody. Two soldiers were dispatched to drive him down to jail in Topeka for "aiding and abetting" a fugitive slave. This was punishable by death and it was the Army's job to enforce this law. On their way to Topeka, the patrol escorting Mr. Richards ran into Governor Geary and a small touring company. They listened to Mr. Richard's story and compared it with the Army's account. Mr. Richards was set at liberty since the soldiers hadn't captured the evidence; namely, the slave. When Mr. Richards arrived here on foot, he told Adda and me that he was released under the legal Doctrine of Habeas Corpus. Well, thank heavens that Doctrine has traveled this far west. Before he left for Nebraska, he said, "By the way, the Army has your horses and the wagon."

October 1, U.S. troops, mounted and on foot, have begun moving into our area. They seem to be establishing a camp near us, just across Pony Creek. It seems to grow a little every day.

And lately, toward the end of the day, a few of the soldiers, and an officer or two, from the new camp have come over to socialize with some of the wives whose absent husbands were with General Lane or in prison with Father at Lecompton. Though most of the women in our settlement are married, there are a few, like Adda and me, unmarried.

We asked one of the young officers why Colonel Cooke would establish a camp here? He explained that they were here to maintain law and order between the proslavery forces and us. They said their mounted troops had been moved from Fort Riley, southwest of us. The foot soldiers were from camps over near the river, north of Fort Leavenworth.

They speculated that their camp in sight of Plymouth should act to discourage any border ruffians, (who are mostly Missourians who have the gall to call themselves the Law and Order Society,) but I am a little bitter that they have come now, after Father and the Town Company went off to fight at Hickory Point. Why didn't the Army know earlier about the threats to us from the ruffians camped over at Iowa Point? And why didn't the Army protect us then, in August and September? It didn't take me long to realize these were very naive ideas. We soon learned Colonel Cooke had established other camps near Lexington and Holton. One was called Camp Sackett.

One of the soldiers told Adda he has carried dispatches to Fort Leavenworth for the Colonel who calls their camp, "Fort Plymouth." He and other soldiers said their scouts are to be on the lookout for a very large heavily armed wagon train coming down from Chicago headed by Jim Lane, loaded with military supplies.

From several days' conversation with the U.S. Army soldiers I think they were put here to intercept our supply trains and to confiscate military supplies, particularly cannons and gunpowder. Small Army patrols seem to be everywhere.

It was informative to talk with these gentlemen. Most had Southern accents. Adda and I were learning all about rank and ratings: They taught us to tell a private from a sergeant or corporal, the size of a squad or a company. A young lieutenant seems to be paying attention to Adda, which she enjoys very much. A handsome captain, who seems reluctant to reveal his name or much about himself, has also been among the callers at our house.

Yesterday we offered these two officers a plate of oatmeal cookies. Mrs. Van Curen admonished us, saying that no good would come from associating with people who believe in slavery. As she shooed them off, the lieutenant smiled, winked at Adda and they both stuffed several cookies in their pockets. The lieutenant smokes a pipe and Mrs. Van Curen also objects to that. Adda and I think they are "dashing."

One warm morning while we were hanging out laundry, Adda said, "Let's ask Mr. Van Curen about the letter from the Governor and the money."

I replied, "Well, won't he lie? The first thing he'll ask us is how we know. Only Mr. Towne could have told us and that makes him a tattle-tale."

"I don't care about that."

I said, "If they turn us out with the Strongs gone, where will we stay? It won't be long and winter will be here."

"Stay? If we have to, we'll stay in the wagon or a tent."

I interrupted and said, "We can't spend winter in an unheated tent!"

Adda said, "Most of the people here are either living in their wagons or tents."

I replied, "About the letter, they will talk it over and he could simply admit that yes, there was some money, but it's to cover our board and room."

Adda admitted, "Well, you've got it half right. We shouldn't be paying these people for 'room.' We have as much right to that house as they do. As for board, we can get a rifle and shoot game.

It's all over the place. As for the rest of our supplies we'll get it from the freight wagons, just like everybody else." But we decided to bide our time.

On the morning of October 10th, as Adda and I were watching additional troops file into the Army's new camp, which has grown to over 300 soldiers, we suddenly spotted our horses pulling Mr. Van Curen's old wagon. They came in from the south, "paraded" in front of our settlement, dropped down out of sight to ford Pony Creek. We couldn't believe our eyes! A few of our boys, who had gone off with Father and the Town Company, had recently begun to return to Plymouth. On the night of September 14th, they had been camped a half mile or so from Father's group and so had escaped capture at Hickory Point, but had been given temporary leaves-of-absence, which was General Lane's way of complying with a recent proclamation from Governor Geary commanding both sides to dissolve their companies and stop fighting.

We asked two of these boys if they would walk over to the Army camp and retrieve our horses. At the camp, a sergeant told them it would be necessary for the owners, to identify themselves to Colonel Cooke to recover the property.

We had never been in an Army camp. I worried that women might not be welcome, that we might be teased and that we might have trouble getting to see the Colonel. We didn't even know how to find him. Adda suggested that we simply inquire of the soldiers when we get there, that we'd probably see one or two that had visited Plymouth in recent days but I thought that since this camp has grown so, it was not likely that we'd see someone we knew, and it would be better if we had one of our men with military experience along and that's the way it worked out.

Adda and I got dressed up and asked Mr. Sullivan from Cape Cod, who was on leave to go with us.

Colonel Cooke

It was a rather pleasant walk. It couldn't have taken more than fifteen or twenty minutes. Adda and I did remove our shoes to cross the creek. The weather wasn't chilly but I wore my shawl, the one that I "forgot" at the Detroit depot. Although that happened only three months ago, it seems like ages ago and Detroit seems like another country. So many events and changes have taken place since then.

At the camp there was considerable activity. A company of foot soldiers was on drill. As we approached them, they whistled and smiled at us. Dozens of dragoons were coming and going on horseback. Three long straight rows of tents with narrow streets between stretched out on the rolling prairie. Off to the north was an orderly collection of big and small wagons. Two large corrals, formed with ropes and stakes held dozens of horses. A second corral contained almost as many mules; both corrals were on the down streamside of Pony Creek, which flows north there.

As we approached on the west side of the tents we inquired of a sentry where we could find Colonel Cooke. He said if the Colonel were in camp, he would be in the middle tent of the second row, which could be identified by the Company's "Guidon" flag. Colonel Cooke's tent was identical to all others, except it did have a little blue flag fluttering on a pole just in front of it. While we were figuring out what to do a soldier came by. We asked him if this was Colonel Cooke's tent. He said, with a Southern accent, that this was not only Colonel Cooke's tent; this was the U.S. Army's headquarters for the Second Dragoons. His manner was condescending as he looked at us "civilians," which is what they occasionally call us. I suppose he thought we were over there trying to sell something or to offer some service, like doing their laundry.

The soldier said that Colonel Cooke was in charge of the entire battalion, which included four other companies of dragoons camped around this northern part of the Territory. Just as he was telling us that our business with the Colonel had better be important a rather tall man, who I assumed was Colonel Cooke came out of the tent. Except for his hat, he was in full Army uniform and very impressive. One of the striking things about the Colonel was his full and rather long beard. I was to learn later that it was intended to make him appear older than he was.

Earlier it had been cloudy, but now the sun was out and it was rather warm and pleasant.

The Colonel looked at the three of us and very politely and rather quietly, I thought, inquired if we had some business with the Army.

I spoke up, saying that we were from Plymouth town site and pointed south. Coming from the big city of Detroit, I was embarrassed to call Plymouth, our camp a town, which has a few houses, three or four muddy streets and one unfinished log fort.

Stating my business, I said that my sister and I saw that very morning what we believed to be our horses parading into his camp and we would like them back. We also thought they were pulling a wagon belonging to Mr. Van Curen of our town, and we wished to reclaim that as well. I was prepared to be a little snippy about the U.S. Army's right to confiscate private property but my presumptuous attitude was suddenly put to rest by the Colonel's formal but courtly manners.

The Colonel spoke again, I thought rather softly for an officer of his rank and reputation. He said, "Miss . . ." and paused, looking at me expectantly and with a kindly interest.

"Oh, I'm sorry, sir. I'm Augusta Stewart. This is my sister, Adda, and this is Mr. Sullivan from Massachusetts. My sister and I are from Detroit."

The Colonel said, with a big smile, that he had over 200 horses and over one hundred mules, that they ate more than the men,

Colonel Cooke

and that he would be more than happy to get rid of any that didn't belong to the Army.

One of the advantages in living in our tight little compound is that information, and rumor, travels quickly. Two or three of our Plymouth men had served in the Mexican War, so they could explain the various military rankings and could tell us about such military details as company, battalion or regimental size, etc. One of those veterans occasionally musters our men out on the prairie to rehearse them on military maneuvers and target shooting. After the drills he often boarded with us. This gentleman was a "rare bird," an abolitionist from Missouri who had served under the Colonel during the Mexican War. It was from him that we learned of Colonel Cooke's military career and the war itself.

I couldn't believe I was actually carrying on a conversation with him. I was so impressed meeting an Army officer with such an illustrious background. I screwed up my courage and asked him if he was the same Colonel Cooke who had fought in the Black Hawk War. He said he was indeed. I asked him if it was also true that he had fought in the Mexican War and that before the major engagement he had carried a letter demanding the Mexican's surrender.

He chucked and said, "That letter was not persuasive, so we had to fight; I commanded a battalion of Missouri volunteers." He asked how it was that I was so well informed and I told him about the old soldier from Missouri in our town. He laughed and asked if this veteran was a Mormon. I said I didn't know. He said his command then included several hundred Mormon volunteers. "Many were with me all the way to California." I was fascinated with his Southern accent. I had seldom heard such a nice accent. He seemed to be such an agreeable man for an officer in charge of so many soldiers, and mostly southern soldiers at that; I'd heard that he had 500 or 600 men in his command, not only those stationed here but also in camps generally in the eastern part of the Territory. I had not met many men (or women) with such pleasant manners. So I pressed on with my questions. I asked him where he was from before getting into the Army. "Leesburg, Virginia," he replied. Then he chided me a bit by saying that people like him didn't just "get into the Army." He was an Army "Regular," he said, and had been since leaving West Point, which he had attended after graduating from public school.

Well, I knew he was a "West Pointer."

"My, what an honor," I said. "What year did you graduate from the Military Academy, sir?"

He smiled, "I was in the Class of 1827." I became a little embarrassed. I was born in 1839.

Sensing that he wished to conclude our business, I tried to continue the talk by explaining that several men from Plymouth was in the Lecompton war camp and Father was among them.

Calling me, "Miss Stewart," oh so politely, he asked sympathetically, "How long has yoah daddy been in that camp?"

"We don't know exactly. Father and a small group from Plymouth were captured at Hickory Point, south of Lawrence."

"Yes, I know about that skirmish. Your Plymouth men were heavily armed and under the command of a Colonel Harvey, but Mr. Harvey is not U.S. Army and has no commission to defend you settlers or to fight proslavery troops on your behalf, and the same can be said for Mr. Lane, who is calling himself "general." I thought he said that in a rather derisive manner.

"The Plymouth Company was taken prisoner by C Company under the command of Captain Wood. *What can you tell me about your father?*"

"Well, Father had the only team of horses in our Town Company, so he volunteered to pull our utility wagon with supplies.

COLONEL COOKE

He and two others left a little ahead of the Plymouth Company but we thought they were on their way to Iowa Point."

"That may be so, but they must have had their plans changed. We know they were involved in a skirmish with a group from South Carolina down on the Kansas River. The Plymouth Company and some of Lane's companies fought several small battles down there and caused a lot of trouble. I believe it was September 13th that they engaged another group at Hickory Point for two days and killed one man and wounded several others. The Plymouth Company was armed with a cannon that fired a six-pound ball. We suspect it and the powder came from your settlement. They also had a large stock of rifles, some of which they had captured from a company from South Carolina.

"We knew there was a company of Southern troops at Iowa Point itching for a fight and we also knew that some of Mr. Lane's companies were heading up there. My orders were then, and are now, to prevent armed conflict. Yoah daddy's company was captured a mile or so south of Hickory Point on the evening of September 14th. And I've been informed that later that night Mr. Lane and Mr. John Brown headed north to their camp in Archer, Nebraska Territory. We don't know the whereabouts of Mr. Harvey and his staff."

So, Colonel Cooke knew about John Brown's association with General Jim Lane. That information was sobering. And it frightened me. I suddenly became apprehensive and cautious. I knew I mustn't say anything to reveal that both General Lane and Captain John Brown are frequently in and around Plymouth. I sensed that our meeting had become less social and that I would have to watch what I said. We'd heard from soldiers visiting from their camp about how skilled, courageous and dangerous the Army thought John Brown was.

I wonder what the Colonel's reaction would be if he knew that Adda and I were acquainted with General Lane and that we had met Mr. Brown, indeed, that he had given us both a Bowie knife—though he failed to explain what it was we were to do with them. Recently when he went north out of the Territory, he was suffering from swamp fever and stayed in Plymouth at the cabin of Mr. _____. After dark they all came over to our place for supper, which Mrs. Van Curen is operating as a boarding house. Adda and I served him his supper. Two or three young men were with him; we later learned from his Plymouth contacts that they were John Brown's sons. My sister and I prepared the last meal eaten by Osawatomie Brown before he left Kansas.[29] It was the last time I ever saw him. Poor old man! He had grief and trouble enough to craze him, no wonder he was ready to fight.

Colonel Cooke said that Father's company and two or three others; over one hundred all together had been marched down to Lecompton and brought before Governor Geary, who has been instructed by Washington to prevent armed conflict. Both the Plymouth Company and the Lexington Company were heavily armed. Since the Plymouth Company had at least one cannon, the Governor felt he was within his rights to imprison them because they had defied his proclamation. "Ah suppose ah could say that we saved some lives by our action, possibly yoah daddy's."

"Miss Stewart, yoah daddy isn't the surveyor, is he?"

"Yes, yes, that's him!"

"Well, I can tell you this much. Your father has been appointed Commissary Officer of the camp. He's allowed to go into the

---

[29] Added to the Journal later, when Augusta felt it was safe to write about this incident. She did not identify John Brown's Plymouth contact in order to protect him. Augusta's account of John Brown's visit was confirmed in "Memories of Addie Stewart Graton," by Alice Graton Kincaid, from the "Kansas Collection," U. of Kansas Libraries KHMS 84:5:13. Alice was the daughter of Adda and was my cousin—MLC

Colonel Cooke

countryside to locate food and other supplies for the prisoners. Water is a problem in that camp. Providing water that is safe to drink and use in the kitchen is also his job.[30] The U.S. Army hadn't planned on running a prison camp, so we lack adequate rations and other supplies. You see, when we captured those two companies, we had no jail, so I was ordered to bring two of my companies to set up a camp and guard the prisoners.

"I got to know several of them, not well, but that's how I know about your father. I was in charge of that prison camp until September 28th when I was ordered up here to Plymouth."

Colonel Cooke said that Governor Geary, President Pierce's new appointment intended for Kansas to be peaceful, and might be held accountable to the North if it wasn't. President Pierce was from New Hampshire.

"There is too much zeal on both sides. In addition to the Yankees," he said, "there were also some proslavery prisoners at Lecompton." Well, that information was certainly no comfort to me. Coming from Michigan I never thought of myself as a Yankee. I suppose he was referring to all the New Englanders around this part of the Territory, particularly those from Massachusetts. At Tabor we had discovered that they were the most fired-up about the abolitionist cause. But General Lane and Colonel Harvey and John Brown aren't Yankee. They are simply very serious abolitionists.

Colonel Cooke asked me if we could identify our horses.

"Certainly. We brought them all the way from Detroit. Both have small brands that Adda and I will be able to recognize."

---

[30] Confirmed in Memories of Addie Stewart Graton from Kansas Collection, U/Kansas Libraries, pg. 8. Note that the author, Alice Graton Kincaid referred to her mother as Addie: though Adelaide Stewart Graton was called Adda by her family—M.L.C.

The Colonel said, almost with a flourish, "Ladies, you have convinced me. I will write a note that you may take to our quartermaster, Lieutenant Henderson. He will help you find your horses and the wagon."

A soldier was coming out of a tent near us. The Colonel motioned for him to join us. "Son," he said, "please escort these ladies from Plymouth to Lieutenant Henderson." Smiling, he said, "I'll tell the lieutenant to give you a bushel of oats or barley in exchange for the use we've had of your horses." I thanked the Colonel for his courtesy and all the time he was able to give us. He said, "Well, we all have to git along an' I want you both to bring over your friend from Missouri for supper one of these nights."

When Adda and I returned to Plymouth, it was a little after noon. It was turning a little cloudy, looked like rain. We tied up the horses and left the wagon in a conspicuous place, I went into the house humming a little tune, girlishly light hearted and very stimulated by our meeting with Colonel Cooke. Mrs. Van Curen asked what made me so "chipper." With self-satisfaction I could barely repress I told her that we had just recovered our horses and her husband's wagon and that we had met Colonel Cooke, which he's not at all the ogre we've made him out to be. He's a polite dashing officer—and I began telling her about our long conversation.

She cut me off in mid sentence, "If you were a little older, you would be less impressed with his social graces and question just what purpose is served by that camp and why the Army needs 300 soldiers between Plymouth and the border. Well, I'll tell you. It's to intimidate us." I waited, expecting her to thank me for recovering their wagon, but she was determined to disparage the Colonel and his intentions. She continued, "Who better to discourage immigration into the Territory than a couple of companies of Southerners in the uniform of the U.S. Army? They've learned to suppress their own people by tarring and feathering them if they suspect them of any softness on slavery. They terrorized Mexico into submission just as they continue to terrorize the Negro and they will make every effort to terrorize us, mark my word!"

Her response was sobering and disappointed me, but events soon to unfold caused me to see some wisdom in her opinion.

"What do you call threats we've had to wipe out our little settlements and the violence and killings down on the Kaw River if it isn't proslavery terror? They've been ordered up here by Leavenworth to be on the alert for trains coming down with arms and supplies like those Preston Plumb brought in here for Mr. Redpath's outfit in mid September. Can you imagine the dust-up that would have occurred if that camp were over there when all that military freight changed hands that day?

"And let me remind you, young lady, it's your friend over there, Colonel Cooke, who ordered the capture of the Plymouth Company and ordered them to be marched down to Lecompton. You surely appreciate, don't you, that he was the gentleman responsible for the incarceration of most of our men including your father." As she spoke, I listened, but I was also thinking.

Her conclusions generally matched the facts, except I think it was Governor Geary who decided on the prison. Though she was adamant in her opinion through most of September and these first few days of October we've all felt more secure. The U.S. dragoons being here have put a stop to the threats from the proslavery camp at Iowa Point.

Well, even if she is right, I decided not to let her attitude affect me. I felt good about getting our horses back—and their wagon even if we got no thanks for it. I think I will try to get a letter through to Father. I know he will be pleased to hear about the horses. I just won't say much about Colonel Cooke and the new

Army camp up here, and I won't tell him the Strongs have moved to Archer.

As Mrs. Van Curen continued her speech, I heard some noise outside.

7.

CAPTAIN HENRY'S STRANGE PROPOSAL,
October 10th to late October 1856

I'm sure Mrs. Van Curen would have continued to lecture me except we suddenly became aware of some commotion outside. A squad of Colonel Cooke's Second Dragoons had come over to Plymouth and were searching through tents and wagons. It had begun to rain.

There was an understanding between the Army and us settlers that each immigrant family was entitled to a muzzleloader for hunting and for protection against the Indians. But the Dragoons weren't here to search for muzzleloaders. They were looking for large caches of ammunition, cannons and particularly Sharps rifles all rumored to be here. The soldiers coveted those rifles because they knew how deadly they were even at long distances. Earlier this month, I had heard some of the soldiers from Colonel Cooke's camp speculate about whether our settlement possessed large weapon caches, maybe even a cannon or two. The soldiers seem to believe that we were all from Massachusetts and suspected that we had more mechanics than farmers in our company. They suspected that the mechanics might have had access to northern armories sympathetic to the abolitionist cause. Some of the visiting soldiers had asked where the "four pounder" had come from, the one Plymouth Company used in the Hickory Point battle. He was uninformed. He was referring to "Old Sacramento," the cannon that General Lane had requested be sent up to Hickory Point from Lawrence. What they didn't know was that Plymouth still had a cannon and four kegs of powder for it.

Just as we heard the search party outside, several soldiers, one officer and a civilian pushed our door open and barged in. The officer was the handsome captain who had been over for oatmeal cookies earlier this week. The soldiers tore-up the floor planks and, lo and behold, found a barrel full of powder (one of the four barrels that Preston Plumb had given us a few weeks earlier.) I thought, "Oh, oh, now we are in for it!" I poked my head out the door and saw ten or fifteen of our Plymouth men being marched at gunpoint by some of the search party squad. I knew one of the soldiers and shouted to him, "What's the matter?" As he yelled, "We found three barrels of cannon powder," a sergeant told him to "shut up." The sergeant yelled to the officer in our house, "Where's the U.S. Marshall?" The Captain yelled back, "He's with us." The sergeant said, "Tell him I'm arresting these settlers." I quickly turned my head around and asked the officer, "What's the meaning of this?"

Pointing to the powder, the civilian answered, "This is serious evidence and I'll have to take all you abolitionists prisoner." Mrs. Van Curen spoke up, "Pardon me, sir, but who are you?"

I am William J. Preston. I'm deputy U.S. Marshall, appointed by Governor Geary. I'm here inspecting Colonel Cooke's camp. He paused and looked around the house. It was obvious he was not impressed with our lodgings. He said, "I've been in this pest hole before, Madam. I was here with a small Army patrol September 15th and arrested Mr. Charles Robinson, the one you abolitionists mistakenly think is your Governor, and two of John Brown's sons." His contempt for us was plain as day.

Moving to another room, the deputy barked an order to Mrs. Van Curen to open those two large trunks.

Since the trunks belonged to Adda and me, Mrs. Van Curen told him I should open them. I had been in the habit of carrying the key to the trunks and some little trinkets on a white ribbon I wore around my neck, I took my "sweet time" pulling the ribbon over my head. I bent over and used the small key to unlock the trunk, opened it and stood up. If I had been three years younger, I would have probably stuck out my tongue. I deeply resented their invasion of our privacy but I felt rather smug knowing that those trunks didn't hold contrivances to make war; indeed they simply contained bedding and some personal effects that on close scrutiny might embarrass them. The Marshall impatiently ordered me to turn them over so he could see the bottom. Feeling rather important from my meeting with Colonel Cooke earlier that day, I said, "No, I won't do it!" He smiled and nodded to one of the soldiers. He turned the stuff in our trunks over and found nothing more dangerous than ladies undergarments. As the search party continued to snoop around our house a soldier came in and reported that they had found and confiscated three Sharps rifles out in the tents and wagons. He was all puffed up, probably because they had found the other three barrels of gunpowder. This sent a chill through me. I knew we had ten to twenty times that many Sharps rifle in our possession, hundreds of tins of ammunition, as well as our own cannon for the fort. I was just amazed that they found the four barrels. We had been warned in Tabor to take precautions. Some of the settlers had hidden their guns and tins of ammunition out on the prairie while others had built false panels in the sides or bottoms of their wagons to enable them to retrieve their rifles quickly in case of an attack, Indian or Missourian.

After the Marshall and the soldiers went out to continue the search, the officer kept himself stationed, unnecessarily in my opinion, in our house. He seemed interested in Adda, or perhaps me. I asked where he was from. "Lexington, Kentucky," he said. I asked him how long he thought they would remain camped here so near to our settlement, and whether they would send the arrested men down to Lecompton. He said, "Marshall Preston might. He really has it in for you people and finding all that powder[31] hasn't helped. Colonel Cooke's job is to prevent fighting." I asked how long it would be before Colonel Cooke would release the men they had just arrested. He said that his camp had enough supplies to last two weeks, adding that Colonel Cooke wouldn't want to feed any more people than he had to.

"Are you really here to protect us from the proslavery troops? All through August it was rumored that they were on their way here from Iowa Point to wipe us out."

"Yes, if the proslavery boys come around, we have orders to disarm them. If they are from Missouri, or from the east for that matter, we are supposed to take them to the river and escort them out of the Territory." He meant the Missouri. Then he added, "We are expecting one of your commanders, a Colonel Eldridge, to come through here soon with a new and armed contingent from the North. We know this outfit has 600 to 700 men. We know they used all the ferries to cross the river. We know it left Nebraska City on the fourth and arrived in Archer. We expect it

---

31 Major F. J. Porter sends a report (October 10, 1856) to Fort Leavenworth that he and his men found four kegs of powder, thirteen muskets and a box of lead at a house (in Plymouth) near the fort. Another report signed by him on October 7, 1856 expected a twenty wagon train from Archer. Nebraska Territory Army records; Fort Leavenworth.

today or tomorrow. With caution and in soft voice he said that's really why Deputy Preston is up here. He believes Jim Lane is with this group and there's reward for his capture." We know Colonel Eldridge is a friend of the Governor, so we have orders to contain his group as peaceably as we can. But we also have orders to search that train, confiscate his arms and escort him to the Governor in Lecompton. We suspect he has some cannons and powder from some Northern armories." I asked him how he knew all this.

"Miss Stewart, there are no secrets out here in the Territory."

I interrupted him to say, "How do you know my name?"

He smiled and said, "When Colonel Cooke ordered me to head up this search party, he told me about your visit and about your father. He said you and your sister had a lot of spunk to walk into an Army camp and ask that your horses and wagon be returned. He also said you were quite well informed about the Mexican War."

He continued, "Our scouts are continually bringing back information. Colonel Cooke gets reports daily about the size of the immigration parties coming in, whether they are abolitionists or from the Southern states. I'll bet Colonel Cooke can tell you to a rifle how many guns the proslavery boys have over at Iowa Point. He knew to the day when your Plymouth outfit would attack Hickory Point. Now I'll admit we didn't know your company had a cannon. That was a surprise."

I interrupted, "Well, if you are so well informed, why didn't you prevent the battle?"

He ignored my question. "Some of Jim Lane's boys," he told me, "have that cannon back in their possession. Now ain't that a kick in the pants?" Before he left, he said if Marshall Preston doesn't send your men to Lecompton, they would "interrogate" them and release them in a day or two. I thought he was a very straightforward gentleman, but I didn't get his name.

As the officer prepared to leave, he pointed to the three Sharps learning against the outside wall of the house. Much to my surprise, he scribbled a note and asked Adda and me to restore the guns to their "rightful owners", which we did. The owners were George Olds, Mr. Boyce and Mr. Littlefield. Adda remarked to me, "Wonder where Mr. Boyce suddenly got a rifle, since he came back without one."

This October 10th is proving to be a momentous day. First, Adda and I had our long talk with Colonel Cooke and got our horses back, then we had Marshall Preston's search party find a keg of powder in our house and three more kegs elsewhere. Now the most amazing event of all: Later in the day the Kentucky officer and I had another opportunity to talk and out of the blue he said he was thinking of leaving the Army and "make for" the Kansas gold fields, and asked if I wanted to go with him. I was aghast. What an impetuous idea.

With a mixture of curiosity and indifference, I interrupted him, "This sounds vaguely like a proposal." I was seventeen years old. I couldn't bring myself to put the word marriage in front of proposal.

"It is", he said, just like he was buying a pair of boots.

Well, I had no idea that my first marriage proposal would be so dry and unromantic. This was a business proposition, not a real proposal of marriage.

Later in the day, he took a moment away from his duties. We spoke again. This time we had maybe ten or fifteen minutes together. We walked toward Pony Creek. He seemed nervous as we talked and kept fidgeting with his sword handle or would twist the attractive brass buttons on his uniform. He seemed unnecessarily alert, concerned, I suppose that we might be seen fraternizing.

He said, as I recall, having made this entry from old, hidden notes long after leaving Plymouth, "Miss Stewart, there's gonna be a war, sure as shootin'. All of us in our Company share this view. I ain't gonna go get killed just to satisfy some plantation owner's desire to own Negroes and work 'em. Most of the men and all but one officer in my Company are from the South. We love the South, but not one of us is from a family that owns slaves. Most of the Northern boys have been transferred to forts out west to separate them and their views about slavery with Southerners. But Northern or Southern, most of the men under me are poor. They just joined for the uniform and three square meals a day. Any opportunity that the Army affords will be more than they'll see at home. Miss Stewart, if you and I go far enough west outside the Territory, we'll be beyond the Law. The Mormons know that. We'll be free to make the most of our efforts."

Just then a soldier came running up and said that "Captain Henry" was wanted by a Major "so-and-so". The Captain left me abruptly. No good-bye, no lingering touch on my arm. In fact, as he turned to leave, his dragoons' scabbard swung out and spanked my knee. I don't believe he was even aware of it. Well, now at least, I know his name.

Sure enough as he expected, about two o'clock an immigrant train began crossing the creek from the north and as it trickled into our settlement I recognized two of the guides. It had continued to rain and the new arrivals were ducking into the tents at Plymouth. This was an advance part of Colonel Eldridge's train and had followed Lane's Trail, down from Archer.

This train was mostly made up of freight wagons, pulled overland by mules since the Missouri River continues to be blockaded. We were happy to see the supplies since we were running low on flour, sugar, foodstuff, and grain for the animals, etc.

Soon there were twenty or so wagons and maybe seventy-five to a hundred people milling around, maybe more, including seven wives who had accompanied their husbands.

Colonel Cooke's sentries, stationed on the outskirts of the woods north of us, saw what was going on in our camp but they delayed coming down until a sufficient number of the new train had accumulated in our camp.

Suddenly a company of U.S. Troops from Colonel Cooke's camp marched into our settlement. These troops were new to me. Some of the mounted dragoons were pulling cannons, six of them! In recent days Colonel Cooke's local force has grown to 300 men, most of them mounted dragoons, the majority of them from Fort Riley southwest of us and from small forts over by the river near Leavenworth. Although the number of soldiers greatly exceeds the number of people we have in Plymouth, it's about half the combined population of the four settlements in our area, which have continued to grow all autumn.

The troops surrounded the newcomers' wagons. Mounted dragoons were stationed on the left. The six small Army cannons were wheeled in to face the new wagons. I couldn't believe my eyes. U.S. Army cannons aimed at a bunch of muddy civilian freight wagons and their drivers. Some of the drivers were still sitting on their wagon's seats; some had gotten off and were holding the reins. Several women, some without hats were standing by their wagons. What a pitiful sight. The newcomers were getting drenched; it wasn't a hard, driving rain but a chilly October drizzle and these poor souls had cannons pointed at them. I was scared for what might happen and I was deeply offended. My eyes searched among the soldiers for Colonel Cooke, thinking he wouldn't condone this shameful behavior. I didn't find him but I saw Captain Henry, and his eyes met mine. He spoke to a lieutenant and came towards me. We were some distance from

Captain Henry's Strange Proposal

the search party, which was occupied with the new train, so our meeting was not conspicuous.

As he approached me, I became more and more indignant, "You and your soldiers ought to be ashamed, pointing cannons at your own people. This isn't the Mexican War, you know!" I told him that most of these people were simply farmers from Iowa and Ohio. "Do you think they are your enemy? Why in the world does the Army need 300 soldiers camped so close to us? You know there's not enough water in little Pony Creek to go around." I was getting so indignant I'd started to sputter—and I was getting cold.

"Miss Stewart, I'm so ashamed by what we've been assigned to do. That's why I'm leaving the Army and I want you to go with me. This stain on the U.S Army will never leave us—and you don't know the half of it." He told me that the Army had increased the number of troops here by abandoning the camps near the river at Fort Leavenworth, giving the Missourians unobstructed access to the Territory, so they can more easily rig your elections in the fall, as they've been doing for the past two years. "Three more companies have been moved to Lecompton to guard the prisoners, who, except for horse thieves are all abolitionists. With all these companies being in this area, the proslavery trains from Georgia and the Carolinas can come in unfettered. They probably have as many guns and as much powder as you all have."

He said that Colonel Cooke[32] and Deputy Preston had ordered his company to search this new wagon train. They ordered the artillery officer to bring the six cannons. Looking askance at the U.S. Marshall strutting around he wondered out loud what

---

[32] Lieutenant Colonel Cooke reports this incident to headquarters at Fort Leavenworth. The train included 240 people, that he planned an escort for this train to Lecompton to see the governor. Kansas Historical Collection, Volume 4, page 516.

he thinks he's accomplishing with this excessive show of force; intimidating, fifteen or twenty women and children wet to their bones and a bunch of farmers with muddy schooners. "I tell you, Miss Stewart, it's humiliating for us soldiers to have to take part in these searches. And all this will not go unnoticed or unreported. Then it will really be embarrassing!" I didn't have to wait long to see what he meant, "not go unnoticed."

"Three days ago," said Captain Henry, "we were over in Lexington searching through a newly arrived train at that camp. Oh, yes, Deputy Preston was there, too, but he drew some very snippy remarks from an English newspaper reporter. They had quite an altercation. I think the Englishman's name was Hinton."

Recalling that Mr. Hinton had escorted an entire train in the same week we came to Plymouth, after "helping" himself to all those Iowa rifles, I thought to myself, "You have no idea who Mr. Hinton really is," but I just smiled and kept my mouth shut.

"Miss Stewart, get me some settlers' clothing. I'll get two good horses and we'll skedaddle out of this mess tonight."

"Where do you propose we go?"

"I don't care—the mountains, Oregon, California. Well, maybe not California. It's part of the Union now. With so many Southerners in California, we all thought it would surely come in slave, so I guess we'd have to avoid California.

My flimsy cotton bonnet was getting soaked. I was shivering from the excitement, the cold and the disgust of it all. Though I was surprised at my curiosity, I didn't have the slightest interest in helping him, nor could I see myself riding off with him. To what? We couldn't stop at Army forts along the way. He'd get arrested. I just wanted to get dry and get warm. There was no affection in his proposal, no concerns about my safety, no plans for the future. He just wanted a companion. Maybe he thought having a female

Captain Henry's Strange Proposal

companion would make it safer for him to travel, helping him avoid notice if he posed as a settler traveling with his wife. Of course, I'm old enough to suspect that his offer contained more than just his desire to desert the Army.

It was now later in the afternoon. As we talked, I could see the soldiers continuing to round up the newly arrived men folk at gunpoint and marching them across Pony Creek toward their camp. The soldiers behind the cannons continued to light long matches, which the rain would quickly extinguish. If it hadn't been so dangerous, it might have been humorous. The soldiers had also rounded up women and children from the new train and made them stand with some Plymouth women clustered together in the rain. The soldiers commenced searching the freight wagons, rather rudely, I must say. The dragoons began throwing bedding and personal things from the wagons into the mud!

The searching and inspection had gone on for about half an hour when Colonel Shalor Eldridge rode in with five other leaders of the train. More wagons continued behind him. I recognized Mr. Pomroy.[33] Colonel Eldridge immediately confronted Deputy Preston, who signaled a lieutenant to join him. Sensing trouble, Captain Henry abruptly left me and joined Deputy Preston. I waited a few seconds, and then followed him. The Colonel dismounted and demanded that the searching be stopped; saying that a half-hour of it should have been sufficient. What really angered Colonel Eldridge was the inconsiderate way belongings were being thrown in the mud. He was a little older and heavier than the U.S. Marshal, but very "saucy" and fairly authoritative in his remarks to Deputy Preston.

---

[33] Samuel Pomroy was an officer of the Massachusetts Aid Society. A firm abolitionist, he had already led a party to Kansas in August of 1854, and had been invited to the White House to witness the signing of the Kansas-Nebraska Act on May 30, 1854. He was the state's first senator when Kansas became a state—M.L.C

The troops had already completed searching the new arrivals. In the end the soldiers only found a few rifles and a keg or two of powder.[34] *Well this is not the "whole" story, far from it.*

The following episode has been constructed from previously hidden notes, mine and Adda's after we removed to Eldorado in the spring of 1858..

By nightfall, after the soldiers had finished their search and went back to their own camp, we were to hear the full account, and glory over it. The previous day, Colonel Eldridge and his men had hidden some cannons up by the Nebraska border. What Deputy Preston didn't realize was that the Colonel had escorted not one but two wagon trains into the Territory, totaling about 700 people, less than a dozen women. He had split the main train a few miles north of Plymouth. The first train of about seventy-five wagons bound for Plymouth, with much needed food and supplies, was a decoy.

During the two hours while the Deputy and the U.S. soldiers were busy rounding up the new arrivals and searching their wagons a rider quietly slipped out of Plymouth to notify the second wagon train, which was hiding in a creek bed north and west of us, to proceed south to Topeka. That train carried the main supply of arms, ammunition, winter clothing, etc., and was not intercepted.

Late that same day, October 10th, all the men from the supply train were released after undergoing questioning at the Army's camp. Colonel Cooke and the Marshall decided the whole outfit was under arrest and would be escorted to the Governor by Major

---

[34] U.S. Marshal William J. Preston later wrote a report about the interception and search at Fort Plymouth on Pony Creek, listing the arms discovered in this wagon train: 6 "five shooters", 26 Navy Colts, 10 Sharps rifles, 230 muskets, 1 1/2 kegs of powder and miscellaneous ammunition. Kansas State Historical Society, Vol. 4, pg. 608.

Captain Henry's Strange Proposal

Sibley and an Army squad, where Colonel Eldridge could file his grievance.

As many of the newcomers who could get in joined us for a makeshift supper. The next day this group departed for Topeka with their Army escort.

Reunited in Topeka, both groups met with Governor Geary[35]. He heard their side of the story and returned their arms. Deputy Marshall was not pleased. They marched on to Lawrence with banners flying to music of fife and drum.

Two days after the events of October 10th, an Army private delivered a small pasteboard box wrapped with a sealed envelope containing a letter from my persistent Captain Henry. This time he was proposing to me in writing. The contents of the letter was so dangerous that I probably shouldn't reveal them in my journal, should the information fall into the wrong hands.

Added later when it was safe to do so: The letter from Captain Henry included his proposal and warned, "Do not betray me" and "Please destroy this letter."

I must admit his letter and our furtive conversations flattered me, but his proposal was utterly impractical.

The little box contained a shiny brass uniform button resting on a pad of gun wadding. The hollow, two-part button, almost an

---

[35] According to the documents of the Kansas State Historical Society, Volume 8, page 305, 306, includes a letter from Shalor Eldridge to Governor Geary, the immigrants presented a list of grievance. They were peaceful immigrants whose only intent was to settle in the territory, armed proslavery men were marauding Northern Kansas, the Missouri River was blocked to Northern immigrants, Shalor Eldridge and his party had been rudely searched and detained in the rain at Plymouth for two-thirds of a day by Deputy Preston and in effect had been taken prisoner by him. The immigrants asked that the property he had seized be returned to them. The six "Conductors" of the train signed the letter. Additionally, Dr. John Gihon, *Geary and Kansas,* quoted in Volume 4, page 604-610, presents both sides of this story contrasting Deputy Preston's view with Colonel Eldridge's view.—M.L.C.

inch in diameter, had an attractive military design pressed into the front. A little round eye protruded from the back, no doubt for the thread. It was identical to the buttons on Captain Henry's uniform. When Captain Henry and I had talked the day of the search, I had been curious about, and admired the elegant brass buttons on his uniform. Calling them regimental buttons, he explained to me that they were new and that only the mounted dragoons were allowed to wear them.

Late in the day Captain Henry came over to Plymouth with a three-man patrol party. Yesterday and the day before it had turned delightfully warm, drying up the mud holes and ruts made by Colonel Eldridge's wagons. Adda asked him to come in but as soon as he saw Mrs. Van Curen, he stayed in the doorway and ordered the three soldiers to look around the settlement for anything suspicious. He asked me to come outside, I assume so that we could be away from Mrs. Van Curen, who was still smarting from the rude search party and the cannon powder nonsense, all of which was under Captain Henry's command and so she blamed him. Adda stepped outside with me. As soon as the three of us were alone, he asked me, "Did you read my letter?" I nodded. Adda looked at me curiously. I was relieved to see he was still in uniform. I scanned his coat for the missing button, but quickly realized that this was foolish. He simply had sent an extra button.

I'm sure he sensed I was not too pleased with him or his Army people. He seemed tense yet anxious to talk. First he apologized for his company's rude behavior two days ago, excusing it by saying that the presence of Deputy Preston had forced them to do it and that he was an officer with duties to perform, whether he liked the orders or not. He wanted me to know that the members of the artillery squad in charge of the cannons were Northerners. He claimed that if they had been ordered to shoot, they would

Captain Henry's Strange Proposal

have fired over the heads of the immigrants. It was Captain Henry's opinion that if Deputy Preston had ordered a battle, half of Colonel Cooke's troops would have come over to "our" side. We've discussed it since and agreed that we should keep Captain Henry's confession strictly to ourselves. Adda[36] was privy to all of this.

The three of us were standing just outside our doorway. Captain Henry took my arm and without saying anything indicated that he wanted to take a little walk. Adda caught the hint and went inside. The October afternoon was warmly pleasant. We walked east beyond earshot of any wagons or buildings. Now and then we'd pause but mostly we walked, and he talked. He asked rather casually if we were harboring any Negroes.

"No."

"Have you seen any Negroes?" He pronounced the word "Negra."

"No, why do you ask?"

"Army headquarters believes Plymouth might be sheltering run away slaves. Our patrols are now going to be out looking for them, so watch your step. We have to enforce the fugitive slave law."

I kept quiet. His warning called to mind an incident that had occurred about a month before Colonel Cooke stationed his troops nearby, probably about the 5th or 6th of September. A northbound wagon, really a small, scruffy schooner, stopped here briefly, long enough to take a late-noon meal at our boarding house. After they'd eaten, the mister made soft small talk with Mrs. Van Curen. She suggested Adda and I step outside. She often did that if she or Mr. Van Curen wished to speak with visitors

---

[36] Confirmed in *Memories of Addie Stewart Graton University of Kansas Libraries, Kansas KHMS 84:5:13*—M.L.C.

heading north. Adda and I had our suspicions but we kept them to ourselves. Outside we noticed that occasionally their wagon jiggled slightly, but there was no breeze to cause it.

After the wagon left, Adda and I decided to take a little walk north. There was something about those people that made us curious. We assumed they would stay on the Lane Trail and walked generally north, maybe a mile and a half to two miles. Pony Creek runs north there and is left of and parallel to Lane's Trail. Up ahead the trail crosses Pony Creek and goes on north to the Nebraska line. Though it's tricky to get a wagon down to the creek bed, the creek is easily forded in that stretch of it. It's the same trail we took down from Archer, so it was familiar.

We'd heard about some caves in the limestone cliffs of Pony Creek in that area. To find them we left the trail to follow the creek. Walking soon became more difficult, as we entered a corridor of shrubs and woods well above the creek, which was ten or so feet below us. In some areas the cliffs were steep and well defined, but in other places, a sandy bank, sparsely covered with small trees and bushes, confined the creek. We used one of those sloping spots to get down to the creek bed. Occasionally there were shallow caves and indentations in the cliffs at varying heights above the creek, some with water weeping from their openings. Most caves were small and inaccessible except to swallows that darted in and out and seemed to prefer the cliffs' upper edges. We walked back generally south along the creek, perhaps a half-mile. Ahead of us on the left we saw a narrow, triangular opening, two to three feet wide at the base, partially obscured by an elderberry bush that had a few purple clusters remaining. Water was oozing out below the bush, slowly trickling into the creek. It was late in the afternoon and the cliff on the west side of the creek was high enough to prevent sunlight getting down to us.

Captain Henry's Strange Proposal

    Without saying anything to each other we pushed the bushes to one side and squeezed our bodies in. Adda was ahead of me. The dark cave was made even more so by our bodies blocking the entrance. We certainly couldn't see how deep into the cliff the cave went, but not six feet from where we were gradually, as our eyes adjusted to the darkness, the vague, lumpy outlines of two human beings materialized, apparently a young man and woman. I almost jumped out of my skin but had enough sense to keep quiet. Since Adda was in front of me, she must have seen them a second or two before me. The slaves were hunched down on the wet muddy floor of the cave. None of us spoke. I put my finger to my lips, which I suppose the world over means silence. Immediately I pulled at Adda's clothing until both of us were outside and standing on the soft sandy, muddy surface of the creek bed. It was only then that we saw the northbound footprints going toward the cave. We walked south along the creek until we could find a convenient set of stone outcroppings and exposed roots, which we used to climb up into the sunlight. On the way back to Plymouth we vowed not to say a word to anybody about what we had seen in the cave. We guessed that the slaves had been on the wagon that had stopped at our house, but we did wonder why the wagon's driver hadn't taken them on to Archer or Rolla. It was generally known in Plymouth, but never discussed openly that those two settlements were stations in the northbound underground railroad. Adda and I walked very briskly out of the woods and onto the prairie and Lane's Trail. If there was to be a late-afternoon rendezvous, we didn't want to be any part of it.

    Needless to say, since the Army has established its camp north of us, I doubt that cave will get much business from here on.

    While I was recalling this episode, Captain Henry had launched into a long speech as we walked. "This might come as a surprise to you but most Southern white folk, mine included, don't own slaves. Just because a person hails from the South doesn't mean he owns slaves. I'd guess only one white in four, maybe one in five, owns slaves. My family certainly doesn't own any and that goes for all of the men in my company. Most of my soldiers are off the farm. Some of my men can barely read and write, some can't read at all. I'm an exception because I grew up in the city and had ten years of public school. I think it's because so few of our boys are educated that I was selected to attend an officer-training course. I did well and earned my commission."

We had walked some distance now from the settlement. Now and then we'd drop into a little rolling depression in the prairie. It was late in the day, with long shadows across the plains. In these little valleys we were well out of the afternoon sunlight, and occasionally we were out of sight of Plymouth. I wondered what my father would say about my being alone out here with a soldier and a Southern one to boot.

"Many Southerners are as opposed to slavery as you are," he told me. "In some of the border states, like Maryland, there are Quakers known for being organized and active abolitionists. Whites in the South who oppose slavery walk a fine line. It's seditious to say publicly that the Negro should be free, even though in the border states, and to a lesser degree in Tennessee and my home state of Kentucky, there are indeed some free Negroes. My state has its own special problem. Kentucky is directly across the river from Ohio and, from what I can figure; Ohio has more abolitionists than any state in the North. They come into Kentucky pretending to be on business but they are actually crossing the river to spread sedition to our Negroes. Anyone caught putting ideas into the Negroes' heads gets punished severely, usually by vigilance committees and gangs. The authorities look the other way."

He told me that growing up in Kentucky, he had the idea planted firmly in his head that the Negro lacked the will and mentality to learn occupational skills.

"Over the years," he said, "I could see with my own eyes that what my relatives told me didn't square with the facts. We had several blacksmith shops in town. In at least half of them Negroes were employed. My own uncle patronized a shop that was owned by a free Negro. My uncle went to him because he said he was the least expensive. My uncle brought all his mules and horses to this fellow. That man did all their horse shoeing, and I observed that those shoes never fell off.

"When I was thirteen or fourteen a large building to house a dairy was built in the south end of town. I'd go down and watch. Negro bricklayers did all the masonry. One of my aunts declared that 'the first good wind' and that building would come down. She was right in most things, so I waited for the dairy to fall down, but by the time I joined the Army, that building was still standing, including the roof, which had also been built by some free Negroes. So it was nonsense about the Negro being too dumb to learn skills. All they needed was opportunity."

What he was saying sounded like something he'd been thinking about for some time. I wondered why he wanted to discuss these things with me. Maybe he was trying to tell me that the two of us had more in common than his behavior at Plymouth would cause me to believe.

Captain Henry told me that in the border states like Maryland and Virginia some slaves began petitioning to get their freedom. He said that before slavery was outlawed in the Northern states, the slaves there had the right to petition the state government for their freedom and often got it. "The idea is catching on in the South, particularly in the cities in the border states. They are encouraged and helped to petition by free Negroes with whom they socialize or attend church. Maybe a quarter of the city Negroes in Delaware, Kentucky and Virginia are already free, and up to half in Maryland, but there aren't any big plantations up there. But I doubt the petition idea will achieve much success in the Deep South. In the first place the Negro isn't even a citizen, so I don't understand how he has the right, like you or me, to petition, and with the Southern legislatures dominated by slave owners you may be sure it won't become law, not in the Deep South!" Much of this news was very interesting to me.

"Most of the slaves are on plantations, they're not in the cities. Anyway, we don't have big cities like you do up North." Captain Henry added that only a small minority of whites could afford to own slaves, telling me that the plantation owners had created resentment among the poorer whites. "The plantation owners are expanding a form of aristocracy that as a country we'd be better off without."

Captain Henry explained that "Since Eli Whitney invented the cotton gin, the South has doubled its land size and has grown the slave population to three and one half million. Before Whitney cotton wasn't important. Before Whitney, for every slave working the fields, ten to fifteen were in the sheds tediously and manually separating seed from fibers; in fact, after the harvest this labor consumed the balance of the year. Whitney's invention freed all those hands to plant more cotton, which has made it the country's most profitable product. Why, some Southern leaders see a corridor coast to coast paved with cotton fields, worked by slaves, connected by railroads. The Cherokee land and this territory are on that plan. They are already planting cotton in Texas and California. But it all needs to be connected with railroads. That's why statehood is so important. The railroads need the protection out here that they enjoy in the East.

Captain Henry's Strange Proposal

"But if the North thinks they can stop slavery, they are crazy. It's simply too important. So, the South will secede, just as the original thirteen colonies seceded and declared independence a hundred years ago and what happened? War!"

I was struck by how much better informed he was than me. I wondered if he learned all this in the officers training course.

"The resentment in the South towards the plantation owners isn't only among the farmers who can't afford to own slaves." He told me, "The strongest resentment comes from the slaves themselves. Sure, there are uprisings, and have been for fifty years, but they are small and scattered and unless they involve murder, they don't get much notice. The slaves get back at the owners in other ways, by tainting the drinking water just enough to make the Massa and his family sick, or they'll serve spoiled meat. Sometimes the slaves won't dry the winter grain, so that it rots, or they will let the cotton bales stand in mud puddles, which stains the cotton and lowers its value. And they have been known to fiddle with the wheels and axles of their owners' wagons to make them look as if they're breaking accidentally. So the slaves take a lot of supervising and policing."

It was a pleasant day, but it was getting late, and I wasn't used to so much walking and talking. I knew Mrs. Van Curen was expecting me to help with supper. I probably had spent more time with Captain Henry than I should have but I was seeing a different side to his nature and I could see why he might want to leave the Army.

Years later, as I rethought those tumultuous days in Plymouth, I wondered why he simply didn't resign. It never dawned on me to ask. I suppose it was because I was so flattered that a handsome Army captain was paying me so much attention. He was also older than I was, maybe by four or five years, and at my age then, that made quite a difference.

Our walk had taken us in a big circle. We had gone east of the settlement and south of the Army camp, but well out of sight of both. We walked back towards Plymouth. Nearing the outskirts of the settlement we had to hop over ruts left by the recent freight wagons and rain. Dodging the ruts, which were now soft but no longer muddy, took some agility. To help, Captain Henry moved closer to me and courteously put an arm around my waist. I didn't resist. His arm was there only a second or two but the gesture did not offend me. He did it in a way that seemed quite natural and helpful. It was the first display of warmth or accommodation I'd received from Captain Henry.

As we approached my house, he said "Miss Stewart, you've been very quiet during this monologue of mine. You've hardly said a word." I thought to myself, he could talk about slavery but I couldn't tell him about the cave episode or the fugitive slaves that I suspected were being transported north. I merely replied, "I was listening to what you were telling me about the plantations and slavery, the importance of cotton, your worry about a war, things I'd never had cause to think much about."

We were now only a hundred or so feet from the house. We stopped. It was really the first time we'd stopped since we began our walk. Looking directly at him I said, "Captain Henry, if there is a war, you're from Kentucky. You'll have to fight for the South."

"Yes."

"Will you leave the Army before then?"

"Right now, if you'll go with me."

"You haven't answered my question."

He paused. "If I leave, will you come with me?"

"No."

Luckily he didn't ask me why not. I was wondering what I would say. How could I explain to my father in a prisoner of war

Captain Henry's Strange Proposal

camp that I had decided to run off with a soldier, a Southern soldier at that, never mind his reasons or that he was an officer. And how would Captain Henry be able to live with the dishonor that he deserted? If I joined him, would I have to share this shame? He is proud of being an officer and he's earned that pride. In time, I thought, he would regret it if he left the Army, never mind his reasons for doing it.

We had come to my doorstep, "Well, I've given you a lot to think about," he said, "I'll try to get over again in a few days." He left and disappeared in the little draw of Pony Creek north of our place.

When I walked back in the house, Mrs. Van Curen was talking with Adda and two other ladies. My appearance stopped their discussion in mid sentence. They must have had a great time speculating as to what in the world was going on between Captain Henry and me out there on the prairie. I could imagine them saying, "Humph! They were gone almost two hours." I admit I enjoyed being a party to this mystery, since I knew the ending. I could hardly wait to begin the journal entry. I wondered how much I should tell Adda.

That was the last I heard or saw of Captain Henry. Occasionally I've thought about the absence of romance in his proposal. I suppose all girls expect their first proposal to contain romance. It wasn't long after that Adda and I removed to Archer (Nebraska Territory) and in the meantime, we didn't see him. I assumed he had been sent to another location for a few days. I've occasionally thought about his contrary opinions about slavery. Maybe he was a secret abolitionist. He'd certainly given a lot of thought to the difference between what he'd been taught about the Negroes and what he had observed of them while growing up. But more than just the wrongness of slavery, I think, as an officer, he'd learned to plan ahead and he saw how distasteful things were in Kansas and knew it would be so much worse if the South really seceded.

8.

A Pleasant and Social Interlude,
Autumn 1856

Father is paroled by President Pierce

In late October, Mr. Strong returned to Plymouth to get some property they left behind when they moved to Nebraska. He had no sooner come into the house than he began to complain about having been rudely stopped and searched by some sentries on the Lane Trail north of us. His bitter remarks about the soldiers and the new Army camp and its size prompted us to tell him about the big October tenth episode, which seemed to increase his aggravation.

Mr. Strong suggested to us that we return with him to Archer, adding that he had room in the wagon for the two of us but not for too many of our household effects.

In a long, fatherly conversation with us he said that ever increasing hostility in Kansas, brought on by the proslavery people, matched and escalated by the Free Staters, is becoming explosive. Our family's experience, he told us, is a good example of what has gone wrong and how quickly. He reminded Adda and me that since August, when we came into Plymouth, we had several alarms that could have resulted in bloodshed, if we had not had the organizing genius of General Lane available to us. That showed the proslavery side that we could hold our own. Then he made a very personal point.

"Where's your father? Is he building his sawmill or surveying out here on the prairie? No, for heaven's sake, he's a peaceable man with no military experience but was pressed into a ragtag army that was so inept or betrayed—it doesn't matter—they were captured. And by whom? The very forces that should be protecting us, the U.S. Army."

Mr. Strong said, "Regretfully, I've come to this conclusion: the Government has taken sides and they are not on our side." He paused for that idea to sink in.

It was his opinion that our Government had invented this scheme of Popular Sovereignty to attract proslavery immigrants to settle in the Territory and build up the population in order to vote Kansas into the Union as a slave state. Worse than that, our own Government had very cleverly and quietly, and without the North realizing it, appointed a proslavery administration from top to bottom including the judges, the sheriffs and six Federal Marshals, not to mention our two Territorial Chiefs of Police. Because these administrators encourage it, this policy contributes to the lawlessness. "General Persifer Smith's record on our behalf is laughable. And so is that of his crony, Sheriff Sam Jones, who led the effort to destroy Lawrence and now runs the prison camp at Lecompton. The authorities turn a deaf ear when we Northern settlers need protection. When the fox is in the henhouse, can the hens expect any protection?"

As an example, he said, look at our postal system.

"It's a sham, particularly if the parcel or envelope is going to or coming from the North. That's because the postal service, what little of it exists, is in the hands of the proslavery people, and they use it as an opportunity to loot our mail, as an accepted form of additional compensation." Mr. Strong also mentioned that we had yet to have a Territorial Land Office, which makes it difficult for Free Staters to file their land claim, but assumes Southern settlers have squatters' rights.

"Augusta," he said, "the crucial test for our safety, well-being, pursuit of happiness, all those plums I left Wisconsin for, was when Mr. Soley, who was leading a train from Massachusetts, went all the way to Fort Leavenworth to petition the Army for safe passage for his company into the Territory. What did the poor man get? An order to get off the fort grounds while he was still in one piece. Now I really don't care about General Smith's sentiments. I have mine, too, but he should be professional enough to set aside his sentiments and do what he was appointed to do—and that's to protect all the citizens of this Territory, not just those who are proslavery.

"No sir, when Soley got turned down by General Persifer Smith, when your father and the other settlers from here in Plymouth were captured and turned over to the tender mercies of Sheriff Jones and his proslavery ruffians running that camp in Lecompton," he paused and said, "do you know, Augusta, that the two judges who found your father and the others guilty of murder are both rabidly and unapologetically proslavery. We're not even sure that Judge Cato, the one who tried and convicted your father, is a lawyer!"[37] They are walking examples of what I said before. They were part of the proslavery administration cynically appointed by the Federal Government in Washington

---

[37] Associate Justice, S. G. Cato tried the men on September 23, 1856 in Lecompton. His superior was the chief of the territorial court, Samuel Dexter Lecompte..—M.L.C.

to run this territory. Run it for whom? For the proslavery people, that's who."

Mr. Strong explained that when he saw and thought about all these things, he realized we Free State settlers had been misled by the well-meaning abolitionist groups in the North. "This place is not safe," he said, "We are in the middle of an uprising aimed at driving out the Free Staters and this part of the territory is its center of gravity. So, Augusta, Mrs. Strong and I didn't need a séance to tell us to move to a safe haven.

"And if you will pardon me for saying so, I hope you girls are a little smarter than your father and will come live with us over in Archer, at least until there is some semblance of law and order in the Territory, or until Old John Brown musters an uprising that liberates the prison camp. You can work in my store or for my missus. She already has a boarding house set up, so she will need help. This is not charity we are offering, though we do care about you girls and continually worry about your safety down here."

He told us that he was going to be here a day or two. "Take the rest of the day to think about my offer, but you ought not to sit around here waiting for the proslavery ruffians to pluck you off."

I'm sure he repeated his concern for us to Mrs. Van Curen that evening, because the next day she turned very chilly towards us. After all, if we left, she would have to find other helpers, helpers so destitute that they would be compelled to work without pay, though they would get board and room, like my sister and me. Isn't that the limit? Father built this house.

Adda and I discussed Mr. Strong's offer to go to Archer, though we didn't know how long that would be for. Aside from our safety, we loved the Strongs, especially Mrs. Strong, so it was an easy choice.

A Pleasant and Social Interlude

That evening Adda and I announced to Mrs. Van Curen that Mr. Strong felt the two of us would be safer in Nebraska. We said that we had given it considerable thought and had decided to accept his offer of work and hospitality in a safer settlement.

Adda and I were concerned about our big wagon, the two oxen, our horses and household effects if left to the tender mercies of Mr. Van Curen. We had already experienced some of his dishonorable behavior, including the matter of the undelivered letter. On another occasion in early October I lacked the postage to mail a letter back to the States. At that time the closest post office was over in Archer, Nebraska Territory. It was also the safest one for us to get to. Mr. Van Curen was on his way to the Archer post office to pickup mail for the Plymouth Company, and I asked him if he would buy and add the necessary postage to my letter. I handed him the pennies and my letter. Weeks later during one of Mr. Strong's visits to Archer, before they moved there, Mr. Strong happened to remark that there was a letter of mine at the Archer post office. The Postmaster knew we lived in Plymouth and he sent word via Mr. Strong that my letter awaited the necessary postage. So much for the honesty of the man who didn't want us to leave Plymouth but hinted that if we did leave, he would look after our team, wagon and household goods.

Adda and I were particularly concerned about Father's surveying tools, most of which we had since moved into that large wagon box, which served as a front seat of the big wagon. We decided to take the two horses and our small wagon with us to Archer. We planned to put the most valuable of Father's surveying instruments into that large box and carry it with us in the small wagon, along with our personal effects. We would leave the oxen and the large wagon in Plymouth. We agreed to let Mr. Van Curen use our Studebaker in exchange for his keeping it until Father was released and we could all return to Plymouth.

Adda and I moved the balance of our household effects into Mr. Shea's covered wagon. Mr. Shea's brother had volunteered with Father and was also in the prison camp. The Shea brothers had come with the Stowell Party from Cape Cod, Massachusetts. They are Irish and left the "Old Country" during the potato famine. Their wives and children were still in Massachusetts. Mr. Shea said he would also look after the oxen.

So, about the last week of October, Adda and I packed our clothing, some personal belongings and some bedding into one of the two big trunks that the soldiers a few weeks earlier had suspected might be full of rifles or cannons or gunpowder or whatnot, and left with Mr. Strong for Archer, Nebraska. We followed his wagon out of camp. Our departure caused quite a stir. Most everybody came out of their tents to wish us well.

We retraced the route we had used to come into Kansas Territory from Archer in August. Archer was less than a day's drive from Plymouth (maybe fifteen miles) and is near a small river nicknamed "Muddy." Although we stayed on the prairie, occasionally we would skirt some woods. It was a glorious dry autumn day. The trees were beginning to turn. The Maples were now at the height of their orange-and-red hair "do."

Towards late afternoon, Mr. Strong pulled his team to a halt, jumped down from the wagon and signaled us to wait quietly. He reached behind his seat box and removed a double-barreled shotgun. Walking ten to twelve paces towards some woods off in the distance he took careful aim at something in the prairie grass. He discharged one barrel with a terrible noise. Fifty or so yards from the wagon three or four turkeys rose in the air but not high. They flew in a large arc just above the grass towards some brush several hundred yards away and disappeared in the tall yellow prairie grass. But while they were still in flight, he discharged the other barrel.

A Pleasant and Social Interlude

Mr. Strong trotted over to where the turkeys had been and picked up the two he had shot, holding them up for our long-distance inspection.

When he returned to the wagon, we got down to admire his marksmanship. He said enough shot hit the first turkey to almost tear its head off. The next day we helped Mrs. Strong prepare a big turkey dinner.

Archer turned out to be a very sociable place. We seemed to have left at the border all of the worry about threats of attack that had consumed so much of our daily activity in Plymouth. The landscape was not much different from Plymouth's. Of course, we were only a dozen or so miles from Plymouth. We had hardly arrived and unpacked our things, putting them away in our room in the cabin that Mr. Strong and his neighbors had built, when we were invited to a ball. Mr. Strong had already started a grocery store in Archer.

Mrs. Strong had several boarders and among them was a boy from Maine and Mr. Peters, a Southerner. George Miller, another boarder, (no relation to the hotel owner) presented Adda and me each with a small but fancy ticket admitting one person to a ball that was to be held at Miller's Hotel, the same hotel where we had dinner on our way down from Nebraska City in August. Although we were flattered to be invited, we didn't know whether we were to be escorted by Mr. Peters and the gentleman from Maine, or whether they expected us to arrive alone; we didn't think arriving alone was ladylike. Mrs. Strong called this arrangement "a strange social custom." Miller's Hotel is about two and a half miles from the Strong cabin. Unraveling this social mystery consumed a lot of time and speculation by Adda, me and Mrs. Strong until Mr. Peters, who was rather shy, explained it this way: Married people were just expected to come without invitation, but young men bought tickets and presented them to young ladies, ladies with whom they would like to dance. Mr. Peters had cleared up only a part of this social mystery; just how these Nebraska Lotharios expected Adda and me to get to the hotel was a mystery.

Mystery or not, the matter was quickly laid to rest by Mrs. Strong. She said she always made it her "business" to know "her boarders" and in this case, she announced, with more than just motherly certainty, that Mr. Peters would not be an acceptable escort. We inquired as to her reasons. She said Mr. Peters is a proslavery fellow and is a "drinking one" at that, and that he continues to use tobacco, adding that any one of these personal weaknesses would be enough for her to disqualify the gentleman as a suitable escort for us.

Her criticism of his tobacco use caused me to recall an incident that had taken place just a few days earlier after supper when the boarders were eating dessert. Mr. Kirk, one of the boarders, and a friend of his, who had been his guest that evening, both took out cigars, lit them and after a few puffs had begun spitting on the floor. Adda and I had both served the evening meal but I was not in the main room when the spitting episode began. Adda was. I came from the kitchen just as Adda said, "Just who, Mr. Kirk, do you think cleans up that mess you're making on the floor?" Mr. Kirk ignored Adda and continued talking to his companion.

Just then Mrs. Strong came out of the kitchen. It was her custom to make a little "small talk" with her boarders after supper while the tea was "steeping." She stopped as abruptly as if she had hit a brick wall. The room instantly became silent. Mrs. Strong assumed a commanding posture. Very erect, with both hands on her hips, she lowered her voice, causing us to strain to get her words. As she lowered her voice, she lowered its temperature to below freezing on the Fahrenheit scale and in cold, barely audible words, said, "You know the rules of this house. No tobacco use in any form, and spitting on the floor is so reprehensible I can't imagine any gentleman, especially a Southern gentleman, doing it." She immediately ordered them to the door, to dispose of their "filthy products," after which they could return. They did as they were told. Then she said, "Adda, find these two gentlemen two old rags and a dishpan of water." Adda went into the kitchen and soon returned with the cleaning materials. "Now, gentlemen, if you wish to spend the night in my establishment, clean that wood floor 'til it sparkles. I'm so disgusted with your behavior that there will be no tea served tonight." Mrs. Strong returned to her kitchen. This incident indicated why Mrs. Strong had decided Mr. Peters would not be an acceptable escort to the ball. As she spoke to us, she put her hands on her hips. Adda and I sensed from Mrs. Strong's posture and the sudden lowering of her voice that his offer was in trouble. With a sharp downward nod of her head and a blink that closed both eyes, the matter of Mr. Peters' invitation had been nullified. Adda and I were already familiar with that authoritative, almost audible two-eyed blink. We'd seen her use it on several occasions in which Mrs. Strong was called on to make a decision, whether about a certain food or who would be joining us for supper or when she and Mr. Strong were arguing about some point, when we all knew the decision would ultimately be Mrs. Strong's to make.

We had learned from traveling with the Strongs that summer that the quick nod meant that she had already reached a decision. There would be no further discussion, no appeal. The quick nod established finality like the closing rap of the judge's gavel. It established in a flash her absolute authority. Regarding Mr. Peters, escorting us to the ball, she did not need to verbalize her opposition for us to know that this conversation was over.

Well, just when Adda and I thought our invitations to supper and the fancy ball were "dashed on the rocks," our social prospects improved considerably. Another young man appeared at the Strong cabin to inquire if he could borrow our wagon for the day of the ball. He said Mr. Miller wanted him to go over to the river to get some "things" for the occasion. I'm sure he meant the Missouri and was speaking of the ferry landing just beyond Nebraska City. This gentleman, who said he was doing some carpentry at the Miller Hotel, was none other than Frank Robinson, the young man who together with Jacob Chase about mid September had brought us news of Father in the Lecompton prison. He said if we would go to the ball with him, he would arrange to come for us and also see us safely home. With the swiftness of a hawk, "Mother" Strong swooped down on this proposition. She hadn't even been in the room; Adda and I had speculated that Mrs. Strong possessed a sixth sense that signaled to her, wherever she was, that her decision-making powers were required. She immediately began an intense, detailed, "lowered voice" interrogation of Mr. Robinson, who found it necessary to lean against a chair for support.

After Mr. Robinson's departure, much to our relief Mrs. Strong announced that Mr. Robinson would be acceptable. We now had to get word to him that he had passed the test: "Many are called, few are chosen." It would be agreeable for the Stewart girls to be his guests if he appeared on time, in a proper manner, properly dressed, and, yes, he could use our wagon to go "to the river," providing it was back at the Strongs' on time.

When the evening finally arrived, we didn't want to be late but Mr. Robinson came early enough. This was the greatest dance I ever attended. Of course, in all honesty, I haven't really attended that many dances.

Supper at Miller's Hotel, which is simply a double log cabin, was ready early. We were so excited that I don't even recall now what was served. Directly after supper we went into the large room where in August our "outfit" had eaten dinner. But the room was different tonight. All the tables and chairs were removed, and three or four musicians were at one end of the room. This was rather new to me, as I had never gone to many balls. Mr. Robinson said he hadn't either, but told us he would find partners if we would dance with them. Mr. Robinson was turning out to be quite a social arranger, which was pleasant for Adda and me since this seemed to be such a special occasion. Soon Mr. Robinson brought a gentleman over, who asked me to dance. I recognized him immediately as the friend of Mr. Robinson who was released because they were young and had come through Plymouth to tell us about Father. As a dancer he was the best of those I danced with, though he was very quiet. I suppose he was concentrating on his dancing. I certainly was. After that dance, Mr. Robinson came over and reintroduced this gentleman as his "friend, Chase." Smiling, and to make conversation, I asked them if Mr. Chase had a first name. Mr. Chase quietly said, "Jacob."

This was a strange conversation that Frank Robinson and Mr. Chase and I were having. I knew perfectly well who Frank's "friend" was. After all, it was only two or three weeks ago that these two boys came to Plymouth. I also knew that Mr. Chase had been with the Lexington Company that had headed for Iowa Point and that he was with Father when they were captured by Colonel Cooke's dragoons. I had always believed, since he and Frank Robinson had made such a "bee line" to Plymouth after being released and were so anxious to leave us for Nebraska Territory, that a judge or one of the prison official had spoken very sharply to them, warning them to get out of the Territory and, for their own safety, to stay out. But I kept this opinion to myself.

So I had indeed met Mr. Chase and remembered him very well. But now in Nebraska, Mr. Chase seemed distant and reserved in my presence and I suppose I mimicked that behavior. But I didn't understand what purpose it served Frank Robinson to assume that we were such strangers with poor memories.

Mr. Chase and I danced again and again during the night but he remained very bashful, spoke little, and while dancing spoke not at all, and I seemed troubled with the same complaint, so there was not much conversation between us.

The next Sunday, Frank came over to the Strongs' (I now believe to see Adda.) Soon Mr. Chase arrived. Neither Chase nor I spoke. Frank noticed this reticence between us and said, "Miss Stewart, this is Mr. Chase. I believe you saw him at the ball, did you not?"

I said, "Yes, I believe I did. Yes, I do believe I've met the gentleman before." Well, I certainly knew well enough who it was. I danced most of the sets with him only a week ago, but I was simply reluctant to speak to him. It wasn't really fear. It was a form of "dumbfoundedness" that seemed to keep me from speaking sensibly. I was, for some strange reason, reluctant to speak. I had for a week thought of that dance and the social pleasantries over and over. What a fine dancer Chase was, and although he didn't talk much, it was to me he kept returning dance after dance, and when other men asked for the "next dance," I took comfort, bordering on snootiness, lifting my chin as I said "My sets are all spoken for"—even though that wasn't always true. I really didn't know from one set to the next whether Chase would leave the group of men, whom he seemed to know, and after the music had started, walk over to me, smile and offer his arm as an indication that we should dance together again. But he did and, Dear Journal, I can tell you in all privacy, when I saw him coming back, my heart danced with joy.

Later, I gave a lot of thought to my behavior toward Chase. I couldn't understand why I was so bashful with him but so comfortable with Captain Henry, even while declining his proposal. And I had no trouble with Colonel Cooke, who was old enough to be my father.

Mrs. Strong appeared and asked the gentlemen if they cared to stay for Sunday afternoon tea. They did. Later in the evening, after Chase and Robinson left, one of the other gentlemen boarders, a Mr. William Lemon, tried very hard to presume enough familiarity to tease me about our gentlemen callers. I ignored him.

Adda seems very taken with Mr. Robinson.

Almost every Sunday, Frank Robinson came to the Strongs' house. The first of December, the Strongs moved to a larger cabin closer to Archer. Of course, we moved with them. Here we could go to socials and various meetings more often. The new cabin was much larger, which allowed Mrs. Strong to increase the number of boarders. Our duties remained the same, except I did more cooking. Mrs. Strong did all the baking. We were all like a family but the family suddenly expanded by four or five.

This morning I had a few moments to reflect on what I shall call "contrasts." I am suddenly struck by the contrasts the rather orderly life we enjoyed in Michigan, compared with the disorderly style we had in the Kansas settlement.

Those settlements are only fifteen to thirty miles south of us, but in comparison to all the building and progress in Archer, they could be a continent away. Here in Nebraska Territory, there is such constructive talk and bustle—talk of spring planting, the best tools for home construction. In Plymouth it was one rumor after another of some impending calamity, an unhappy combination of do-nothing one day and great commotion the next. None of it was very pleasant, none of it constructive.

Thinking back on it, Mrs. Van Curen was right in believing that Colonel Cooke's Army camp was there to oppress us. Father, Adda and I didn't have the slightest idea of what was in store for us when we left Iowa City in our gleaming white prairie schooner.

After Adda and I moved to Archer, we remained in constant communication with our friends in Plymouth. The safest post office closest to Plymouth was Archer, so two or three times a week there was someone coming from Plymouth to post mail or pick it up. Thanks to these sources, we stayed current with events in Kansas Territory. After we left, we heard that in October, a large party of immigrants who were bound for Kansas Territory was arrested by my friend Colonel Cooke. Colonel Cooke's dragoons escorted this group to see Governor Geary, who lectured them to be peaceful or they would all be put into Lecompton, and then released them. Our informer did not tell us where this group settled.

In late October a visitor from Plymouth stayed overnight with the Strongs. He had some recent Eastern newspapers including the *Tribune* (I've since forgotten whether it was a New York or a Chicago paper) and the *Boston Traveler* (dated September 22, 1856), which contained an article by Richard Hinton with the names of the 107 Free State prisoners at Lecompton, some who had been arrested after the Battle of Hickory Point. Father's name was on the list. To see his name appear in such a way was chilling. There were several editorials deploring their imprisonment and suggesting that the states that sent immigrants should send their militia to Kansas Territory to free the men and to make the Territory safe for all immigrants, not just the proslavery element, which our Federal Government seems to favor over the Free State people. The most scathing of the editorials was written by the Governor of Iowa, who said his legislature was agitating to send the Iowa militia to Kansas Territory to maintain the peace.

A Chicago paper carried a story about immigrant trains being rudely detained and searched in Plymouth, Kansas Territory, by a Colonel Cooke, U.S. Army. This obviously referred to the episode on October 10th.

A Pleasant and Social Interlude

In November, a Wisconsin relative of the Strongs sent a letter with a *New York Tribune* article that included a long statement about the conditions at the Lecompton prisoner of war camp. Most of the prisoners had signed it. We wondered if our English friend, Mr. Hinton, the newspaper journalist from London, wrote that article while he was visiting these parts.

Also in November, we heard that Father was one of forty Free State men at Lecompton who had been moved to a prison camp near Topeka called Tecumseh, because Lecompton was too full to hold more. That information turned out to be false.

In mid-December, a friend of Mr. Strong, who was visiting, said at supper time that land sales are now beginning in earnest. He had news that the Governor had appointed a Surveyor General and had set up an office for him and the surveyors under him as a territorial land office in an old abandoned log cabin at Lecompton. They collected monies for the land sales after the surveyors did their work.

According to Mr. Strong's friend, Governor Geary had reported to President Pierce that he had received $440,000 for the recent sale of 880 sections of land. This gentleman said to Mr. Strong that he did not think this was a particularly large land sale. Father must be very upset knowing there will be all this surveying work and he can't get to it. The gentleman added that 209,000 acres of land equals 1,300 sections, near the town of Leavenworth had sold for $450,000, or about $2.25 per acre, but he and Mr. Strong had a good laugh over the news that 320 acres in town had failed to sell at the posted price of $30 an acre, or $7.50 per city lot. Everybody around this "neck of the woods" knows that there are only about 2,000 people living in the town of Leavenworth, and that's not counting soldiers or Indians. So it will be a long time before enough people move in to buy up those lots.

A taffy (candy) dance was planned for Christmas night at Miller's Hotel. The hotel also lodged the Archer post office. Mr. Miller is the county judge as well, so his premises serve as the local courthouse. Archer is the county seat of Richardson County. Frank Robinson came to fetch us. We had quite a merry time. Mrs. Miller made the candy. After the taffy had cooled to the point where it could be tolerably held, each couple at the dance was given a chunk about the size of a fist. Mrs. Miller demonstrated how to pull and twist the candy into a rope, folding it over and braiding it to make it thick again, then pulling it again and so on.

This process makes the taffy take on a light amber color. After considerable pulling, each couple put their pulled-out taffy on a table, where it was cut into small pieces and dusted with powered white sugar. Later, as we danced by the table, the custom was to pause and pick up a piece of taffy. We certainly chewed a lot of taffy that night.

Mrs. Miller had also made fudge with Black Walnut meat in it. There was some white candy containing roasted Hazel Nuts. There are large stands of Black Walnut here in Nebraska and along the river there are "patches" of Hazel. Some people call them filberts. Mrs. Miller said her family owned a fancy candy shop in New York City before her family moved to Albany, where she met and married Mr. Miller. She said Mr. Miller had wanted to own a hotel but could not afford an Albany location.

Mr. Chase was not at the "taffy" party. He had gone to a ball in Barada about nine miles north of Archer. Well, I must admit I had a fine time anyway but I missed seeing Mr. Chase. He would have enjoyed the Miller's party since he likes to sing and has a rather nice voice. Every so often the dancing would be interrupted by a round of Christmas carols. Everybody sang.

A Pleasant and Social Interlude

We were led by a lively young woman, Miss Catherine Samuels, who teaches in Archer and has only one arm. Her school is called a "subscription" school and, according to Mrs. Strong, it gets some assistance from a church in the East. I discovered later that some of the candy for this party was provided by Mrs. Sally Dodge, a friend of the Strongs, who is a nurse and acts as the local doctor in Archer and surroundings.

Earlier in the week some of the boys had gone over to the River, found a pine and felled it. The top eight feet or so was used as a Christmas tree, which the Millers placed near the door to the kitchen and decorated with garlands of popcorn and little loops of colored paper.

In Archer, we were invited to about one party a week, sometimes more often. At one party at the Cooke's all the old folks and babies were there. A Mr. Potter introduced a Southerner to me, a Mr. Kirk. This was the same John Kirk who had been so severely reprimanded by Mrs. Strong a few weeks ago. Now he was exceedingly polite and didn't mention the spitting episode. Mr. Potter told us a few days later that Johnny Kirk asked him, which of the two Stewart girls was it that Frank Robinson was paying attention to, saying that he was coming to see the other one and would marry her! Well, fat chance that I would ever settle for a skinny, cigar-smoking Southern spitter, like John Kirk.

The day after Christmas, Frank Robinson dropped in. Mr. Chase was with him. It was so nice to see Mr. Chase again but I felt I could not let on that I was pleased to see him. He too was very quiet, though that night he played the violin. Mr. Kirk was put out by the arrangement. He complained to me that Mr. Chase and I seemed to be on familiar terms and that was unfair to him. I exaggerated a bit by explaining that Mr. Chase and I were old friends from Kansas Territory, and that we had been settlers there together, but I didn't tell Mr. Kirk about Mr. Chase being captured by U.S. troops in September.

On New Year's Day, we attended a party in St. Dervin, Missouri. It had snowed hard all day and got dark early. We returned to Archer late in the afternoon. The Strongs had planned a ball and we were glad to be back in time for it. Two men came in shortly after we got home. One of the strangers bowed to me, the other went behind the stove, I presume to warm up. I paid no attention to them. We were accustomed to people coming and going at the Strongs.' Mrs. Strong always had boarders and it was hard to keep track of them all.

Presently, Emma Strong came into the room and said, "Augusta, don't you know these gentlemen."

I was provoked at her for asking me such a direct question in front of them. "No."

"Well, they are Plymouth gentlemen from the prison where they are holding your father."

Regaining my composure, I admitted that one of them did look like Mr. Kerr of Plymouth. It was Mr. Kerr and he burst out laughing. I told her that I didn't know who the other one was, the one in the shadows behind the stove. At last that one spoke up and said, Adda and I were a couple of "smart chickens" not to recognize him. Sure enough, it was Father, but so much heavier and fleshier it was no wonder we didn't recognize him.

Adda just exploded, "You escaped! We knew it was just a matter of time."

"No, girls, I didn't escape, though I could have any time I pleased. No, I was pardoned by President Pierce.[38] Seventeen of

---

38   (According to the executive minutes of Governor Geary, President Pierce pardoned the prisoners and signed March 2, 1857. Governor Geary's release signed March 5, 1857, freed seventeen Free State prisoners, convicted of manslaughter in the attack on Hickory Point.

A Pleasant and Social Interlude

us are on what they call a parole. We will get the official pardon early this spring." Father said that the group included him and Mr. Kerr and two or three more men from Plymouth Company, and Frank Swift (a soldier we would get to know in Lawrence.) "Adda, you remember Alonzo Crawford, one of the guides who led us down from Nebraska City to Plymouth last August. Well, Alonzo and two or three more men from Plymouth including Kerr are among those who were released just a day or two after Christmas." Said Father. "In all, eighty of us will be pardoned."

Adda, "Sure I remember Alonzo, but you said eighty!" Augusta and I counted 105 names in one article we read in a Chicago paper. And the article by Richard Hinton in the Boston Traveler listed 107 names. What happened to the other twenty or so?"

"Well, about a dozen or so did escape, but I'm afraid the rest died. Mr. William Bowles from Missouri, who owned a gallery[39] in Lawrence with his brother, was not well and he simply couldn't withstand the primitive conditions at the prison. One of the Shea brothers from Massachusetts also died."

Adda and I began packing our things. The three of us planned to leave the following Thursday, January 8th. The Strongs said they would give a farewell ball in our honor on the night before we left. I hoped that Mr. Chase would hear about it.

By chance, Frank Robinson and Mr. Chase came to Archer for a visit on the night we learned about the ball and were surprised to see Father. Mr. Chase, who had some carpentry work in Rulo, seemed to know Father better than Frank. I succeeded in putting Frank up to telling Mr. Chase about the farewell ball that next Wednesday.

---

[39] A studio for the new process to produce a "Likeness". The term photograph had yet to be invented.—M.L.C.

The days before we left Archer were joyful, festive days but Adda and I also had ample time to talk with Father about exactly what happened after his departure from Plymouth last August 25th and about the hardships in the prison camp and what really happened to put him there.

I have shortened and assembled the various conversations that we had, many of which concentrated on Father's opinions on the political struggle in the Territory. He said that during the three months he had spent at Lecompton,[40] he had come to realize by talking with the various prisoners, particularly George W. Deitzler and some proslavery official "up on the hill," that it was a political struggle between the abolitionists and the proslavery settlers that was driving the armed struggle. He said it was complicated but stemmed essentially from the fact that we have two incompatible political forces, each striving for dominance and its own version of statehood. Therefore we have, simultaneously, two governors and two state governments, neither recognizing the legitimacy of the other.

Each side has a town designated as its own state capital, Topeka for the abolitionists and Lecompton for the proslavery people. Both sides have crafted their own set of laws and a constitution. Both have sent their constitutions to Congress requesting statehood under "their" constitution. And we know that Congress and the President are sympathetic to a proslavery state, yet they must face

---

[40] The prison camp was located directly below the proslavery capitol building. Governor Geary would occasionally allow leaders from the prison camp to petition. It was in this fashion that Sam Stewart was allowed to leave the compound with a government horse and wagon to solicit food, blankets, etc. when in their petition it was pointed out to the Governor that Sheriff Jones and the U.S. Army were not providing adequately. Until early October Colonel Cooke and two companies of Dragoons were stationed at Lecompton and knew of the prison situation

the fact that they invented Popular Sovereignty for use as a local solution. "Now that the Northern immigrants can out vote the Southerners, they choose to deny that reality. The proslavery people here in the Territory won't recognize the dual reality that their policy of terror and intimidation has failed and they have lost the immigration contest, so they've lost the vote."

"We have here two huge, irreconcilable differences, two equal but opposite imperatives. The Ancient Greeks knew that those were the elements that precipitate tragedy," he said.

"However, during this entire long and bitter struggle the antislavery people who in time have come to outnumber the proslavery population have remained the political underdogs because slavery remains the law of the territory, deriving from the "law of the land" and their interpretation of property rights."

Because there have been two distinctly different political bodies, they both have felt morally justified to have their own separate militia. And it's been only recently, that is since mid-September, that the U.S. Army Forces have been used to prevent bloodshed on both sides. Until Governor Geary, the U.S. Army was proslavery and viewed the Northerners as invaders, our peaceful coming in an "insurrection." His use of U.S. Army troops to prevent the two sides from each using their own well-armed militias was both his invention and was his downfall.

In the summer of 1855, the proslavery political party meeting in the Shawnee Mission chose Lecompton as their capital. There were several other candidate cities but Lecompton was their choice by vote. They persuaded Congress to appropriate $60,000 for their capitol building.

While the new capitol at Lecompton was being built, the Shawnee Mission was charged to establish a legislature and a body of laws, including a constitution. For the most part it was copied from the Missouri constitution, which, of course, called for slavery, etc., severe penalties for meddling with the slaves, to speak out or print (editorials) against slavery was illegal, etc. These laws were imposed on all citizens of the territory including "Free Soil" advocates who resented them bitterly and dubbed them "bogus."

But bogus or not, they lent legitimacy to proslavery violence delivered by an armed militia, which included the springtime destruction of Lawrence. By then Lecompton was a military stronghold, defended by a large contingent of U.S. troops commanded by "my friend" Colonel Cooke, who had been assigned to prevent any new threats from General Lane and his Free State militia.

The Free State response to the Shawnee/Lecompton "Bogus" Constitution of 1855 was made in August 13th and 15th of that year in Lawrence. A Resolution was passed authorizing a Free State Constitutional Convention to convene in Topeka[41] on September 19th.

Jim Lane was appointed chairman. He set up a form of revolutionary government to embrace the entire state; i. e. not just Lawrence. Jim Lane had served in the U.S. Congress, so he had some "Government" experience.

The "Topeka" Constitution, specifying no slavery in Kansas when awarded statehood, was carried to Washington by Jim Lane who together with Acting Governor Reeder were both elected to the U.S. Senate by the Free Soil Party in March of 1856. Lane presented the Topeka Constitution to the U.S. Congress. Senator Douglas (Illinois) took offense, resulting in an argument, which

---

[41] In forty-nine cities and towns, representing eighteen districts, 2,849 votes ratified this Constitution and elected Reeder and Jim Lane delegates to Congress. Estimate put Free State population (October 1855) at 15,000 and proslavery at 5,000. Ref. Kansas and Kansans, Volume 1, Connelley, p. 480.

Jim Lane suggested could be solved with a duel. Well that didn't advance our cause any.

President Pierce and others in the Federal Government viewed the Topeka constitution and its Convention as a form of insurrection, Father told us, and were so concerned they notified Colonel Cooke and Fort Leavenworth to put down any rebellion by the abolitionists.

This in effect set the tone for our own civil war in Kansas later. Of course, being an abolitionist document, the Topeka Constitution attracted wide and sympathetic attention in the North, especially among Congressmen, editors and public speakers, particularly the Protestant preachers who were using slavery to fuel a new wave of religious zeal, which grew so passionate that Congress responded by ordering the U.S. Mint to put the motto "In God We Trust" on all coins from about 1855 on. For a young nation anxious to avoid the old European alliances between church and state, this was quite a departure from the Country's official position. In the meantime several meetings were held in Topeka (now the new, Free Soil Capital) to elect state officers. Of course, Topeka became the "other" capitol.

These acts so offended the proslavery elements that they called for the arrest of all Free Soil officers and legislators. The Lecompton legislators empowered marshals and sheriffs, aided by U.S. soldiers to carry out these arrests. The "Free Staters" or abolitionists wanted the capital in Lawrence. Their elected governor, Charles Robinson, wasn't even recognized in Washington and as Father told the story, by spring and summer of 1856 was himself in prison, in Lecompton, charged with treason.

In the spring of 1856, before we left Michigan, the territorial government appointed by Washington issued warrants for the arrest of several prominent Free State leaders, among them, Governor Charles Robinson, George W. Deitzler, Gaius Jenkins, two of John Brown's (older) sons, George and John Jr., seven prominent Free State political leaders. Father said that at various times from spring to summer all these arrests (and more) were made, all imprisoned in Lecompton. This action legitimized the sacking of Lawrence the same month. Father said he was to get to know the prisoners and came to a better understanding of the political reality that motivated the use of proslavery arms in the territory to carry out what amounted to Federal Government policy.

Undaunted, the Free State Legislators reconvened last summer on July 4th. However acting under orders from President Pierce in Washington, General E. V. Sumner appeared at that convention with a force of U.S. troops and in an elegant speech to the gathering, ordered them to disperse.

Keep in mind that among the Free Soil people there was a strong but unconfirmed opinion that their population by summer of 1856 exceeded the proslavery count. To pursue that opinion, the Free Soilers met again later that summer that is, those who weren't in jail and authorized a census.

To further abrade the proslavery policies of the U.S. Senate and President Pierce, in August 1857 Congress was reminded of its own doctrine of Popular Sovereignty and was again petitioned to admit the new Territory as a Free State. Father said that on September 5th, shortly before he and the Plymouth Company men were jailed, he learned that there was quite a jubilation in the camp. General Lane and a militia of about 500 Free State, well-armed soldiers who formed up on one of the hills overlooking the prisoner of war camp. The town population became very alarmed. There were also murmurings in the prison camp that if Lane attacked, the guards would be ordered to kill all of the abolitionist prisoners. The prisoners, those who were "political" and not criminal, let it be known that a number of Sharps rifles

A Pleasant and Social Interlude

and some Colt Repeaters had been smuggled into the camp, so it might not be so easy for the guards to kill them.

However, the proslavery boys had failed to appreciate that Lane could rally such an opposing force. Lecompton had only 150 soldiers available. To a man they knew that Lane had the "drop" on them. All Lane's men had Sharps rifles. And several cannons were now wheeled in place all pointing at the "Capitol" building.

Smiling at me, Father said, "Your Colonel Cooke commanded two companies of soldiers that acted as guards, but those soldiers drank most evenings and there weren't enough of them against General Lane's 500 men. And it's a well known fact that if you can see 500 of Lane's men, it is prudent to assume, due to his military training, that he had in reserve, out of sight, another 500."[42]

"Colonel Cooke and the (acting) territorial Governor Woodson and a U.S. Marshal by the name of Preston rode up the hill to "parley" with Lane.

Hearing the name Preston, Adda interrupted Father and gave him a quick report on the October 10th fracas at Plymouth where this rascal was involved. "The upshot of the conference," said Father, "was that Lane agreed not to attack the Capitol if the political prisoners were released unharmed. Colonel Cooke was to be in charge of the release." Father said, "Not all of the prisoners were set free. George Deitzler was held on 'other' charges; namely, treason.

"Then, ten days later, our company of Plymouth boys was captured and marched into the same camp. Several of the

---

[42] Lane actually had a force of 1,200. The proslavery guards numbered about 100 to 200. Colonel Cooke participated in the negotiation. Kansas State Historical Society Transactions, Volume 8, p. 340.

younger men, like your friends, Mr. Chase and Mr. Robinson, were released, and some of our company also escaped. Later that winter, he added, some died, too.

"I know now," Father said, "that in the interval between September 5th or 6th, when Governor Robinson and some of his associates were released, and ten days later when we were imprisoned, the number of skirmishes with the proslavery militias escalated, with upwards of 2,500 Free Soil men in the field under Jim Lane, all prepared to fight or, indeed, already fighting."

"While all of this was going on," Father said, "a larger number of immigrants had begun coming into the Territory from the south, particularly South Carolina, Georgia, Alabama, Virginia and Kentucky. They formed camps fairly close to our Free Soil settlements and stepped up their harassment. They didn't know, though, that the North was supplying us with more men. Lane was building up our army faster than theirs. Nevertheless, the Southerners increased their tactics of terrorizing our little settlements, often carrying out several well-planned attacks the same day. After hearing that John Brown planned to attack the prison camp and get us released by force, some of the Kentucky boys reinforced the capital at Lecompton. He insisted that an adequate force could open-up the prison camp. They were just as determined not to allow Lane and John Brown to free us and we were now probably about 200 men in the camp."

Father said that when he volunteered for the Plymouth Company, he had become part of Lane's effort to respond to the Southerners' growing aggression. "In late August, after our company was mobilized, we didn't go straight to Iowa Point. Lane ordered us to go south to surround a group of Roughnecks who had recently arrived from North Carolina and were threatening Oskaloosa. We removed them of their guns, two supply wagons and several horses.

"Two days later, over at Franklin, we taught a camp there a little respect for Northern attitudes. That same week we captured the armory at Fort Titus. "General" Titus was in that engagement. After seizing the armory, we took the guns, ammunition and powder to Lawrence. General Lane was moving north and east with his troops and planned to confront the rascals at Iowa Point who kept threatening to attack Plymouth and our other new settlements along the Nebraska border. We heard that there were 200 or so of those Ruffians. We planned to be part of the attack but we never got there. Colonel Harvey was put in charge of three or four companies, including ours, so he had about 250 men altogether, and ordered us to surround Hickory Point, which was on our route to Iowa Point, and we've covered that fracas before."

January 7, 1857, this is our last night in Archer, the evening of the Strongs' ball. Last Monday or Tuesday, Mr. Chase dropped in and Mrs. Strong invited him to dinner. She joked with Mr. Chase, saying he was always welcome to stay for dinner if he "continued to bring the dinner." We wondered what she meant by that. We discovered that earlier that day Mr. Chase and Mr. Robinson had come in with two fat turkey hens, which we later had for supper. The last night in Archer Adda and I planned to stay up all night.

Tonight, for the ball, the Strongs served a festive supper, which was followed by an entire night of dancing and singing. Although it was great fun, there was considerable sentiment attached to the evening. Several of the men and boys—some of them boarders at the Strongs', came by to speak to us, either to say they would miss us or to ask if it was really true that we were so foolish as to return to the troubles in Kansas.

In the wee hours of the morning, the dancing and music-making still continued. Though I had danced with Mr. Chase most of the evening, he began occasionally to dance with Adda. But he did speak to me, acknowledging that we would be leaving in the morning—when we had this conversation, it was morning!

About daybreak most of the guests took their leave. Mr. Chase left without saying a word. I can't understand him. I was so pleased to see him and so happy that we could be together for so many of the "sets." Then he "ups" and leaves without a word. I don't know what to make of him and his strange social behavior. I was, I guess, looking forward to a more conventional good-bye, maybe a more romantic good-bye. Father said some people don't like farewells and try to avoid them. He thinks that's what happened to Mr. Chase.

Frank Robinson came over and we shook hands as old friends and he bade me good-bye. Then he went to Adda. He stopped as if to whisper something in her ear and kissed her. I saw this and it made me suspicious that things were more serious between them than they had been pretending.

During the last few sets, Mr. Potter came over to dance. I refused each time he approached me. I thought it would be obvious to him that I usually danced with Chase. I guess you could say I preferred to dance with Chase. When Chase danced with Adda, it gave him an opportunity to make his fond farewells with her. Why hadn't he said them to me, too? On those few occasions, Mr. Potter swooped in; he had observed for those sets that I did not have my usual partner. So to be rid of his pestering, reluctantly I agreed to dance with him. The last time we danced, he pressed my hand with his thumb and forefinger several times, which so provoked me that I withdrew my hand. I really had an aversion to this man. I saw him on several occasions at the Strongs' and he always seemed to make a nuisance of himself. Later I expressed my indignation with Mr. Potter to Frank Robinson, who is trying to become something of a brother. Well, as we were discussing this bit of unwanted familiarity who should walk up but Mr.

A Pleasant and Social Interlude

Lothario himself, Mr. Potter. Joining our conversation, he said Frank Robinson wasn't familiar with the Southern gesture he'd made. "When a man gently presses a lady's hand," he explained, "it's a pretty sure sign of love," and he gave me, what I suppose he felt was his most affectionate smile. He was missing two teeth. Teeth or no teeth, he repelled me. I didn't return his smile and I have all my teeth—aversion is aversion. After we put on our winter coats, scarves and gloves, and prepared to leave, Mr. Potter held back and would not say good bye. I shall not miss him.

But I will miss Mr. Chase, though I found it strange of him to leave without saying good-by: such manners. And he claims he's from Boston; well, Massachusetts.

It came time for us to take our leave of the Strongs. We thanked them for their hospitality while we were in Archer. Father hitched-up our two horses, and Adda and I climbed aboard. The three of us set out for Kansas.

It was a bitter cold day and snowing on the prairie. To return to Plymouth, we took the old familiar Lane Trail, noticing that the occasional stone markers along the trail were still there but with the heavy snow the landmarks seemed different and sometimes hard to find. The distant woods were barren of leaves and seemed to be farther from the prairie trail than they appeared to be when we came to Archer a few months ago under such pleasant autumn circumstances.

By 4 PM, it was almost dark. Adda and I told Father there was a makeshift road somewhere nearby, which had been left by the military wagons of Colonel Cooke's troops. We knew we were close to Plymouth, but we had to drop down into Pony Creek and cross it, to get to the settlement and we guessed that Pony Creek was somewhere ahead of us beyond the thick timber that we were in.

As we came out of the timber, I think we were on the trail. It was snowing hard and blowing with such a force it was hard to see. Pony Creek, frozen over, was below us. Beyond that was a steep hill to negotiate before we could get up on the plateau. Father had, with help, removed the wheels from the big wagon and hinged down the sled runners, which incidentally had been bolted to the bottom of the wagon since Father's purchase of it in Detroit. We now had the hoops up and the cover on, so our "ship of the prairie" was on sleds rather than wheels.

Adda and I were in the wagon-bed hovering behind Father, close enough that we could speak to him but covered in heavy buffalo robes. Some of our other belongings, including the big trunk and the box of Father's surveying equipment, were piled in rather loosely. The four big iron-rimmed wheels were in the back of the wagon, but not tied down. Though we had some of our goods in the wagon some of our possessions were still in Plymouth, which was one reason for our returning to Kansas Territory.

Climbing up out of the creek bed, which was steep, my sister and I suggested that we get out and walk up but Father said, "Stay right where you are." It was snowing very hard and the accumulated snow was deep and had drifted to various depths.

The horses made two or three attempts to get up the hill, all of them at a slant towards the creek's bank, but it was so slick that the horses could not get a foothold. Each time we got a few feet up the slope the whole contraption, horses and sled, would all slide back to the bottom.

Father was pretty resourceful. He unhitched the horses and led them up on foot to the flat, open prairie above the creek. Then he led a rope from their harness down to the tongue of the wagon, (now a sled.) That put the horses on level ground and they began to pull and we went steadily uphill, but just as the sled approached the crest somehow the rope slipped off the tongue and we went back down that sloping bank lickety-split. The heavy sled didn't want to go straight down the hill, perhaps because it didn't come straight up the hill. The sled was making an awful clatter as it bumped over little dirt clearings where the wind had blown away the snow. Each of these little snow-free patches changed our downward direction so that in its travel the sled was leaning precariously downhill. Adda and I and the buffalo robes were bouncing around like two potatoes. Some of the bumps caused the wagon bed to lift to such an angle with the hill that we temporarily traveled on the downhill runner only. I knew that one more bump and a little more speed would cause the load to shift and the whole contraption of several tons would roll over. I also knew that if it rolled once, it was likely to roll again. To make matters worse much of the load was free to slide towards the downhill side of the wagon, and that included Adda, me and the buffalo robes, the trunks, the big iron-rimmed wheels and miscellaneous cargo.

Halfway down the hill, as the sled teetered and lifted from side to side, we came to a violent halt. The wagon had come to rest with its back end traveling halfway up the trunk of a large cottonwood tree. This threw us, with the cargo, all smashing forward. Then the sled slid back down along the tree trunk, but we had stopped. We were leaning sharply downhill but luckily both sled runners were on the ground and miraculously nothing had tumbled out of the wagon bed. Half of a wagon wheel was on top of me. Adda, still in her robes, was on top of that. Suddenly she began to laugh hysterically. Though I was relieved that we had halted, I saw nothing to laugh about. If we had upended or rolled over, as we came close to doing, I'm sure that would have been the end of us, the load had been put in so loosely.

Father raced down the hill to where the wagon was resting. His face was as white as the snow. He was relieved that we were still in the wagon and not in one of the snowdrifts. "Well, I guess you had better get out," he said. "We'll put the buffalo robes up on the hill. I'll cover you up and we'll take another stab at pulling the sled up." First Father and I carried the robes, and then we helped carry some of the freight to lighten the load for the horses. When Father secured the rope the second time, he ran the rope down through the metal yoke that the wagon tongue hinged on and this time we got up the hill. On the prairie there was no sign of Colonel Cooke's camp, though I could envision its three neat rows of tents and the corrals as though it were yesterday.

It was almost nine o'clock and we had some distance to go before reaching Plymouth. On the prairie trail the snow was heavily drifted. One long drift was so deep Father had to unhitch the team again and walk the horses through the drift to break a path before the horses could pull the sled through. And it was so cold. Well we finally arrived at "Van Curen's" house, our house, that is, which Mr. and Mrs. Van Curen had taken over. They had turned the garrison into their home and they were still "keeping" boarders. They weren't pleased with us blustering in almost Midnight with cakes of snow on our clothing.

The wood fire had gone out, but Father soon got it going again. When we finally got warmed up, he whispered to me that it was strange that after all these months this cabin still had a dirt floor. I quietly explained that there wasn't much point of having a wood floor when the Army kept coming in and ripping it up, looking for cannons and gunpowder. I quietly told Father that I'd later tell him about the rainy October 10th episode with six cannons when the Army found a whole keg of powder under the floor of this cabin, near where he was standing, and they arrested all the Plymouth men. I also mentioned that we never received

A Pleasant and Social Interlude

the letter from Governor Geary that he had given to Mr. Van Curen to deliver last September.

We stayed with the Van Curens what was left of Saturday night and all day Sunday. Mrs. Van Curen was not too friendly with Adda and me. I suppose she had not forgiven us for denying her our free service when we left in October. The Van Curens had four paying boarders, but I don't know where they all slept.

Would you believe it? Sunday morning Mrs. Van Curen asked Adda and me to help make and serve breakfast, which, of course, we did. After the meal, she went in the "front room" to talk with the men; as she left the kitchen, she asked us not to use too much hot water in rinsing the dishes, unless we wanted to fetch a few buckets, which would mean breaking some heavy icicles at the spring. Well, nothing much as changed here in the Plymouth settlements: "Our" old house, which had been converted to a garrison, is now the local boarding house and there is not another house in the settlement; also the fort is still without a roof. What a contrast Plymouth is to Archer.

Early Monday morning we left for Lawrence with a planned stop in Lecompton. Father wanted to visit with some of his friends, who were still in the camp, particularly Mr. G. W. Deitzler and Captain Cracklin. He said he wanted to begin to organize a Company for the purpose of laying out a town, but far enough west to create our own voting district. He also explained that we'd be taking a circuitous route down to Lecompton, making familiar stops at all the Northern settlements to solicit food and anything else the settlers wanted to donate for the prisoners.

9.

THE PRISON CAMP VISIT,
January to March 1857

WE GET A JOB WITH MRS. GATES

On Monday, while we were still in Plymouth packing and making arrangement for the oxen, Father told us that on our way to Lawrence he planned on visiting some of his political friends who were still in prison waiting for parole.

Some had expressed interest in joining him in a town company. He said, he needed to start raising money and making plans for a sizable land purchase and he needed to recruit people to go with him: farmers, craftsmen, tradesmen and families to populate these towns. He said he expected to spend the balance of the winter and all spring in the organizing and persuading process. He said it was important to remember that the one hundred or so who were captured, and he got to know several of them, was a very small fraction of Lane's Army. It will be from those veterans and other immigrant abolitionists that he will recruit. He said Mr. Deitzler advised him of the political need to establish towns in newer, generally western counties, or counties yet to be established so that their vote would be predominately abolitionist from the start. Many of the eastern counties and voting districts were controlled by proslavery administrators and voters.

Father was resentful that he and his friends had missed out on the first land sale in November, and said that some of his fellow prisoners had been bitter about their incarceration. "By keeping 200 of us in prison the Territorial government in effect stopped us from voting and also kept us out of the land market. The Southerners want the word to get back up North that this prison could be the fate of other Kansas-bound settlers."

Father said, through visitors and Governor Robinson's office that he and Mr. Deitzler and others suspect massive fraud by Missourians coming into Kansas, claiming land, actually staking it out in many instances, and then returning to Missouri. Some of their claims are on treated Indian land. One of the Lecompton prison administrators is an officer on loan from Fort Leavenworth. He has claims on land in the Delaware Indian Trust and will either settle on it, when his enlistment is up, or will sell it. He's trying to get it surveyed now.

Father added that Mr. William Kerr, the Plymouth settler, paroled with Father who came up with him to Archer, also intended to develop some town sites in the Territory. Father said that Mr. Kerr was originally from Iowa. "He told me about administrators and voters. several settlements in Iowa, that have grown into towns and county seats. First, the developers started, by buying one whole section, or 640 acres paying $800 for the land. One of the first things they did after they filed their plot plan with the nearest land office was to raise money and put up two major buildings: a hotel and a building suitable for a county seat, which would soon be turned over to the new county, establishing a county seat. Then they'd start the surveying, dividing the section into as many as 5,000 town lots, which included business lots.

The Prison Camp Visit

Those Iowa lots sold for as little as $100 each. But, girls, that amounts to $500,000 when all the lots are sold off.

"Of course much of that money goes to building the city, laying out its streets and so on. I'm going to use Mr. Kerr's Iowa model when we finally settle, but I'll make sure we stay clear of the land already on the books for the Indians. While I was at Lecompton, I discovered that the treaty system is much more complicated than the descriptions of it in the Quaker tracts, that we read over in Tabor last July. They said that twenty or so tribes had been assigned about five million acres along the Missouri River. Well, I've learned that the Government has also assigned 60,000 acres along the Kansas River, a little west of Lecompton, to the Pottawattamies."

Father said he was particularly looking forward to discussing all this with his friend, Mr. George W. Deitzler, a very bright man, a staunch abolitionist, who, by the way, was a friend of John Brown. Mr. Deitzler had been arrested back in May, along with a group of John Brown's followers. Charles Robinson, the Governor, was included in this roundup! These seven men, including Brown's oldest son, John Brown, Jr., were charged with high treason and denied bail by Judge Lecompte, the Chief Justice of the Territory. Some of them including Governor Robinson were released last September 5th when General Lane brought a battalion of militia to the Capitol building and negotiated their release. However Mr. Deitzler continued to be held under a special charge of treason. That very week most of Lane's Companies were in the field badly beating the Southerners in maybe a dozen battles and skirmishes. Of course nine days later parts of Plymouth and Lexington companies were captured and imprisoned, but that was a small piece of Lane's Army.

I asked Father, "What in the world could the elected Governor of this Territory do to be charged with treason?"

"Judge Lecompte is a very patriotic but rather poorly educated proslavery lawyer, and he's very loyal to his Southern roots. His strictly legal stance is that slavery is allowed not only by Territorial law but also by the Federal Constitution that protects property. Slaves are property and to tamper with slavery is to tamper with property. So, to oppose property law by conspiring to free the slave without compensation is equivalent to stealing it or 'take' it, which he claims is the essence of the abolitionists' intent. In his view that is illegal.

"According to our current laws, resisting slavery is not only unlawful but also treasonous.

"Lecompton, the territorial capitol and the site of the prison camp is about sixty miles generally south of Plymouth.

The first night after leaving Plymouth we stayed with Artemus Parker in Lexington who had been paroled with Father. He was originally from Massachusetts. With Father, he acted as a commissary volunteer for the prisoners at Lecompton, going out into the countryside to shoot game, fetch barrels of fresh drinking water and return with other provisions, that they solicited on the prisoner's behalf. From sundown 'til bed time Father, Mr. Parker, Adda and I "made the rounds" asking for food and clothing for the prisoners and was pleased with the generosity of the Lexington settlers, considering their primitive conditions. The second night Father, Adda and I repeated those solicitations at Holton, collecting several large hams, some molasses, 100 pounds of green coffee beans and three 100-pound sacks of cornmeal.

Crossing a creek bed south of Holton, one of the original five settlements formed last summer; we watched several adult doe drinking. They ignored us, so Father had plenty of time to aim and shoot one. We dressed the doe immediately and threw its carcass into the back of the wagon. Adda asked Father where he got the Sharps rifle. He laughed, "I got it from Mr. Strong before we left Archer. Didn't you know he was a rifle 'distributor' for the southbound settlers?" We didn't. We spent that night in one of the two newest settlements, Albany or Jackson (I've forgotten which).

Continuing south, after less than a day's drive we arrived at a Christian mission school for Indians, located north of the Kaw River. The missionaries all seemed to know Father, so he must have called here before. Their donations included two 100-pound bags of flour (grist), several hundred pounds of frozen buffalo meat, a rick of dry firewood, which filled up the back of the wagon, and six skinned and frozen rabbits. It had been cold and blustery since Holton and the doe in the wagon was now frozen. Needless to say the prisoners will be glad to see us. The meat and other supplies we are bringing will provide them with extra food for a while. Many of the abolitionists in these settlements had friends or relatives in the camp. That they remembered Father from previous visits contributed to their generosity.

From the north bank of the Kaw River we could see the ferry on the other side but our waving didn't bring anyone out of the little shed. Father fired his rifle and that brought out the single ferry operator.

While we were waiting for the ferry, Adda asked Father what sort of mission was it that we had just visited. He said, "It is one of several Quaker missions, though every Christian denomination in North America has a mission for Indians out here generously supported by their eastern churches." The mission system, and there are now about thirty missions in the Territory, are loosely supervised by the Indian Bureau in the Department of War. This mission was moved here from Ohio or Indiana by the Army under the supervision of a commissioner from the Indian Bureau.

Some Quaker missionaries were assigned to accompany this tribe of Indians who had treated their land back east. The Army moved them here and is supposed to enforce their treaty. They may have been located for several years someplace before they got here.

This mission provides education and considerable effort is made in all the missions to teach them to speak some English and some of the youngsters learn to read. They get medical and general Christian guidance. The Quakers don't try to convert the Indian to their church but try to lead them to be better people by Christian principals of hard work, honesty and peaceful love of one's neighbors, all through example and education. The second building they built when they arrived in the 1840s was a schoolhouse.

The Quakers were the first to teach the manual arts to the Indians. Boys learned carpentry, blacksmithing, the sawyers trade, animal husbandry and general farming skills. The girls are taught to sew, knit, weave, and spin wool and cotton from fibers into thread, to cook and bake and care for children in more sanitary ways.

This Quaker Mission, like most of them, is self-supporting. They generate some cash for textbooks and other necessities beyond what the Mother church provides by milling grain. This mission is capable of grinding 300 bushels of wheat or barley or corn per day. This mission and two others contract with Fort Leavenworth to provide it with corn meal, wheat and barley grist.

Midafternoon, (Monday, January 12th) we boarded the steam ferry and crossed the Kansas River right at Lecompton. The river was partially frozen over, but not at the ferry site. We are about fifteen miles west of Lawrence. Both cities are river ports for stem-and-stern-wheelers from St. Louis and other river towns.

Just as it was getting dark, we arrived at the prison camp and asked for permission to enter and to have supper with the prisoners. The guards recognized Father as one of the trustees

The Prison Camp Visit

who had been allowed to forage in the countryside for supplies to augment the Government's meager rations. When they inspected our wagon, one of them pinched a gallon jug of molasses and the six frozen bunnies. In a soft voice, Father said that is one of their more tolerable forms of corruption.

This so-called prison camp is simply a big Army camp, a tent city of fifty or sixty dirty and patched-up tents of various shapes and sizes, within sight of the two-story capitol building, which is on a little hill above the camp. At the camp, there were large bonfires, every 100 feet or so, which Army soldiers guarding the camp were using to keep warm. Father said all of the men chosen for this guard duty are Southerners, though there are plenty of available Northern soldiers. One of the guards told us that there were now about 200 prisoners; about half are prisoners of war and those are all Yankee abolitionists. Richard Hinton's article in the *Boston Traveler* listed the names of 107 Northern prisoners and where they were from. I had shown it to Father when we'd had our reunion in Archer. He and Mr. Kerr had read every name and had made some anecdotal comments about several of them. Father had been amazed at the article's chilling accuracy. Now here we were at this Southern contrivance—this pesthole. There are a goodly number of horse thieves, murderers, crooks of every description, riverboat gamblers and squatters. These squatters had been imprisoned for settling on a preempted claim, particularly if it was determined by the Territorial court that the so-called squatters were on land that was part of an Indian reservation or a town site or a claim made previously by a proslavery settler. Father said, "You'll find no Southerners incarcerated on this charge. Only Northerners are judged to be claim jumpers or squatters." Father added that there are no Southern militiamen in this or any other Territorial prison. "Governor Geary has issued warrants for some of them, but to my knowledge, none ever served," he said.

Many of the men from Plymouth, Walnut Creek, Lexington and Holton, a disposable remnant of Lane's Army of the North, were still in prison waiting their turn for parole consideration."

We had supper in a large smoky tent with about ten of the prisoners, including Jeremiah Jordan, whom Father hopes will work for him when we get our sawmill running. We recognized Alonzo Crawford immediately. He was one of the four young armed guides who escorted our outfit down from Archer last August. Adda sat next to Alonzo during supper. The only levity of the evening was Alonzo and Adda's recalling their turkey shoot last August in Plymouth. Our supper group also included the prisoners George Deitzler and Alphesus Gates. During supper Father arranged with Mr. Gates for us to stay that night at their house on our way to Lawrence.

Father seemed to have a lot to say to several of the prisoners but mostly he was organizing a party to accompany him farther west to establish town sites. He invited some of the prisoners, like Mr. Deitzler, to become investors in the venture. These men are all to be released and pardoned in the next three months. It's all expected to be completed sometime in March, by orders of President Pierce.

The prisoners seem quite concerned that earlier today the Second Territorial Legislature had convened here in Lecompton to continue writing the constitution by which the Territory is expected to be admitted as a slave state. Father and Mr. Deitzler, in particular, are offended that this ultra proslavery legislature includes very few Free Soil representatives. The legislators are expected to be in session more than a month. Some of the prisoners complained that even when the legislators are not "in

The Prison Camp Visit

town" food is scarce. Now they are concerned that their rations will be even smaller. One proslavery citizen with a contract to feed the prisoners has already quit because for two months the governor hasn't paid her.

The current Territorial Government arrangement is very strange. Washington has appointed Governor Geary, who is generally expected to represent the Federal Government's sentiments, which are proslavery. At the same time we abolitionists have our own elected Governor Robinson, in our Free State stronghold of Lawrence; he and his extended family are all in the Territory entirely out of their antislavery convictions. So, the Territory has two governors simultaneously and two Capitols. Washington does not recognize Governor Robinson, even though he was elected by vote and we resist recognizing Lecompton as their Capitol.

Father inquired of one of the guards, about the prison's warden, Sheriff Jones. The guard said Sheriff Jones had just resigned in mid-December but since Governor Geary wouldn't commission his proposed replacement (a Mr. William Sherrod), Sheriff Jones was still "running the show." In a soft voice I asked Father, "Is he the warden who ordered the balls and chains for you?" He said, "That's the one." Father asked the same guard the whereabouts of Levi Hampton. The guard addressed Father with the same snarly contempt that he used when he spoke to the prisoners. It seemed strange to me that he couldn't make a distinction between Father the prisoner and Father the freeman visitor. The guard drawled, "You mean old softhearted Kentucky Hampton?"

"Yes."

With obvious satisfaction, the guard replied

"Well, Sheriff Jones fired him a long time ago."

Father told us that he would have either starved or frozen to death if it hadn't been for Levi Hampton.[43]

Later I asked Father who Mr. Hampton was.

Father said, "He was the only guard who behaved halfway decently towards us. He was from Kentucky and was called, "Kaintuck." When he first arrived, he was a proslavery Southerner but in time he met Jim Lane and other such men and experienced a conversion. Of course, he only revealed his new attitude to us Free State prisoners, and we all thought highly of him.

"We later learned that Kaintuck[44] was appointed 'Master of Convicts' to guard twenty-two prisoners in Jefferson County, except there was no provision for a prison or jail in that county.

The Lecompton prison had no facilities for a decent night's lodging, indeed we had heard that the place was infested with lice and other "vermin" so we were glad when, after the long supper, Father announced that we were leaving.

Before we left the prison camp Father gave D. H. Montague, one of the prisoners and a friend from Plymouth, a list of prospects in the area for donating provisions. Mr. Montague is the new commissary officer for the prisoners. Adda said she remembered

---

[43] A Kentucky resident, Levi Hampton, went to Kansas to vote on behalf of slavery. Although he had abolitionist relatives, he was proslavery but changed his politics after long conversations with "General" James Lane (whom Hampton was assigned to assassinate!). *Kansas & Kansans*, Wm. E. Connelly, Vol. 11, p. 640.

[44] Before he resigned in March of 1857 Governor Geary was in such disfavor with the "Slavers" that he used the last seventeen or eighteen incarcerated abolitionists as bodyguards. Old "Kaintuck" was their company commander. (General Persifer Smith had refused to send over an Army bodyguard from Leavenworth.) After Governor Geary's resignation, a proslavery committee at Leavenworth rescinded Hampton's appointment as master of convicts. His dismissal is reported in the Territorial Dispatches to and from Governor Geary, Vol. 15 Kansas State Historical Society p. 628.

The Prison Camp Visit

Mr. Montague from Plymouth, that he was a veteran of the Mexican War.

After we left Lecompton, Father said Mr. Deitzler told him that about 180 men, mostly Free Staters, whom Governor Geary had inducted into the U.S. Army in the late summer, that by late November these men all petitioned the Governor to be dismissed, and they even received pay for their time in the Army, though they had to go up to Leavenworth to collect it.[45]

We drove the ten or eleven miles southeast along the south bank of the Kaw River on a portion of the Santa Fe Trail, locating the Gates House about a mile west of Lawrence. We woke Mrs. Gates about midnight of January 12th. She came to the door with a candleholder. Otherwise her parlor was dark. Even sleepy, she is a very attractive woman. Her auburn hair, which is quite long and abundant, could be called chestnut colored. At first Mrs. Gates was cautious and a little put out about being roused in the middle of a very cold night, but her face lit up when she saw Adda and me. She said she was so happy for some female companionship. At breakfast she offered us both a job. "Doing what?" asked Adda. Mrs. Gates explained that she had a contract to feed a local company of militia two meals a day and was short of help in the kitchen and dining room. She shot a glance at Father and asked if we were interested, adding that most of these soldiers were single and good-looking.

Father hadn't explained what the two of us were to do in Lawrence, so after a hasty conference we accepted and went to work for her that day.

---

[45] Confirmed by the Governor's own records, Executive Minutes of Governor John W. Geary circa Nov./Dec. 1958. Kansas State Historical Society, Vol. 4 p. 650.

Adda and I had in effect been employees at Mrs. Strong's boarding house up in Archer all through the fall. So we had learned how to do this line of work. But life in Archer had been so social that I hadn't really thought of working for Mrs. Strong as a job. And before that, from the end of August to October, we had worked for Mrs. Van Curen, though her boarding house had no "regulars," just a steady procession of north and southbound travelers. So we had a pretty good idea of what Mrs. Gates would expect and knew we could do the job.

Father left for Lawrence directly after breakfast. He said doing what he had to do would be more convenient if he stayed in Lawrence. Had Father joined the soldiers out here for his evening meals, observing Mrs. Gates' unconventional behavior, (which I will describe shortly) would have been embarrassing for me. We soon learned he was staying at a small hotel called the Whitney House.

Directly after Father left, Mrs. Gates began showing us around. We were to share a nice bedroom upstairs.

We met Aggie Rourke. She didn't say whether Aggie was a Miss or a Mrs., but she's Irish, very friendly, about Father's age and is the chief cook. She has an assistant whose name I didn't get but sometimes helps in serving.

Mrs. Gates explained how things work between the kitchen and the dining room, how she wants the tables set, where the china and the flatware are kept, etc.

We had barely unpacked our things and Mrs. Gates called to say that we should come down in a few minutes, " . . . because our boys will soon be here for the noon meal and I want to put the soup out." When we came down, she asked how we would like to be addressed by the soldiers.

It was really some time before we heard them stamping the snow off their boots on the porch.

The Prison Camp Visit

When they were all seated, Mrs. Gates clapped her hands and the room became very quiet and in a very gracious way she introduced us, explaining that Father had recently gotten his parole from Lecompton, that her husband, who would also soon be free, was a friend of Father and that we would be helping her while Father would be in Lawrence organizing a party to go west to establish a new town site. Though the work kept us very busy, for the next several months, it also exposed us to some very interesting people.

Perhaps I should explain a little more how this job came about. Father had met and become friends with Mr. Gates in Lecompton. He was from Worcester, Massachusetts, and had been captured with the September 14th group, at Hickory Point. In prison, Father made an arrangement with him allowing the three of us to stay with Mrs. Gates at their farm while Mr. Gates remained in prison. He was due for parole sometime after this month. Mr. Gates had entered into an agreement (in prison, I'm told) to buy a partnership with a Mr. John Mack who owned a small hotel in Lawrence, called the Cincinnati House. He planned to expand and run this hotel after his release. Last night when we arrived, Father assured Mrs. Gates that her husband was well and in as good spirits as his situation in Lecompton could allow.

Although Mrs. Gates has a daughter in Massachusetts, whom she says, she misses; she is far from lonely on her farm. We soon learned that her "boarding contract" was with the Immigrant Aid Society, which had hired her to feed the Stubbs Company one of General Jim Lane's several standing companies of Free State militia. Mrs. Gates provides the meals, but not the housing. Some of the soldiers stay in camps and others are quartered in homes. All of the Stubbs boys were housed between here and Lawrence to protect it against another raid by the proslavery ruffians. These soldiers are not U.S. Army troops but are part of a larger well-trained militia of almost 3,000 Free State boys. This Company's officers were Captain Joseph Cracklin and Mr. Frank Swift. In the next several months, Adda and I got acquainted with both gentlemen and took comfort in knowing that their troops were near Lawrence, and the Gates' place for that matter, in case the proslavery roughnecks decided to return and finish Lawrence off, as they did last May. Rumors are that remains their intent.

Captain Joe Cracklin and his men helped scare off an imminent attack by a proslavery militia of about 2,700 men last September 14th, the same Sunday evening that Father and the Plymouth and Lexington companies were captured. Adda and I were to hear many stories of this standoff at Lawrence, some of them quite exaggerated, I'm sure. But the fact remains, Captain Joe Cracklin's men averted another raid. Certainly most of this was due to the presence and the bravery of the well-armed and well-trained militia, plus having John Brown and his company close by. You may be sure that they are all "heroes" in Lawrence.

Frank B. Swift[46] had been released from Lecompton shortly after Father. In Captain Cracklin's frequent absences, Mr. Swift assumes command and usually joins his boys for dinner or supper at the Gates' place. In conversations with Frank I discovered that he was in the Lexington Company, which had joined the Plymouth Company in the "Famous" Battle of Hickory Point

---

[46] Added in 1886 by Augusta: "I had been invited to attend but couldn't arrange it, a Kansas Quarter Centennial, held in Kansas City January 1886, thirty years after our arrival. Someone later sent me the bound transactions of that celebration. I note from one of the speeches by John Speer, one of Lawrence's early pioneers, editor of the *Lawrence Republican*, author of the Life of General James H. Lane, in his speech he refers to Father, Hoyt and Jones as 'Martyrs to Freedom.' He said, 'There were giants in those days' and included such gentlemen as John Brown, George W. Deitzler, G. A. Jenkins, and a few more: included in his list was Frank B. Swift." The bound book referred to became the first volume of the Transactions of the Kansas State Historical Society, Vol. 111, p. 343.

The Prison Camp Visit

last September. He, too, had been captured and had spent several months in Lecompton. Frank is about two years older than me and we enjoy exchanging a few words when there is occasion. Of course, I see him most every day as he takes two meals with his Company. I might add he is a very handsome man who is a Yankee from Brunswick, Maine, quiet, of medium build, broad across the shoulders. I'd guess he's about a six-footer, and very mature for his age.

I don't exactly know what the circumstances were that led Frank Swift to say to us one evening that it had finally dawned on him that we must be the same Stewart sisters who were the daughters of Sam Stewart, whom he knew very well from their time together in Lecompton prison. He had always been polite with us but after that particular evening he went out of his way to be friendly and to offer help or assistance if we needed it.

Of course, Mrs. Gates occasionally spoke to Mr. Frank Swift about her husband, who remained a prisoner.

This company goes by several names which at first was confusing: the Stubbs Company (sometimes the "Stubbs Rifles"), the Oread Company, Company A and the Soldiers. The proslavery militia calls our boys "Jayhawkers" or "Jim Lane's Jayhawkers," but I seldom hear our boys refer to themselves as "Jayhawkers." On the other hand our soldiers call the Missouri soldiers "Bushwhackers" and amongst themselves refer derisively to the Southerners as "Pukes", "Missouri Pukes", "Kentucky Pukes" and other names not suitable for print. I've noticed that my gregarious sister seems to enjoy using some of these foul-mouthed terms when bantering with our soldiers.

Some of these young men are from Ohio & Michigan but most are from Illinois and Massachusetts; three or four, including Frank Swift, are from Maine. Mrs. Gates' favorites are from around Springfield, Massachusetts (where she used to live) and

Maine. One of the Maine boys speaks French and occasionally she engages him in a little verbal banter in French.

Her family came from Maine up near the Canadian Border. They were originally French: Amboise was her maiden name. Mrs. Gates on several occasions told us of her maternal ancestor who came to Quebec as an unmarried girl from Normandy. She came with a large company of single girls, subsidized by King Louis XIV and sent to Canada to help settle the New Country. They were known as Filles du Roi (Daughters of the King.) This form of French pioneering went on for several years. In this way the Filles du Roi established a strong French maternal culture and, of course, brought with them the French language. It was the intent of the French, having discovered the Canadian part of North America, to populate it rapidly. However, when the men originally got there, they complained about the shortage of women. To solve the problem several sympathetic French politicians appealed to the King to send females for these lonely French pioneers. In spite of his wartime needs Louis XIV asked the archbishops in the coastal provinces for female volunteers, and it was believed that the best and largest group came from Brittany, sailing out of St. Malo, Dieppe, Dunkirk, La Rochelle, etc. Of course, many of the men then in "New France" were also from that area of Old France.

Mrs. Gates said that there were religious problems in France at that time (anti-Catholicism, etc.), with the Huguenots, who were French Protestants, getting most of the blame. So one of the tests of virtue for a Fille du Roi was that she must not be a Huguenot. The King wanted only Catholic settlers in Canada. (She added, "You'll recall the English in New England weren't so choosy.") The other requirement was a letter from the girl's archbishop verifying that she was—unmarried.

Mrs. Gates is a very interesting woman, at times all business and yet also warm, open and generous. She is curious, genuinely curious, about her friends and acquaintances. She certainly treats Adda and me like family, and has since our first day been solicitous about our welfare and anxious to help, whether we need it or not, but in running her boarding house she can be very businesslike.

However, in the presence of men her whole personality changes and sometimes her behavior seems to be, well, unconventional would be to put it mildly. Her demeanor with men is entirely different than with women. With men, she will punctuate her conversations with a friendly jab, or slap on the shoulder, or elbow poke in the rib. She moves around a lot when she talks. In her charming way, with those big brown eyes and long auburn hair, she seems to dominate the conversation; that is, if it's her intent. Though she's outspoken with her political opinions, I wouldn't say she's "all fired up" over the Abolitionist Movement. (According to Father, that's Mr. Gates' department. He's a little younger than Father, but joined one of Jim Lane's companies not long after Lawrence was burned the first time, months before Father joined the Plymouth Company.)

The Gates' parlor is the largest room in the house, large enough for three tables: two seat six, one five. Captain Cracklin or Frank Swift sit at her table. A little hallway near the stairwell can accommodate a long skinny table set up against the wall and three or four soldiers can eat there all sitting on a common bench. That's the "overflow" table. The three round tables in the parlor all have proper chairs. Against the west wall is a large chiffonier with a huge beveled glass mirror. It gets daily use as a serving sideboard. She keeps the "silverware" in its three drawers. Coffee cups, saucers and miscellaneous china are stored in it. Large plates and bowls are kept in the kitchen. The chiffonier is the most elegant piece of furniture I've ever seen, having short fat carved legs, carvings on all the door panels and carved figures that support a high shelf above the mirror. Mrs. Gates said they freighted it out from their Springfield hotel. Before that it was her grandmother's wedding present from France. The grandmother lived in Old Quebec and it was her ancestor who was one of the Filles du Roi.

Mrs. Gates takes all her meals at the table seating five. She eats heartily but will often interrupt her meal to get up and walk over to one of the other tables to be friendly with a soldier, often tousling his hair or rubbing his scruffy neck, all the while talking to him. She knows the first names of every soldier in the company and the last names of most, as well as a few personal facts about each. She will inquire, "What do you hear from Wooster, Charlie?"[47] She'll ask Clyde if he's heard from his girlfriend in Springfield lately. These little table visits seem to elevate for a few minutes the social status of the soldier she's chosen to speak to. She will occasionally banter in French with Frank Swift's friend from northern Maine, though she is not affectionate with that one.

Sometimes she'll bend over the table to speak to one of the boys and I've noticed that when she does she'll often place one (usually bare arm) on his neck and with the other hand reach under the table and rub or grasp his leg, which often produces a surprised gasp or giggle. When I first observed this, I thought her motive was rather base and certainly unladylike but I've mellowed this judgment. Mrs. Gates is a very engaging, outgoing creature and has probably socialized with males like this since she and Mr. Gates ran their small hotel in Springfield; maybe even before that as a girl growing up in Boston.

Once or twice a week she will clink her water glass with a fork. The room will get quiet. Sometimes she'll rise, other times she'll speak while seated. Usually she's speaking to pass on some news

---

[47] "Wooster" is the pronunciation for the Massachusetts City of Worcester

The Prison Camp Visit

or make a political remark condensed from an editorial. Both she and Mr. Gates are concerned about local and national politics.

Some of the Stubbs Boys call her "Mammy" though she is only a few years older than most of them. By no stretch of the imagination could Mrs. Gates be old enough to be considered motherly by this crowd. The Stubbs company boarding contract allows each soldier to eat at the Gates House twice a day, seven times a week, so that keeps us all pretty busy. All the boys have hearty appetites and occasionally engage in raucous behavior. In addition, a select few of them seem to participate in an interesting, certainly novel (for me) social custom—they greet Mrs. Gates with a big warm hug and from a "select" few a lingering kiss when they come into the house. Part of the strangeness of this ritual is that, in my opinion, she looks forward to it and encourages this adolescent-male attention, and her enjoyment and reciprocation of it seems to go far beyond just motherliness.

Before they arrive, she rearranges her hair, applies a little rouge and becomes a bit excitable. She is a beautiful woman and is "well-endowed," as my stepmother once jealously remarked about a neighbor. She busies herself before their arrival, but not with important matters like the food or the table settings. She's taken care-of that earlier. I don't mean to imply that she is not careful about details; she doesn't miss a thing. She's just so well organized that the food preparation and the table settings have all been arranged well before mealtime. When she "expects" her boys, she's prepared to be the perfect hostess. That's her job. Our job is to serve the meal and cleanup afterwards and the cooks' job is to prepare the food, which they start doing at sunup.

Once or twice a week, after a quick inspection of the kitchen to check on the food's readiness and the parlor to make a sweeping glance at the tables, Mrs. Gates will excuse herself and in a few minutes reappear, dressed as though she had been invited to appear at the court of Louis XIV. About twice a week at supper she wears a special crimson velvet party dress, using a shawl to cover her shoulders and upper arms. After most of the boys are seated she'll stand using an excuse to retrieve a cup or piece of silverware from the chiffonier. As she returns to her table she will casually remove the shawl, exposing her white shoulders and upper arms. This makes a striking scene in the candlelight and, I might add, every eye in the room is on her and she revels in that knowledge.

With the shawl removed, the dress, which is V-cut in the front, also displays her white and fetchingly adequate bosom.

This entire process takes several minutes and involves some small talk. Usually she walks around visiting the other tables before returning to her own. Occasionally as the boys file out after supper she will stand and while talking to a favorite, commence unbraiding her hair, letting it cascade in russet waves over her shoulders. Even the girls appreciate this act and they'll linger a bit in the after-supper clean up to join her male admirers.

I must say, she carries herself like an actress and this casual loosening of her hair makes her even more attractive. And the effect is not lost on whichever swain she's addressing.

When she hears the soldiers coming up the road, she will excitedly exclaim, "All right girls, now, here comes our boys. I'm sure we are all ready." She nervously posts herself at the front door, peering out through the small diamond-shaped leaded glass panes. At the sound of their boots on the porch, she will swing open the door with a flourish and a rather deep, graceful bow—but not so deep as to obscure "the view." She maintains this posture until several of the boys are well inside the room. Most of the boys are simply intent on getting to the table to start eating, but three or four will take their "dessert" with Mrs. Gates, in what Adda and I call her hugging and kissing custom, before they take their seats. I'm just amazed at her range of hospitality.

The Prison Camp Visit

She manages to greet every soldier individually. When a favorite comes through the door, her technique is to slip one arm around his waist, resting the other arm on his shoulder or neck. In this way they are face-to-face.

She smiles quickly, maybe whispers something in his ear. Maybe she'll playfully remove his hat. If another soldier is following that one through the door, she will free one arm to shake hands or in some way greet him as well, then immediately turn her attention to the gentleman she's embracing by giving him a long affectionate kiss. Sometimes the greeting is frivolous and the soldier responds with a little pinch in some part of her upper body or he'll tickle her ribs and she'll emit an audible giggle or a mock shriek but more often her embrace seems lingering and promising.

I swear, sometimes, especially at supper, we get considerably into the meal before all this romance is completed. Two, sometimes three of the boys, will be lined up waiting their turn, which, of course, delays their being seated. And it all takes place in the Big Room, so that those who are not engaged in the hugging and rubbing and kissing are watching it. Of course, they are eating and watching. There seems to be an understanding among the boys that not all of them participate: just her favorites. But they're in ample supply.

This greeting process, as curious as it is, makes serving a little easier on us in that it slows down the rush to the tables. By the time each soldier is seated, we are ready to begin serving the soup course.

A large china tureen, full of the *soupe du jour* has already been placed on a platter on the chiffonier, which is near Mrs. Gates' table. Also placed there are two or three stacks of large heavy plain white soup bowls. Mrs. Gates expects us to put a bowl of soup before each soldier within a few seconds of his being seated, but not before he's seated. The three of us, Adda and I and the third serving girl, can serve eighteen to twenty soup bowls in a matter of three or four minutes. And it usually takes longer than that for all the soldiers to get past the romance inside the front door, remove their coats, hats, etc. This soup course, "starter," as Mrs. Gates calls it, is very important to her. Adding to our efficiency she has us use a metal ladle large enough to fill the bowl with a single dip.

To promote a family atmosphere, "seconds" are encouraged. It is the acceptable custom for the soldiers who want a second bowl to get up and help themselves. And just as often they will simply signal to one of us that they'd like another bowl, if it's inconvenient for them to get up or if they are engaged in conversation.

The three of us have usually eaten before we start serving. Holidays or special occasions we'll eat after they leave, but before cleaning up the dining area.

Mrs. Gates is very fussy about the food she serves. She's continually in and out of the kitchen tasting the food, making suggestions about details like keeping the rolls warm or preparing the butter, which is always served in little decorated shapes, made that way by rolling or pressing a piece of butter between two small wooden paddles with designs cut on their surface.

Some meat, or "chops," is served at each meal together with potatoes. They'll be boiled in chunks, mashed, occasionally baked. Gravy is part of every meal and there is seldom any left.

Though I never see her do any of the cooking or baking, there's never any doubt that she knows her business and is in command. She's always attentive to the soup, and I must say, it was invariably good. Seldom, even on warm days, did any of it go to waste.

Mrs. Gates had brought several, maybe two dozen, soup recipes with her from New England.

The Prison Camp Visit

She must have a dozen recipes just for bean soup. Mrs. Gates has the cooks use a small white bean to make one especially delicious soup, a creamy soup flavored with onions and ham hocks. She has a black bean soup that contains chunks of bacon or ham rind with fat still clinging to the brown smoky skin.

When she can get "good" potatoes, she has Aggie and the other cooks make a thick, onion-flavored potato soup to which they add warm cream just before we serve it.

The cook keep two large kettles in the kitchen into which all bones, meat scraps, bacon and ham rinds, etc., are tossed. Called "stock," this is the source of all her soup. Some of it cooks for five or six hours. Noon or evening, "her boys" get soup as the first course. I've never heard a single complaint—ever. Quite the contrary, the Stubbs boys will occasionally get up (while we are collecting the soup bowls and carrying them to the kitchen, or returning with the main course plate on trays) go over and tell Mrs. Gates how good the soup was. She'll often reply, "You just march into the kitchen and tell that to Aggie." And they do. I suppose it was this homey atmosphere, sprinkled with her genuine charm and motherly hospitality that generated the idea that they should call her "Mammy".

After one supper, when all the boys were gone and Adda and I were clearing the tables, she was unusually solicitous of us, engaging us in conversation. On this evening she had worn a very attractive dark green velvet dress, again low in the front, which Adda, with a twinkle in her eye, refers to as one of her "cleavage dresses." She seemed to want our understanding and, perhaps, approval of her interesting social behavior. She asked if Adda and I were "seeing" any of the Stubbs boys, as though living here and working here seven days a week gave us the time. I did mention that Frank Swift had been imprisoned with Father and her husband and that we occasionally exchange greetings. I tried to be polite. After all, she is my employer. I said, "No, it's my impression that of these boys behave like billy goats." Before I could soften my observation, she said, "But, Augusta, some of them are such nice billy goats." She didn't take offense at my remark. Then she paused and looked at me, "Augusta, there is no harm in extending these boys a little affection. They are all so lonely, all they desire is a little warmth and assurance that we care for them." She reminded me that these boys saved this town and they deserve all the gratitude that we can muster. I suppose in this way she was trying to let me know that a little more friendliness, or maybe familiarity, was part of my job, and Adda's, in helping her run her place, one of the many busy boarding houses that season in Lawrence.

Later in the evening, after we had finished cleaning up, one of the cooks made a pot of tea, and we had time to sit down. Mrs. Gates seemed to want to continue the discussion that we'd had earlier. "It's so lonely out here. In Massachusetts we had such a full social life. The travelers and drummers[48] were such interesting people. But life out here is so bleak. We aren't farmers. I don't know what we're doing out here on a farm. But Mr. Gates says it is safer out here away from Lawrence. He expects that the border ruffians will sack Lawrence again. They tried last September and were gallantly repulsed by my brave boys, my boys from Massachusetts,"(though some are from other states) and bravery is not peculiar just to Massachusetts.

To celebrate Valentine's Day Mrs. Gates, Adda, myself and a new part-time girl busied ourselves with some extra decorations. It was mid-February and had gotten dark early. We lit candles along the reflecting wall sconces, to which we tied large flouncy red velvet ribbons. We also lit the three or four hanging coal oil

---

[48]   traveling salesmen

The Prison Camp Visit

lamps, which were also festooned with red velvet ribbons and bows.

We then cut small hearts from bright red paper and placed them on the soldiers' plates. Mrs. Gates had purchased some little Valentine's Day hard candies, pieces of which she arranged on the paper hearts on each plate. She also brought down a box of chocolates and offered Adda and me one each, encouraging us to sample the candy before supper. The four of us shared a moment of friendliness, nibbling at our Valentine's chocolates. We were amused to find that as we bit into their centers, the cream was a soft pink rather than the usual white.

Before the soldiers arrived, Mrs. Gates slipped upstairs, donned her crimson party dress and tied her auburn hair with a large bow of the same red velvet ribbon we had used for the decorations. She asked me to adjust the bow in the back, which I did. Being so close to her while I fixed her bow, I couldn't help but admire her features, particularly her red auburn hair: The ribbon had gathered it together at her neck, below the band of red velvet her hair cascaded out almost to her waist.

Back in Detroit, we had several large Chestnut trees on our street. A particularly remarkable tree was a Red Chestnut. In the early summer when those Chestnuts blossomed with their large white cone-shaped flowers, this particular Chestnut had large red blossoms. In the fall when we collected the fallen Chestnuts, the most prized nuts came from the tree with the red blossoms. Peeled from its prickly shell, the nut shined a deep reddish brown. The locals called that color chestnut. It would be a fair comparison to characterize Mrs. Gates beautiful hair as chestnut.

When the soldiers arrived, the front-door greetings followed the usual formula of hugs and long lingering tender kisses, except the soldiers' spirits were a little higher on this night, as were our own, from anticipating Valentine's Day.

When the meal was over, one of the new officers from Massachusetts rose and made a very nice toast, thanking Mrs. Gates in particular, and also Adda, me and the new girl, for our efforts at providing them a bit of warmth and "homey" good cheer on this special day. The soldiers all stood up and said, "Hear-Hear." Some of them raised their glasses to us. Though we don't serve spirits, Mrs. Gates doesn't object on special occasions, if the boys bring some of their local "Missouri Moonshine" or a bottle of rum. That seemed to be the case tonight.

Mrs. Gates signaled that she wanted the three of us to join her on the side of the room near the staircase.

She looked especially attractive this evening. She had encouraged us to join hands as we stood there, to imply that we had shared being hostesses for the evening party. As the boys rose and shuffled to find their coats and hats, preparing to venture out into the cold February night, four or five of them, including the officer who made the gallant toast, and Frank Swift came over to express their personal thank-yous. Adda and I enjoyed a little small talk with Frank Swift.

I must say, it was unusually nice. The new girl, hired for tonight's supper, asked me if it was always like this.

Our small talk with the departing soldiers was soon exhausted and Adda and I knew that we had to get back to work. Clearing the tables, sweeping up and helping in the kitchen would quickly become incongruent with this unusual role of sharing in the evening's merry-making. The men, one by one, drifted away, leaving the officer and Mrs. Gates. They had casually put an arm around each other's waist and as Adda and I stepped toward the kitchen door, Mrs. Gates loosened her arm and took the officer's hand, "Francis, come upstairs. I want to show you a letter and an ambrotype of my cousin Sarah. You remember her from your Wooster Catholic School." They walked up the stairs together.

The Prison Camp Visit

Though it was her usual custom, Mrs. Gates did not come down to the kitchen that night. After we had cleaned up, the cooks went to bed. Adda and I and the new girl began setting the tables for tomorrow's noon meal. The officer came down, retrieved his topcoat, scarf and hat, all of which he put on without a word to us. As we were busying ourselves he quietly crossed the room, paused at the door, tipped his hat, bade us a pleasant good night and left. He failed to latch the door. The new girl did, saying it had commenced snowing.

Perhaps, as Mrs. Gates says, she is lonely while her husband is in prison. Adda and I discussed this matter several times and from different points of view and Adda thinks I should keep my opinions to myself—and I shall. But her advice does not keep me from sharing my opinion with you, Dear Journal.

Mr. Gates was released on the 9th of March. That night he joined all of us at the farm for a festive welcome home dinner party, with lots of speeches and toasts from the soldiers, many of who knew him. Father came out from town for the celebration. (He had been in Lawrence to raise money for the land he planned to buy, and lining-up prospective settlers.) Several of the soldiers, like Frank Swift and Captain Cracklin, who had both fought in the Battle of Hickory Point, and at least another dozen soldiers all acted as a welcoming committee for Mr. Gates.

Mrs. Gates was particularly beautiful that night and was simply overjoyed with having her husband home.

10.

THE FOUNDING OF ELDORADO,

March to July 1857

Three days after Mr. Gates was released Adda was asked to move to town. By March 19th Mrs. Gates, the kitchen staff and I had moved into the Cincinnati House, with a recently enlarged dining room and kitchen. Aggie Rourke became the chief cook. The Gates simply took their boarding contract with them to the Cincinnati House and the boys all came into town for their meals and ate with the hotel's regular customers. Although the work was harder in town, we had more help. Adda and I were assigned to share a rather cozy guest room on the second floor. We had a window facing north.

In a few days there was another festive party, this one at the Cincinnati House, attended by many prominent people, all of them wishing Mr. Gates and his partner, John Mack, well in their new venture. Of course, all the soldiers attended plus others from General Lane's companies who knew Mr. Gates.

Among the guests were Governor Charles Robinson and his plucky wife, Sara, who was subject to some good-natured teasing about her stay last year with her husband in the same jail of which many of the men at the party were alumni: the Lecompton prison.

I noticed that, if the men teasing her had also been a prisoner, she accepted their good-humored remarks, often with an anecdote of her own. However if a merchant or a soldier, who had not been in Lecompton prison, presumed familiarity, she became aloof and would by conversation or by physically moving, distance herself as though this person lacked credentials to be so personal.

One of the men complained that he'd been unable to find a copy of the book[49] she'd written, while she was in jail with her husband. She took a little pad of paper from her pocketbook, jotted something down and indicated she would get him a copy. I was really impressed to learn she'd written a book and equally impressed with the straightforward way she offered to help this gentleman get a copy.

Well, after seeing this outstanding woman I simply must read her book. I'll bet Mr. Willmarth, a local bookseller, can find me a copy.

Later in the evening I was standing by Mrs. Gates, Mr. Gates and others while they speculated as to where General Lane was this evening.

Mr. Gates made a complimentary remark about him. Sara Robinson said she'd studied the man and his successful career, adding she thought he was ill suited to be the sort of leader we will need. She said he had been a guest in their home many times and she had been with him during political affairs and also said she was speaking phrenologically.

I was struck by her use of that word, a new and popular idea that predicts character from facial or cranial features. I've read a few magazine articles on phrenology, which some in the east think is a new science. I was impressed that she was familiar enough

---

[49] Sara T. D. Lawrence, Kansas: Its Interior and Exterior Life, published in 1856.

with it to pass judgment on her associates. She is obviously an outstanding woman.

While this group was all together, Sara Robinson interrupted the small talk and said to Father, addressing him as Mr. Stewart, that she had heard about his expedition west and said we need all the new voting districts, we could muster. Father responded that a new district was part of their plan. The Governor's wife got in the last word by saying she certainly admired their courage.

About midnight, as the festivities wound down, Mrs. Alfred Robinson, Father, Sara Robinson, Adda and I all had an opportunity to be together. Mrs. Alfred Robinson rather casually asked Adda if she would consider working for her? She said she was sure Adda was enjoying the social hustle and bustle of the hotel but their household and children would be a more homey atmosphere, and Adda would get Sundays off. Mrs. Robinson said she wouldn't be surprised if the pay wasn't better.

Later that night, after we were alone, Father encouraged Adda to accept Mrs. Robinson's offer, noting that the two Robinson families lived next door to each other and were important and respectable people. He said that "Sara Robinson is the sister of Amos Lawrence, the eastern industrialist who had financed the start of Lawrence. She is already a very influential woman. She has argued our case with both Congress and the President." I chimed in with "You know, she wrote a book about the problems out here during the three months that she was in Lecompton with her husband and the Free State prisoners." Adda said she didn't know that.

Father added, "I worry about you two working in this hotel among all these men, every one of them older than you." Adda replied that she was flattered by the offer, but undecided. She told him that she liked working for the Gates and really enjoyed being around the soldiers, and she seemed to me mildly disdainful when Father suggested that the social atmosphere in the Robinson families would be an improvement over the hotel crowd. "Father," she said, "here at the hotel I am somebody. I know everybody and they know me. Sure the work is hard, but it's fun, and I'm good at it. At their place I'll just be a nursemaid to their children."

A few weeks later, in April, Adda told me that she had spoken with Mrs. Robinson again, met the family, which included a "tea" with the Governor's wife, Sara, and was inclined to take the job. As much as Adda likes the associations at the hotel, working seven days a week has been a bother. At the Robinson's she'll get Sundays off and an occasional evening. She wants to go to church, she told me, and have a little more time to socialize.

When she explained her reasons for leaving to Mr. Gates, he quickly arranged for the two of us to have a day off but it was too late. Toward mid-May, after Mr. and Mrs. Gates found a replacement, Adda moved her things to the Robinsons' house.

Mrs. Gates was disappointed to lose Adda and said so, adding that the one that will really miss your sister is Aggie Rourke. Adda's departure caused quite a stir. The soldiers all wanted to know what had happened to Adda. There was concern that she had come down with small pox. One dinnertime regular, a Mr. Sutliff, who owns a clothing goods store near the Eldridge House, said to me that the only reason he ate here was to see Adda. He laughed and said "I owe your sister a pair of shoes" (I wondered what that was all about.) Mr. Wilmarth, a rather scholarly merchant, gave me a book for my sister "Out of the Depths." The inside cover said it was a woman's story. Perhaps I'll read it myself. Priced at seventy-five cents, I didn't want to ask if Adda had ordered it or if it was a gift. I asked him if he'd located a copy of Mrs. Sara Robinson's book. He said he was working on it.

Mr. Finley, another regular and an Irish friend of Aggie Rourke gave me a small bottle of ague pills to be delivered to my sister: a concoction of their local firm. The main attraction of their store is a large supply of hard liquor, such as gin, whiskey, sweet sherry, which comes into town by the wagonload. A sign in their store says it's only available for medicinal purposes! Mr. Finley claims to be an abolitionist but I have my doubts.

A young clerk at Thompson Dry Goods asked me to tell Adda that the shoes she wanted are in. She must have been shopping for shoes. These comments went on and on. I had no idea she was so popular.

I remained at the Cincinnati House with Mrs. Gates, who has become more discreet with "her boys," but I observed that her ardor has only slightly diminished. With Mr. Gates now home, she simply is not as conspicuous as she was last winter, though she continues to act as evening hostess where about half of the guests are Stubbs boys. Mrs. Gates seems to be managing the whole enterprise. And I must say, the two of us have become rather friendly, almost sisterly. And now I have a whole room to myself—The guest room I shared with Adda is now all mine.

All spring Father was very busy with meetings at the Eldridge Hotel, the Whitney House and the Cincinnati mealtimes here. Occasionally Adda would get an evening off and we would linger at their table when we could, as we often knew his guests. He not only was looking for investors but also for men who would join him in an exploratory trip west, planned for May.

A.D. Searle was one who accepted and E.P. Harris, as well. Father knew Mr. Harris from the Plymouth Company. We were to get to know A.D. Searle and discovered he was a spellbinding storyteller. He was one of Shalor Eldridge's lieutenants in Tabor, and we had met him when our train was briefly camped there. He had been involved in the escape of Governor Reeder, helping to disguise and hide him when the proslavery mobs demanded his arrest.

Mr. Searle told us that the Free State leaders planned to hold a convention in Minneola in the late spring to draft a Free State constitution. In March the group that Father was organizing elected him to be a delegate to this convention.[50]

Later that summer Father and his company founded Eldorado[51] and, according to plan formed a new voting district, number 17, but it wasn't certain then which county[52] it was in.

One evening in early May, before he and his party left Lawrence, Father explained to a group of associates during mealtime at the Cincinnati House that his general plan was to intercept the Arkansas River some distance southwest of Lawrence and to follow it until they could find a site that met several requirements, such as abundant farmland unattached by Indian treaties, fresh water, timber, both for fuel and for building, flat stone, ample grassland for fodder for the animals. I recalled how the night of the prison visit had been consumed by Father and his friends, discussing several of the characteristics of a good city site. Now these plans all seemed to be coming together. At one of our suppers, Father said that although he'd been able to examine some military maps at Fort Leavenworth of the area between Lawrence and Santa Fe, he would give a year's earnings for a published map of the Territory. This was the first time I had heard that he wanted to go so far beyond Lawrence. He guessed it was at least one hundred miles.

May 11th Father and a company of seventeen or eighteen local men headed southwest on the Santa Fe trail to begin locating some town sites. Captain Cracklin was the senior military member of

---

[50] C.V. Mooney's *History of Butler County*, p. 237.

[51] Augusta Stewart used Eldorado as the spelling of the town. It was later changed to El Dorado.

[52] Samuel Stewart was the delegate for the new western voting District of Butler County, the area where he planned to establish his first town site.

that group, leaving Frank Swift in charge of the Stubbs Company. So, after almost nine months of disappointment, unwarranted incarceration, civil strife and generally unchecked lawlessness, Father and a small band of perseverant Free State settlers have commenced to do what we came out here to do in the first place.

In late June, Father came back to Lawrence and stayed at the Cincinnati House. He told Adda and me that his group had been successful, had laid out one town, which they had named Eldorado, and had scouted several other sites. He said we could plan on his coming back for us, but it wouldn't be until Fall. We took several meals together, sometimes just the family—other times with people who seemed to have been or will be investors or are prospective settlers.

At one evening meal, attended by a select group, some of them with financial interest in his venture, Father reported that his group did as planned and followed the Arkansas River all the way to the area called the Big Bend but decided it was too remote, too far west. too far beyond the frontier—the commercial definition of the frontier—to be suitable. The party then returned generally eastward. They camped alongside a river they called White Water, but soon rejected that area as well. They then set a northeast course until they found a location they liked on the west bank of the Walnut River, camping there for several days while they scouted the area. Father gave me his surveyor notes of the Eldorado town site, which Captain Cracklin had named. They are so significant I have committed them to the Journal. In Father's listings, I noted the not-so-subtle interest of the sawmill operator.

Elm Creek—wood and water—8 miles
Common Spring—7 miles
Gost or (Goat) Spring—no wood—5 miles

To Cottonwood—wood—15 miles
Big Turkey Creek—no wood—18 miles
Little Turkey Creek—no wood—8 miles
Owl Creek—wood and water—6 miles
Little Cow Creek—wood and water—6 miles
Big Cow Creek—wood and water—3 miles
stands of Black Walnut, Hickory and Oak
Osage encampment—wood and water—6 miles south 15 miles east
Walnut Creek—wood and water—8 miles
 stands of Black Walnut, Sycamore and
  three kinds of Oak on Walnut Creek and
  river ample, flat prairie for settlement
  and farms.

Father reported to the investors in his company, who usually meet with him at the Cincinnati House, that his party came into the Eldorado site on June 6, 1857 which was along the west bank of the Walnut River and had laid out the town.

A good-sized group had joined Father in May, but other investors, remained in Lawrence. Some of the investor had been a prisoner with Father, such as George W. Deitzler, Frank B. Swift and E.P. Harris, who had been a member of the Stowell Party, which formed the Plymouth Company. David Upham, J.P.S. Otterson and Thomas Cordis, the blacksmith, were all in the "locating" party, which also included Jeremiah Jordan, whom we call Jerry. Father has offered him work on our syrup mill and sawmill when we get them up and running.

John A. Wakefield was also in this party. He had been a judge and a Territorial candidate for Congress in 1855, but he was defeated in the election by a proslavery candidate because the proslavery voters were then still in the majority. The election was bitterly fought. Not content with winning, a proslavery

The Founding of Eldorado

mob continued its hostility by burning Judge Wakefield's house here in Lawrence last May. That was the same raid in which the Missourians set fire to the big stone hotel built by the Eldridge brothers and burned the printing press for Mr. Elliot's newspaper the *Herald of Freedom*.[53]

Other early settlers in the Town (Eldorado) Company were Mr. Sumner Rackcliffe, later joined by Mrs. Rackcliffe. John Snow, R.A. Watts, who built the first boarding house in Eldorado (using timbers from the Stewart sawmill), E.R. Zimmerman, another friend of Father's, A.D. Searle, who was also a surveyor,[53] E.B. Whitman, William Crimble; William Partridge; J.P.S. Otterson; T.L. Whitney; S.B. Prentis; Norman Allen; and John Dame. In Chicago, Father had told Adda and me that he would be the first mayor of the first town he'd found in Kansas. He was elected by the gentlemen I've listed above, as the president of the Eldorado Town Company.

My records don't show who the Secretary or Treasurer or Auditor were for Eldorado but I'm sure they were chosen from the list above.

Father and his group also scouted several other sites in the area, at least four of them, all within a day's ride of Eldorado.

They located a town site where the Walnut and White Water Rivers intersect. Some wanted to call it Arizonia, others Orizonia. My records for the names of the officers of this town are better. The officers were:

    Sam Stewart   - President

---

[53] *Mr. R. G. Elliot had bought another printing press and had it running again by the spring of 1857. By then there were several "Free State" newspapers in the territory, including the Crusader of Freedom owned by the Stewarts' friend, James Redpath.*

[53] *A. D. Searle later surveyed Topeka and parts of Lawrence. He also served as a judge during a number of elections in Lawrence.*

J.P.S. Otterson   - Secretary
T.L. Whitney   - Treasurer
S.B. Prentis   - Auditor

The group founded another site nearby, which they called Buffalo.[55]

The Officers were:

G.E. Deitzler   - President
Frank B. Swift   - Secretary
Sam Stewart   - Treasurer

Eldorado was located on the west bank of the Walnut River where the Arkansas-California Trail crosses the river. Father said he wanted the Eldorado merchants to get that business. That's a good idea. There was a constant stream of wagons going west on that trail.

Eldorado was originally in Hunter County, but that county has been subdivided in such a way as to include a new county, Butler. Eldorado is supposed to be in Butler County but it's still not certain yet which county it will finally be in.[56]

Captain Cracklin told Adda and me that their arrival at the Eldorado site following June 6th, all the members of the party spent several days establishing their claims, with Sam Stewart doing the surveying. Father put the information down in legal fashion suitable for registering the claims with the Land Office—

---

[55] In later years Indians claimed the Buffalo town site and drove-off the settlers. The town was abandoned.

[56] Augusta noted later that this question was not resolved for several years: Eldorado became part of Butler county "but not until the territorial legislature in Lecompton authorized it in the fall of 1859. Samuel Medory was Governor: our ninth!"

The Founding of Eldorado

just as soon as they could discover the location of the official Land Office.

The settlers had some concern as to whether the officer in charge of the Land Office would honor their claims.

All of the founders of Eldorado were Free State people with various shades of abolitionist zeal, so they reasoned that it was entirely possible that any land claims they filed might be ignored or destroyed if the Government Land Agent was proslavery, which was certainly likely. Most of the proslavery settlers believed that the doctrine of Squatters Sovereignty meant that Kansas was, defacto, a slave state.

When Father returned to Lawrence in late June, he said that on June 17th[57] the farmers among the group unloaded their "breaking plows" and with great ceremony broke the prairie for the first time. They replowed it at right angles to break up the big clods and planted their first crops, mostly corn. Father estimated that he and Jerry Jordan put in about 100 acres of corn on our claim. Those crops were the first ever planted in Butler County.

I'm pleased and proud to report as a witness to the autumn harvest, that the land produced an abundant crop, over one hundred bushels of corn to the acre. That grain and the abundance of wild game saw us through the first winter.

Several of the men said that upon arriving at the Eldorado site they did have one disappointing discovery. They found to their surprise that in an old trapper's cabin or one built and used years ago by buffalo hunters a little south of the town site by a creek was a squatter whose name was Hildebrand. He had "squatted" there since May, coming to the area a month or so ahead of Father's group. To avoid a future conflict, the officers of the new Eldorado Township used some of their funds to purchase the claim from

---

[57] *Butler County's Eighty Years*, page 11.

Hildebrand. He moved into an old lean-to cabin built earlier by buffalo hunters and took a new claim south of Eldorado.

Father and three others also laid out another town site nearby, which they named Eureka.[58]

Those officers were:
- E.B. Whitman — President
- Norman Allen — Secretary
- A.D. Searle — Treasurer
- Trustees:
  - Sam Stewart
  - J.P. Otterson
  - J.H. Snow

During Father's stay at the Cincinnati House, in June, I would see him engaged in long talks with Mr. and Mrs. Gates. I guess I hadn't realized what good friends Father and Mr. Gates had become in the prison camp.

In the late afternoon, well before supper, when I was busy setting up for supper or working in the kitchen Father would walk right in the kitchen and strike up a conversation with Aggie Rourke, the head cook. He and Aggie would shake hands like old associates. When I teased and queried him about this familiarity, he said, "that a fellow prisoner with him and Mr. Gates, was Jason Connelly, who was an old friend of Aggie Rourke.

Before Mr. Connelly joined Jim Lane's army, he had enjoyed a special "relationship" with Aggie Rourke, beyond just their both being Irish, but when pressed for details, Father wouldn't elaborate about their class of friendship except to say rather mysteriously that whenever he was allowed to come up to Lawrence to solicit food

---

[58] Located on the Fall River, Eureka was sometimes also called Fall River by the town's early settlers

and provisions for the prisoners, Aggie had always been a kind and generous lady. She would invariably send a separate package for Mr. Connelly. Sometimes it was a single large onion that Aggie had boiled in sweetened milk, which she put in a small glazed terra cotta crock to keep it warm. When teased about the onion, Mr. Connelly would only say that the onion had mysterious Irish power. He encouraged Adda and me to get to know her better. Father said Aggie's generosity and her ability to influence others in Lawrence had helped keep the prisoners alive last winter.

One evening, I asked Father how many settlers it would take to make Eldorado successful, since it seemed to be so far west. Father answered with some encouraging news. He said that as he was preparing to come back to Lawrence, he spoke with an "advance scout" who had come to their Eldorado camp. The scout said he represented a small party that was en route from Lawrence and would arrive in early July. The scout said his group wanted to get away from the on going strife in eastern Kansas. He thought that the Eldorado area, which had wood, plenty of water and plenty of raw land, land free of any claims by Indians, would suit his group and that his people would do well there. And he liked the idea that two major westbound trails, the Arkansas and the California intersected at Eldorado. As an inducement, Father told the scout that if his group settled in or near Eldorado, he would survey their claims and file them with the appropriate Land Office as part of the purchase price of the land, just as soon as a Land Office was established in the "western" counties.

The scout agreed. The July caravan included two Irish families named Bemis, Mr. and Mrs. Henry Martin from England (they were a bit younger than Father, very formal but friendly), Jacob Carey, William Crimble, and ten other families.

By founding Eldorado so far west, Father believed he had defied the advice of the Pennsylvania demographer that had predicted bankruptcy for any company established along a new frontier line. Eldorado was the farthest west civilian outpost of Kansas Civilization.[59] Father's town site was the New Frontier and Adda and I took great pride in that status and his accomplishment.

In late June, Father and a few of those who had returned with him left Lawrence to go back to Eldorado. He said he wanted to be in Eldorado to celebrate their independence on the Fourth of July. This notion of independence has always seemed so important to him.

Father said he planned to return for us toward the end of October and that we should be preparing to move.

---

[59] "Kingdom of Butler," Stratford and Klintworth, published by Butler county Historical Society, p. 15.

11.

AN OUTBREAK OF SMALL POX,
July to September 1857

In late June, while I was working at the Cincinnati house, I received a letter from a young gentleman in Nebraska. I never expected such a letter but was both pleased and astonished when I saw it. It was signed by my bashful dancing instructor from Massachusetts, Jacob Chase, the man of few words but many talents.

It was composed of such welcome pleasantries. He recalled the gay social life in Archer, the many "balls" we had enjoyed together. He inquired as to my health and other personal matters. I thought it was a rather forward letter for such a shy young man and I suppose I was still nursing my indignation that he failed to stay around to say a proper good-bye when we took our leave from the Strongs, considering that we had not only danced most of the night together but we had during those months in Archer attended several balls together and he had also been a frequent guest at the Strongs, since he was one of the few on Emma Strong's approval list. He inquired if I was engaged. Though I was flattered to receive his letter and confess I reread it several times and found satisfaction each time, I couldn't bring myself to answer it for some time and it wasn't because I was too busy. I've since wondered what motivated this procrastination and my own strange behavior toward Chase. His letter and its warm sentiments, and the flattery of his personal interest in me buoyed me up for several days. I have since wondered what the source of that buoyancy was, vanity? Flattery?

Whatever were my innermost reasons, I postponed responding. I was certainly either well-occupied with cooking and baking, helping with the laundry, which occasionally included a few pieces of clothing I knew belonged to the Stubbs "Rifles," waiting on tables three times a day, but in all honesty, when I did have time to write, I refrained, reasoning I hardly knew the man. Yes, I danced several evenings with him the previous winter, but we had hardly exchanged a dozen words between us. His reticence fueled a similar shyness in me. But with others, I'm not so shy.

In mid-July, Mrs. Gates sent for her little girl, and in August Fanny arrived with a small party of relatives from Massachusetts. They all moved into the Cincinnati House. No sooner did Fanny get here than she developed a high fever, vomited, and seemed, to my inexperienced eye, to be occasionally delirious. Two of the recent young arrivals, both adults, took sick with the same general symptoms as Fanny. When I could get away from my chores, I'd go up to the family rooms to see if I could help.

On the third or fourth day the doctor came around. He said it looked like Fanny and the others had Small Pox or Chicken Pox, adding that we had better hope it was the latter. It seemed to me that Fanny had gotten it from Mrs. Gates, who had taken sick just before their arrival. The doctor said Mrs. Gates had varroloid, which he also called variola, and said it was the adult form of small pox. But there was something about his demeanor that failed to convince me that he was sincere or sure of his diagnosis. I had trouble matching her symptoms with variola, as explained

An Outbreak of Small Pox

in my Gunn's Book of Medicine or my *New Guide to Health* by Samuel Thomson. She was nauseous in the morning and didn't have a fever; I didn't see her body, so I didn't know if she had any red rash, which is an early symptom of small pox, but had no red spots on her face or neck or arms, and I looked. Maybe she got whatever it was from all that body contact with her favorites in the Stubbs Company. Since little Fanny came down with it shortly after their arrival, it's likely that they brought it down with them from Massachusetts or they contracted it in the North or on their two-to three-week journey.

After five or six days, little red spots on Fanny's body filled with a fluid that turns yellow. Some of the blisters were, I thought, quite large, as big as a pea, and Fanny wanted to scratch them. Her neck, face, forehead were almost covered by these red pus-filled blisters. On one occasion the doctor opened and drained one of the blisters and seemed to smell his little scalpel, which I found strange. When I questioned him, he said that small pox pus just before the scab forms, has an odor so distinct that when a doctor smells it, he never forgets it. It helps him distinguish it from chicken pox or simple skin eruptions.

"Does this smell like small pox or chicken pox?"

"I haven't seen enough cases of small pox to be sure, but I will never forget this odor."

It was obvious to me that the doctor was concerned that this disease was contagious and would spread to the soldiers. He told Mr. Gates he would have to post a quarantine sign on the Cincinnati house.

This posed a problem. We were feeding the Stubbs Company at the Cincinnati House. Fanny and the two others from the Massachusetts party were all sick upstairs with a contagious disease, and they were all in contact with her parents, who were in contact with the public, (including the soldiers and the hotel guests, as well as those of us who worked at the hotel.) "Thank goodness Adda is over at the Robinsons," I thought. If the doctor were to post a quarantine sign, the hotel guests and soldiers would have to stay and eat elsewhere.

Mr. and Mrs. Gates quickly discussed all this with Captain Cracklin and they came to a complex arrangement, which proved satisfactory enough for the doctor to post no quarantine. It was decided that Fanny, Mrs. Gates, the two newcomers and I would move back out to the farm and that I would be their nurse, do the cooking, laundry, etc., to which I agreed. I was to see them all through this small pox/chicken pox trouble. This new job presented quite a change. I had by then been given more responsibility at the Cincinnati house. That is, I was now helping Aggie, the chief cook, in the kitchen, as well as continuing to serve meals, which I now supervised, but I was also getting Sundays off. In hindsight, nursing was lighter work, but I constantly worried about my ability. After a few days of this worrying and anxiety, running up and down the stairs from the kitchen to their bedrooms, carrying food up and bedpans and slop jars down, I was more than willing to go back to my old job, but I had to keep my word.

At the farm, as the nurse for all four of them, I would be working seven days a week again. Mr. Gates, agreed to visit at least once a day and bring out groceries when needed. Since Mrs. Gates was not as seriously ill as the others, she was soon able to return to town and her duties at the Cincinnati house, though she continued to spend about half her nights with Fanny and me at the farm. The Stubbs boys continued to eat at the Cincinnati house and I missed the social contacts with them.

Well, I had my hands full. Though all three were bedridden, Fanny was by far the worse off, while Mrs. Gates, in my opinion had been hardly affected; she only needed to stay in bed in the mornings. I attended them all. Little Fanny suffered so, and yet her mother, who was sick, but not nearly as sick as Fanny, seemed reluctant to attend to her. The doctor came out almost every day. He instructed me to wash out the bedpans with boiling water, which meant I had to keep hot water "on" all the time, so I couldn't let the wood fire in the kitchen stove go out. I worried that I'd have enough wood. I had enough to do without chopping wood. He also told me that on sunny days I was to air out their bedclothes, etc. Beyond those orders he seemed powerless to really help my patients. He just said, "We'll have to let it run its course." Well, it was certainly on its way. Whatever this disease was, it was definitely on some kind of course. My patients were terribly sick. Little Fanny had such a fever it burned my hand. She seemed to have developed this fever as soon as she had taken sick. She also vomited everything I fed her. The doctor said that was normal.

Fanny also called out and moaned and cried all hours of the day and night. I was lucky to get one or two hours of continuous sleep. I was haunted by the memory of the canvas outfitter's wife over in Iowa City who had nursed her child to no avail and in the end lost her and had to bury the poor little soul in that city. To this day I can see that mother's eyes—eyes that, as she told Adda and me the dreadful story, never seemed to focus on anything.

On his third or fourth visit, I asked the doctor if I could catch it. He paused, "I'm afraid so, if it's small pox. It is one of our most contagious diseases. Epidemics of small pox have been studied for years, yet we know very little about the disease. In Europe they are trying to find a vaccination against it. When I was a medical student in Philadelphia, we learned about the research of a German doctor who had actually measured the contagion of small pox during some epidemics in Europe. He found that for every one hundred people exposed to the disease, sixty would get it. So your chances of getting it from Fanny are about sixty percent."

"Of those sixty who came down with it, how many of them died?

He didn't know but would look it up for me, he said, adding, "We know these numbers. I just don't carry them around in my head." (If he looked it up, he never told me. I think he knew how serious this was but didn't want to add to my worry.)

After the doctor left, contemplating these facts, all alone in the house except for my patients, was very sobering. It hit me like a bolt that Fanny could die from this disease and I had a 60 percent chance of catching it myself, never mind what would happen to me after that.

Late that afternoon, Mr. Gates paid us a visit and brought some food including a large pot of Aggie Rourke's thick soup, which saved me the trouble of cooking that night. She sent a short but sweet note of encouragement and said they all missed me. He tried to cheer us up but left about twilight. I could see how worried he was when his daughter couldn't recognize him. As I returned to my very sick patients, his fear had now made me even more scared that Fanny, who was "hit" much worse than the others, would die under my care. Her fate seemed to be more in the "hands" of the disease than what the doctor and I could do. I constantly worried that she'd die and I constantly prayed to God that she wouldn't. If she died, would they blame me? What would I do then, leave town? It would be a burden I would carry forever.

At this stage of the disease her eyes were swollen shut and held that way by a yellow "exudation" that hardened and seemed to glue her little eyelids shut. Both of my medical books said that this was to be expected and used that word "exudation." Several times a day I would put a small rag, wet with warm water, on her eyes to soften the glue. Her little lids would open and flutter, but within two or three hours they would be stuck shut again. Beyond

An Outbreak of Small Pox

the usual sour urine smell that bedridden people get, she along with her bedclothes, developed a rancid odor from the blisters as they broke, which was a symptom of the disease. The doctor visited us less often and, when he did, he seemed more engaged with Mrs. Gates, if she were here, than with Fanny.

I looked forward to her visits. Her kindness and understanding were about the only comfort I got, and it also cheered me to see her because she, of my four patients, was the only one getting better.

When she stayed overnight, she would vomit in the morning, but she never got the rash and she was only sick in the mornings. By midmorning she would be her old jolly, friendly, outgoing self again. I don't think she had any class of small pox.

Well, I was relieved, grateful to God, and so pleased when little Fanny slowly began to recover but no thanks to the doctor. All he did was attempt to identify the disease, and failing to do so, would wring his hands, cock his head to one side and cluck his tongue. He had at least eight ways to cluck his tongue and from my observation not even one way to help his patients, though he could add such profound observations as "well, well" or "hmm, such a pity," then more clucking. When he had bad news to recite, I could always tell it was coming. He had a way of turning down the corners of his mouth; he would pause, then deliver the bad news.

This doctor seemed reasonably skilled at observation but so void of remedies that I seriously wondered if he really ever attended that school of medicine in Philadelphia—or maybe he had just failed to complete the portion of his studies that dealt with cures and remedies.

Fanny's two relatives recovered a few days ahead of her and moved back to town. Mrs. Gates also got better. No sooner had she recovered, so that she was able to be up and about, than she left for St. Louis. She told me that she would take a river steamer all the way. Since she was a Northerner, I worried that the riverboat would be safe for her. I learned later that the boat's captain was an abolitionist and a frequent visitor to Lawrence. Isn't it impressive that a person can get on a boat in Lawrence and not get off until St. Louis? That must be 300 miles. Of course, there are over a dozen riverboats, mostly sternwheelers that call on Lawrence. The "shallow-drafters" can go all the way out to Fort Riley.

She was very mysterious about her trip, but I must say that she waited to time her departure until after the doctor pronounced Fanny recovered. He cautioned that her daughter would still be weak and would need nourishment, and added that it would be my job to take care of her. I felt proud that both the doctor and Mrs. Gates had such confidence in me. The morning Mrs. Gates left, one of "her" Stubbs boys came out to the farm, dropped off some local newspapers, picked her up, and drove her though Lawrence down to the small steamer docks on the Kansas River. Although she was pale, as usual she looked beautiful. I helped "put up" her auburn brown hair that morning.

I later spoke to the Stubbs soldier, who told me that she boarded the sternwheeler *Emma Harmon*. I've seen that boat on the river. Its captain is J. M. Wing. He had occasionally taken meals with us at the Cincinnati house, though he usually stays at the Whitney house, which is closer to the docks and is also a well-known gathering place for abolitionists. They say that when Old John Brown is in town he only stays there. The captain is an old friend of Mr. Deitzler's (one of the cofounders with Father of Eldorado.) A year or so ago when the *Emma Harmon* brought some cargo to Lawrence, among the packages were boxes labeled "Books." Although they were destined for Mr. Deitzler, they had been addressed to a Mr. Simpson. I've heard that Mr. Deitzler's boxes contained one hundred Sharps rifles, which he had ordered

An Outbreak of Small Pox

when he was in Boston speaking on behalf of the abolitionist cause.

After Mrs. Gates left, I suddenly found a little time for myself and as I began reading one of the local papers I noticed a schedule of newly elected state senators and representatives. Among the latter was Father's name, noting that he'd gotten 221 votes from our district, to which they'd added some new counties. George Deitzler received 1,003 votes from his district.

A few days after Mrs. Gates left for St. Louis, I took sick. I was so disappointed. Even though I was tired and had lost some weight, I had so looked forward to going back to town. I told Mr. Gates that I was afraid that I'd contacted small pox, reciting the sixty out of 100 number the doctor had told me. I suggested that he move Fanny to the Cincinnati House, which he did. And I also asked him to take a note to Adda over at the Robinsons, asking her to come care for me if I should take a turn for the worse. I was worried about the pus pimples, and like Fanny, having my eyes glued shut and not being able to see. Mr. Gates obliged and also sent the doctor around that day.

The doctor checked my neck and chest for a rash or red pimples. Finding none he said I should be on the lookout for any pox indications, adding that by now I should be an expert on those symptoms. But I continued to have some serious doubts about this doctor. I explained that I had a mild sore throat and that I was occasionally nauseous, but only in the mornings. He asked me if I was married.

"No", I said, and asked what marriage would have to do with being nauseous, but he only smiled through his mustache. He asked me if I had vomited and I said I had, and that I had trouble digesting my food and had pains in my abdomen. I said no to his question about diarrhea.

He commenced sniffing around my bedclothes. Finally, and with some irritation, I said, "Doctor, excuse me, but do you suppose I have a disease that you can identify by its odor?"

He sat down on the edge of my bed to take my pulse, and chuckling said "Certainly, don't you remember I told you about smelling the small pox pus just before the scab forms? A good many diseases identify themselves by the patient's odor."

At first I took offense at this, but then he went on to say that all the doctor can go by is what his five senses tell him, so he couldn't afford to neglect any one of them. He said that when he was studying medicine in Philadelphia his fingers had become as sensitive and as accurate as a thermometer. An old German doctor, a professor of pathology at the school, even went so far as to taste a patient's urine and other "body juices." Of course, he spit it out, the doctor added, but the professor said it helped him in making a diagnoses and measuring the progress of the treatment. I wonder if that Philadelphia professor is still alive!

During this examination the doctor poked around on my back and asked me if I was "tender" there. I had never heard that word used in that fashion. He said he was looking for swollen areas near my kidneys but hadn't found any.

I later said to Adda that I thought this doctor took some undue liberties in his examination as he poked here and there.

This aroused Adda's curiosity and she said, "Oh yeah, tell me about it," but as soon as I said it, realized that Adda misinterpreted what I said, so I changed the subject.

After his first examination, the doctor said my symptoms caused him to suspect a liver problem, telling me that by poking my back in the vicinity of my liver, he could perhaps isolate the cause or location of my sickness. He said my symptoms were similar to a summertime sickness he had occasionally seen in Philadelphia when he was a medical student. The problem was caused by eating oysters that had been harvested down on the Chesapeake Bay. Without adequate ice they sometimes spoiled slightly by the time they got to Philadelphia, but not so badly that they couldn't be washed and sold by the cynical—or perhaps just ignorant—oyster dealers.

"Well, you may be sure I've had no oysters out here on the prairie," I said. I asked him if the oyster disease was ever fatal.

"I'm afraid so. In its fatal stages it's now called hepatitis."

I asked him if any other food could contain the germs of hepatitis.

"Yes, if it's unclean or spoiled. The disease destroys the liver and in the process the patient's skin turns yellow. We think hepatitis results from unclean or unsanitary conditions."

Well, every day besides checking for red spots or little pus pimples, which, thank heavens, never appeared, I checked my skin to see if there were any signs of yellow.

On his third or fourth visit he said, "Augusta, you are tired. You are exhausted from the month or so you spent nursing Fanny, Mrs. Gates and the others. I doubt that you have hepatitis. I was worried about your handling all those bedpans and bedclothing—in hospitals they occasionally are a source of hepatitis. But you don't seem to have it. I think you have a case of bilious fever, in addition to your just being run down." Before he left, I asked if there was a treatment for bilious fever.

"Oh yes", he said, then proceeded to recite the treatment. I couldn't believe it—the man actually had a cure for something. He left me a small bottle of medicine and gave me instructions for how to take it.

I'd been sick in bed now for almost two weeks and feeling lonely. I was a little put out that although Adda visited me rather regularly, she avoided me on her day off and I wondered what she did with that day. On one of her visits she brought me a pair of used slippers, which were more like soft buckskin moccasins than slippers. They were very attractive, and were decorated with small beads and smelled of perfumed talc. I asked Adda where she got these slippers and she laughed and said "Just don't ask." My concern was that Mrs. Robinson would miss them. Later Adda said they came from Sarah Goss, one of her friends. Adda likes to create a little mystery.

On the twelfth day after I took sick, the doctor came "round" to check on my progress. I was feeling some better. Adda was with me. On this occasion the doctor brought an associate. He introduced him as Dr. Lamb, visiting from Brooklyn, New York. The older doctor made flattering remarks to his associate about my nursing, telling him that I had brought Fanny Gates and the others to a healthy recovery. Then he said I must be very healthy, having been exposed to three serious cases of contagious disease and not contracting it. Addressing me, he said, "With a resistant constitution like yours, you should consider nursing."

Adda asked Dr. Lamb if he planned to stay in the Territory. "No, I've come to Kansas on an assignment from an Eastern firm that is interested in new sources of medicines."

"What sort of medicines do you expect to find out here?," I asked him.

He said he'd only just arrived but had been asked by the firm to look for several plants that were reported to be growing in the Territory. He mentioned goldenseal, adding that I should have some interest in that plant myself in that it was a good remedy for bilious fever and other liver ailments.

He went on to say that on his trip west he had checked on reports that a plant called "feverfew" was being grown and used in Missouri. When refined, he said, it was used in the treatment of serious and recurring headaches, including migraines. I must remember that medicine. Father occasionally has migraines. Dr.

An Outbreak of Small Pox

Lamb added that he'd heard that some tribes in Iowa and Missouri also used the plant to relieve aches and pains of the joints, arthritis. It never dawned on me that medicines could derive from various parts of plant roots, tree bark, etc., even though on occasion as a child I'd been given castor oil, which came from the castor bean for a "physic," and also a medicine called "cascara," which also was a laxative. It was made from a plant's root.

As poorly as I felt, this young doctor seemed to me to be a balm in Gilead, so polite and full of information and possessed of such a pleasant willingness to explain things, and so good-looking.

Before they left, the older doctor told me that his young associate had been a student of Ralph Waldo Emerson in Boston and had gone on several Christian missions in various parts of the world and on each assignment had brought back medicinal raw materials and had identified their sources, though that wasn't his major assignment from the church.

As soon as they left, Adda said, "What a handsome young doctor." We both hoped he'd stay in the Territory, and of course, we wondered if there was a Mrs. Lamb back in Brooklyn. But it was inappropriate to ask.

About the fifteenth or sixteenth day after I took sick, the older doctor came round again. Adda was with me. He said he'd consulted with Dr. Lamb and together they had agreed on a prescription. He handed me a small, flat, three-ounce bottle. The contents seemed slightly cloudy. "Augusta," he said, "I want you to take a spoonful of this medicine three times a day: early in the morning, at noon and before you go to sleep at night. And I want you to drink two glasses of warm water each time."

"Do you mind my asking what this medicine is."

He smiled, "Not at all. It's an extract of ginseng root sweetened with a little glycerin, and it was made by the New York firm that is sponsoring my young associate's trip here.

"In consultation, we have both decided that you are run down from your nursing effort. This medicine will address that condition. And I haven't given up on my diagnosis that you have bilious fever or some other kind of liver ailment."

Getting ready to leave, he said, "I'll be back in a few days to see how you are coming along. In the meantime get rest and take this medicine with the warm water."

He paused. "I noticed you've moved your bed."

I had moved my bed, which had a big metal headboard, closer to the window. "Yes, I wanted to catch better light, and I can read longer. I'm a big reader."

No sooner did I hear the front-door latch click shut, I popped out of bed, put on my robe, slipped into my "new" soft slippers, went down to the kitchen and was relieved to find the big enamelware tea pot was still hot. I filled two glasses from it—I simply couldn't wait to taste my new medicine. I mixed the medicine with some of the warm water, took a sip by the kitchen stove and then walked out into the big empty front room, where Adda and I had served so many meals last winter. All the round tables were arranged just as they had been when we were so busy feeding those hungry soldiers. I sat down in Mrs. Gates' chair and slowly drank the rest of the warm medicine, reveling in the luxury that I'd not have to jump up to refill a soup bowl.

I don't recall ever having tasted Ginseng before. It was rather pleasant and when I went back to bed, I became drowsy. I couldn't keep my eyes open enough to read my book, *Life in the French Court of Louis XVI and his Bride, Marie Antoinette*.

Within five or six days after the doctor dropped off the ginseng medicine, I began to feel much better. I was able to get out of bed, but still seemed to need rest, and for several hours a day I would sit in a rocking chair, in my robe, reading by the window. Adda would come by, but couldn't spend the whole day. Mrs. Robinson was growing impatient with her absences.

A week or so later the doctor came by again, accompanied by Dr. Lamb. The older doctor proceeded to give me the same examination as his first one. He inquired if my appetite was coming back, if I had assumed regularity and suggested that I eat more red meat.

I wanted to make conversation with Dr. Lamb, so I thanked him for his consultations and the ginseng prescription. Dr. Lamb said that this medication had been used for centuries to treat fatigue and to build up the body's defenses against infection.

He suggested that I continue with the medicine 'til it was gone. Reaching into his little medicine bag, he asked the other doctor, "Would it be all right with you if I left a second bottle, for her medicine chest?" The older doctor nodded.

Dr. Lamb picked up my biography of Louis XVI and with a mischievous smile asked if I knew what had finally happened to "this" gentleman. Well, yes, I knew but I thought it would be more fun if I let him tell me.

Instead of divulging it, he said, "Next time I visit you, Miss Stewart, I'll bring you something else to read." My curiosity about his medical research persuaded him to spend more time with me. He asked the old doctor if they were pressed for time. He replied, "No," so he pulled up a small stool and proceeded to tell us this story.

Immediately after he finished his divinity studies (he had already taken a year long course of medicine in Boston, as well as some additional medical classes in Philadelphia), he was asked by his large and prosperous New York church to become a foreign missionary. His first assignment was to convert the natives of several islands in Asia to Christianity. He was warned that it had been reported some of them practiced cannibalism.

According to church dogma, he told me, it was believed that once they converted to Christianity they would put those pagan practices behind them.

He was gone for over a year on that mission, after which he was recalled by the church and made his report. It was his opinion that the church elders were pleased with him because they asked him to go on another similar mission in South America. Again he was gone for another year, after being warned, once more, about cannibalism.

He was gone four years in all, he said, and on the long sea voyages to and from these destinations had gradually compiled a book that described his scientific findings, which boiled down to this: After the natives learned to trust him, he had often prescribed medicines, delivered babies, repaired broken bones and occasionally attended their "sick" animals, but after these two missions it was his conclusion that Christianity was no match for the native culture and their ancient practices, which among the elders included an ongoing tendency toward ritual cannibalism.

Without consulting his church, he had sought and found a publisher for his book, dealing with *Locations of Cannibalism in Mid-Nineteenth Century*. In time his book came to the attention of the church. Several elders expressed deep concern that his findings did not comport with church doctrine. On the other hand, he told me, two of the church's elders were medical doctors and had encouraged him and any other missionaries who were physicians to use their medical skills while on their missions and to be alert for new sources of medicinal raw material. Pending the church's inquiry, which is under way, he had been suspended from missionary work. In the meantime, he said, he had been contacted by a prominent firm in New York, a manufactory of

An Outbreak of Small Pox

medicine, and was now being sponsored by that company here in the Territory. He had been familiar with some of their products from his days in medical school and on both of his missions, when he had continually been on the lookout for additional sources of medicine, had stayed in touch with them.

After finishing his story, Dr. Lamb wished me well and took his leave, along with the older doctor. I was impressed that Dr. Lamb was so young to have already had such an exciting life. This interesting gentleman had gone all over the world, and he yet was on a probationary status with his church for being more interested in medicine than in fulfilling his Christian mission. Probably the cause for his "probation" was that he had written a very controversial book, which his church elders were now studying.

Adda visited me rather regularly. I continued to get better, though slowly. Each week Mrs. Robinson would send a note, not to inquire about me but to see when Adda was coming back to work. I was sick for four weeks and if it was bilious fever, which I doubt, I don't have the slightest idea how I caught it, or if it's contagious: Adda certainly didn't get it. She's as healthy as a horse. But I must say, I am grateful that somehow I didn't get the small pox, chicken pox or hepatitis. I have since seen Fanny and, although she is certainly her mother's child, and so is beautiful, she has some serious small white scars on her face and neck.

I impute my recovery entirely to Dr. Lamb's prescription: an extract of ginseng, bed rest and six glasses of warm water a day.

12.

PREPARING TO LEAVE LAWRENCE,
October 1857

In mid September after my recovery, I moved back to the Cincinnati House to resume my old duties. It was so nice to be back with the old gang. I was pleasantly surprised to receive so much flattering attention that stemmed from nursing the small pox cases, particularly little Fanny who is, of course, back here with her parents.

The first night back on the job, one of the soldiers offered to start the supper with a prayer (which of course is not uncommon) and he thanked the Almighty that I'd been spared the disease and that I was back among friends.

About this time I received another letter from Mr. Chase. He said he was returning to Kansas with Frank Robinson, who, he said, was carrying on a correspondence with Adda and wanted to make sure we were in Lawrence. In a few days they did arrive.

Frank and Adda came over from Robinsons' to see me but without Mr. Chase, though Adda said he had been with Frank when they arrived. I suspect that he was miffed because he had not received an answer to his June letter. But if he were so "miffed," why would he bother to come all the way from Archer to Lawrence? His actions leave me both flattered and mystified.

His was a nice letter and I'm ashamed that I waited so long to answer it that he probably never got it. And even if he did, it wasn't "much" of a letter. When I discussed this with Adda, she said, he's just shy."

While Adda was working for Mr. and Mrs. Alfred Robinson, the Governor's brother, we visited each other regularly. Now and then Aggie would give me an afternoon off and we could go shopping and just walk around the city. We both had Sundays off and appreciated being able to attend church services.

Father returned in mid-October. The first day he was back Adda was able to get off and we all had a noon meal together, though now and then I had to jump up and wait tables. Knowing all the customers and her way around the kitchen, Adda made a show of helping and thoroughly enjoyed serving some of her old friends, though I thought some of them were more friendly with her greeting than their renewed acquaintance required, but it seems to be Adda's outgoing style to encourage them. I just hope she doesn't begin to emulate Mrs. Gate's—generosities.

Adda asked Father if he had gotten back out to Eldorado in time for the Fourth of July celebration.

"Yes, indeedy. It was the first such celebration in Eldorado. Judge. Wakefield delivered a rousing patriotic speech."

By visiting Adda at the Robinsons, I got to know much more about his brother, Charles Robinson, the Governor, at the time the only territorial governor elected by "popular" vote. By "popular," I mean he was voted in mainly by the abolitionists of this town. He is not at all popular with the proslavery folk outside of Lawrence and even in Lawrence there are abolitionists openly critical about Dr. Robinson's excessively radical response to slavery and his unwillingness to compromise with a more moderate group of Free Soilers. As radical as they think he is, he's really quite peaceable compared to Jim Lane and Old John Brown.

From what I can tell he doesn't believe the slavery issue will ever be settled by abolitionist talk or compromise. He thinks it will take a revolution. Feeling the political pressure two years ago the Governor was advised to leave Lawrence. He did and was apprehended in Lexington, Missouri, charged with treason by a grand jury, returned to the territory and jailed in Lecompton together with George Deitzler, John Brown, Jr. and others. Seven days after his arrest while he was in prison, Missouri Ruffians burned his house together with much of Lawrence. The Grand Jury, which is simply a rubber stamp for the proslavery mob also indicted ex Gov. Reeder.[60] Indeed, he was among the seven abolitionists, rounded up in May[61] last year and taken down to Lecompton. As a prisoner also charged with treason, he was kept in prison for most of five months until General Lane, together with 1,200 men, most from Lawrence including many of my friends in the Stubbs Company, demanded on September 5th that the Governor be released. When the Southern soldiers saw several cannons aimed down at the camp from the hill site above it and the so-called Capitol Building, they released them.

The houses of the two Robinson brothers were next door to each other. Their families were inseparable. Although Dr. Charles Robinson was elected Governor, where other territorial governors have been presidential appointees, Dr. Robinson was never acknowledged by President Pierce or Congress, except as being involved in a treasonous insurrection. Dr. Robinson was known to be such a staunch abolitionist. It's my opinion that popular sovereignty was originally an acceptable substitute suggested by Senator Douglas when the Missouri Compromise didn't work. According to the original Senate plan, Kansas was intended to

---

[60] Kansas Historical Collections, Vol. 7, pg. 530
[61] Kansas State Historical Society Vol. 111, p. 203

be brought in as a slave state. For the past three years, Congress ignored the abolitionists. We had to increase our "popularity" and we did. And the country needed to get Buchanan out of the White House and we did that, too.

About once a week, I visited Adda at the Robinsons' house and, just as often, she visited me at the Cincinnati House. During these visits we shared the gossip of our employers. Mrs. Robinson was an open, warm, hospitable Yankee, very affectionate with her family and generous to others and treated Adda as a daughter, though a daughter expected to work. She called Adda, "Dear", though pronounced it "Deah." It was true, the Robinson's paid better than the Gateses, so we both found some humor in the fact that my work was harder. Her people and the Robinson's clan had all fought in the Revolutionary War, which they referred to as the War of Independence. When she began her employment at Mrs. Robinson's, Adda explained that our great grandfather, John Stewart, fought as a lieutenant in the War of Independence against the British and grandfather Charles, also had fought the British in the same war. Charles reenlisted, after the war was over, to fight the Indians, particularly against those tribes in New York and surrounding states that had for over one hundred years been on friendly terms with various branches of the English government. When the colonists declared their independence from England, the English maintained their contacts with these Indian tribes, particularly the Iroquois and Cherokees, and paid the tribes to them to fight with them against the colonists.

After the War of Independence, some of these old animosities toward the colonists remained with certain Indian tribes. Adda said our common family history seemed to create a bond between herself and Mrs. Robinson and, during my visits with Adda at the Robinsons' residence that friendliness was extended to me. However, Adda had warned me if we spoke of Plymouth days to be careful about praising General (James) Lane in their presence or speaking too highly of him, that she had learned that both Robinson families held deep seated animosities toward John Brown, so we never mentioned our acquaintance with that fine old gentleman we knew briefly when we were in Plymouth. The Robinson's see Jim Lane as too militaristic, too willing to fight against the proslavers. Of course, Governor Robinson has exactly the same reputation among more moderate abolitionists. Adda also suspects there exists simple political competition between the Robinsons and General Lane.

Their family was very involved in the abolitionist's cause and they knew all its leaders. What isn't common knowledge is that, Governor Robinson and his brother, Alfred, were related to President Pierce. There was a constant flow of personal letters and reports between these families and the Pierce family. They were all Yankees. The Robinsons and their wives were from Massachusetts and President Pierce was from New Hampshire. Mrs. Robinson was particularly sympathetic for the President after they moved to Washington, DC. On the train ride to the Capitol, an axle broke on their parlor car, the train derailed and their young son was killed.

Governor Robinson, was well-grounded in the humanities, studied medicine and became a New England trained medical doctor. He came from a long line of Yankee abolitionists. He had a practice in Belcher Town, Mass. and later opened a hospital in Springfield, Massachusetts.

In early 1840 he was struck by two tragedies. His new practice, plus the administrative load of the hospital, put heavy demands on him. His health failed, and he was forced to curtail his medical practice. This was followed by the death of his wife of barely two years, Sarah Adams, a Boston Adams. They had enjoyed a long and lovely engagement while he established his medical practice.

These two calamities caused him to consider going west both for his health and as a distraction from his bereavement.

In early 1849, he was asked to be physician for a group of California bound New Englanders. He accepted. They traveled mainly by rail and riverboat to Kansas City (then Westport Landing) but kept going until they got to California, arriving in Sacramento in the fall, which was swept up in the California Gold Rush. With hundreds of others, he became a squatter on Mr. Sutter's lands. When Mr. Sutter's officers served notice to vacate their claims, Dr. Robinson took-up the squatters' cause in resisting first their legal, then their physical attempts to evict.

Sutter and his party had been there since 1837 and represented the "establishment" including law and order. Sutter's holdings included a large Mexican Land Grant that embraced thousands of acres in the vicinity of the Sacramento and Feather Rivers (land that included the present site of Sacramento, the state capitol).

Though the boundaries for Mr. Sutter's holdings were not well-established, he clearly held title to the land.

Dr. Robinson led in the struggle for the settlers' and miners' causes. The settlers, squatters and miners had flocked in by the hundreds, ignoring previous claims, putting down tents, shanties, lean-tos, etc. all on Sutter's land, which of course, included the newly discovered 1849 gold strikes, so it was natural for him to resist this invasion. His attempt to eject the squatters precipitated a riot. Dr. Robinson took up the cause of the underdogs, (some of them, no doubt, were his party from Massachusetts). Sutter had him arrested, which Dr. Robinson resisted and was shot. Jailed on a prison ship, he was released on bail. He was acquitted of all charges. Undaunted, he ran for and was elected to California legislature, which was then at San Jose. But he tired of "government" and sailed for New England. The ship was wrecked off the coast of Mexico and he came back ultimately to New England via the overland route at Panama. I believe by then they had the railroad across the Isthmus.

By 1851, his health fully recovered from the wound he received when he was shot in California, he was back in Massachusetts. After his return to New England, Dr. Robinson remarried. He wed Miss Sara T. D. Lawrence, a younger sister of Amos Lawrence, the financial backer of Lawrence, Kansas. He got swept-up in the increasingly popular cause of abolition. In 1854, the Massachusetts Emigrant Aid Society invited him to be the physician accompanying the first group of Kansas bound settlers, whose emigration to the territory was sponsored by the Society. His brother, Alfred, and Alfred's family joined this group.

The group left on June 28, 1854. En route, cholera broke out on his river steamer and Dr. Robinson was asked to treat those who had "come down with it." True to his character, he soon took charge of the group, which arrived in Kansas on July 31, 1854, two years ahead of us.

At that time, the South still believed that the territory would become a slave state by popular vote within weeks following of the passage of the Kansas-Nebraska Act and this certainly began to happen. Proslavers from Missouri moved into the territory. But the Southerners vastly underestimated how politically offended the North was by the act, which over-threw the Missouri Compromise. They certainly underestimated the organizing zeal of the Kansas Central Committee and the implementation of that zeal by thousands of Northern immigrants willing to bring their varying degrees of abolition, coupled with their considerable mechanical and agricultural skills to the new territory.

Of course, the north-south competition didn't stop there. The South became more belligerent, more aggressive in their forays into Kansas. Overarching all that was the South's new determination to have their own nation stretching from sea to sea with their own culture, whose economic underpinning was the institution of slavery. Their progress in this matter was a major topic of the day. Not only did the South want the Kansas Territory in as a slave state, but they were bitter that in their attempt to get California admitted as a slave state, they had failed. Forty percent of the people making up the "California or Bust" migration were Southerners. Anti-abolition sentiment was strong in California. Most newspapers in Los Angeles and San Francisco endorsed the idea of secession for all southern states.[62]

As for the Southerners' plans for a new nation with slavery from sea-to-sea, they had already acquired several states from the land bought in the Louisiana Purchase by President Jefferson in 1803. Only nine years after the purchase, Louisiana, the first state cut out of the purchase was admitted as a Slave State. Missouri followed in 1821 (Slave), Arkansas in 1836 (Slave), Texas, a part of which had been in the land we bought from Napoleon, entered the Union in 1845 as slave.

As for our side, Iowa came in free in 1846 but there was so much proslavery sentiment and resistance to abolition that only a handful of its towns and villages supported the Underground Railroads, which was mainly used by Missouri slaves seeking freedom.

California, when it was finally admitted in 1850, came in a free state.

Although father was eager to participate in the settlement of Kansas Territory, after his experience in the Lecompton prison, his goals expanded beyond establishing and surveying new town sites. He planned to join the Legislature, and he hoped to help write the Free State Constitution.

---

[62] "The Civil War in the American West" by Alvin M. Joseph, Jr., pub. Alfred Knopf, NY

Preparing to Leave Lawrence

During October, after Father had returned to Lawrence, Adda came over as often as she could and we had nice family chats about his plans. Father's description of Eldorado made us anxious to head out there before it got too cold. Adda asked why we needed to be so far west, and wondered if we weren't taking some business risks by being out so far ahead of the "Frontier."

"By establishing several towns out there and advertising the available farm land and city lots we'll create our own frontier," he replied.

Though Father had lots of business to attend to in those waning days of October, he seemed to be in very good spirits: he had won a seat in the Legislature.

Father told us that District 17, which includes the Eldorado town site and Butler and Hunter counties, had polled about seventy-five settlers in the October election, which had taken place on the 17th. Sixty-nine of the settlers were Free Staters.

"Girls," he said, "your father now represents District 17 in the Territorial Legislature and my name has been put forward to work on the Free State Constitution." Adda and I were happy for Father and impressed with his popularity.

"You see," he added, "these Free Soil positions for territorial legislature are already filled here in the Eastern Counties, so by establishing our own voting district, I'll have a better chance. Since we've been here, I've also realized just how well-established in all the government positions the proslavery boys are, including postmasters, land agents, official surveyors, etc. To avoid being at the mercy of the proslavery people, "We Free Soilers need to increase our representation."

Father went on to say that, "Of the fifty-two total seats now in the Territorial Legislature, by my count of Free Soil members after the October elections we control thirty-three of them, so, when we need it, we have a seven man majority and I'm proud to say that I'm one of the thirty-three. Of course, it will require my being gone off and on this coming year, more than I prefer, and we'll have to put the finishing touches on our own constitution."

"Will you be involved in that?," asked Adda.

"Well, I hope so. I've been nominated for the committee but, as usual, there are more nominees than places on the committee."

And I asked Father if he thought most of the fighting was over.

He said he hoped so, but we could expect on-going sporadic trouble as old animosities get settled and there will be more lawlessness as we try to get the territory organized to operate under the rule of law. Father added that from what he had heard the October 17th elections were generally clean and not interfered with by the Missourians who previously seemed free to come over and mess with our polls without restrictions, had not interfered with the October vote.

Although the elections had gone well, Father said that we northerners would have problems to deal with. The process of filing a legal claim is still murky. Little of it had been settled, and it wasn't just because of proslavery obstructions. "We don't know from one month to the next how much of the Indian land has been freed up by Mr. Manypenny, the Indian Affairs Commissioner, and occasionally when it is available, we discover it's already in the hands of some Missouri speculators."

He produced a circular that said Mr. Manypenny had obtained agreements with nine or ten of those Indian tribes to sell or trade for land farther west or in Nebraska, accounting for over two and a half million acres or half of the land, that the Indians have had for twenty-five or thirty years. Father went on to say that squatters had already claimed much of that land. He said he had met a Mr. George Crawford, who had written a formal letter to the appropriate land office in Washington, DC, asking them to accelerate the arrangements with the Indians who own two of the larger reservations: the Miamis and the so-called New Yorks.

One noon meal in late October, Mr. Wilmarth, the scholarly book dealer, signaled me as he came into the dining room. He handed me a book wrapped in paper and said, "You'll be pleased, Miss Stewart. I've found the book by Mrs. Robinson that you asked for last March. I had to order it from the publishers. Apparently she or the publisher has ordered a second edition."

I thanked the gentleman and began to walk to the kitchen. He coughed to get my attention and said, "That will be sixty-five cents including the postage."

I guess I was so elated to get the book I forgot that I would owe him money. I can't wait to begin reading it. I just can't get over that I have this book by the (elected) governor's wife who wrote of these events, some of which we have in common and I've met her, and my sister sees her frequently, as she visits next door where Adda works for the family of the governor's brother, Alfred. According to Adda, although Sara Robinson enjoys her brother-in-law's children, she is quite formal with them. Adda thinks that's because she has no children.

I continued working at the Cincinnati House but was pretty well packed up for Eldorado. Father had returned and one evening was taking a meal here with some of his "prospects," including Mr. Jones, one of our "regulars". After dinner I was able to join them for tea. When Father was distracted by another guest, Mr. Jones quietly pulled his chair closer to mine and in a soft voice asked if we could take a little walk. I knew from his previous comments why he wished to speak with me and I resented it. I guessed "what was coming" and excused myself to go upstairs, where I waited until I was sure he had left. Because it was my job to feed him, or anybody else that came in at supper I was always friendly and polite. I suppose from my hospitality he over-exercised his imagination or his presumptuousness.

Father said the next morning that I seemed to have evaporated after serving tea. I fibbed and said I was making beds. I didn't want to explain my reasons to him but he had his suspicions. Father did say he thought there were better ways to deal with gentlemen like Mr. Jones, than running upstairs. Father went on to say that out here in the Territory there will be more men than women, so I might as well get accustomed to these social conditions—and enjoy it. Father explained that some men were lonely. Perhaps they hadn't learned to appreciate their own company and they would be overly attentive to available girls, like Adda and me, and rather than be offended by their behavior, he suggested humor or a contained friendliness and he quoted proverbs, "A soft answer turneth away wrath." I told him I could handle wrath. It was overly presumptuous men that I needed to "turneth" away. I told him that I had experienced many of those male traits over in Archer and in the several months I had worked for Mrs. Gates with the Stubbs Boys. I enjoyed this quiet talk with Father, though there were some questions I would like to have asked him about men, but I didn't. I'm sure these would be conversations I could have had if my mother had lived. I had a lingering desire to discuss Mrs. Gates and her attractions to the Stubbs Boys but couldn't bring myself to begin. I'm still trying to sort out how it was that such a beautiful, successful, married woman with a ten year old daughter could provoke and relish the attention of "billy goats" and in her womanly-talk with Adda and me, explaining it as all part of the "birds and the bees." Adda had advised me to keep that episode to myself, and I have.

At one of the suppers before we left Lawrence, Father asked, "Do you remember Sam Pomeroy?" I said, "I certainly recall the rainy episode of October 10th last year in Plymouth when he and

Mr. Eldridge rode in with their supply train and quickly put a stop to the rude searching of the new wagons being directed by Marshall Preston."

Father continued, "Well, as a measure of how the tide has turned in our favor, Mr. Pomeroy has just purchased the old 'Atchison Squatter,' the proslavery newspaper over in Leavenworth." He laughed and said, "I suppose we'll see quite a shift in that paper's editorial content." Adda laughed and asked, "Think he'll change the name?"

So the deed was done! Goliath, this nine foot tall puffed-up proslavery bully, who for several years strutted around our territory in the uniform of the U. S. Army, fattened by a Federal bureaucracy, encouraged by the U. S. Senate, sanctified by our Supreme Court, was by the close of 1857 dead, laying out as horizontal as the prairie he intended to dominate, killed almost accidentally by the stone of Popular Sovereignty, hurled by Little David the immigrant, who slyly figured out he could form a state free of slavery by infringing on the Senate's patent of "Popular Sovereignty." Bobby Burns should have included politicians with his two bungling planners: "mice and men." The irony, of course, is this: the unintended man is dead. Goliath's plan all along, from 1854 was to stifle, oppress and kill Little David, the abolitionist.

On November 2nd (1857) we left for the Promised Land.

13.

Eldorado,
November 1857 to February 1858

This chapter of our adventures was to bring out strengths, talents and bursts of resourcefulness we didn't know we possessed. And we also developed a virtue of interdependence and mutual help, both within our family and with our new friends. Staking our claims in Eldorado really commenced our pioneer life. In Plymouth and Lawrence we were always waiting for something. Our lives as pioneers were always impending. We were like actors waiting to go "on."

We left Lawrence for Eldorado on November 2nd with the big wagon, pulled by the pair of oxen that Father had bought in Iowa two summers ago and named them with such laughter—Tempus and Fugit; time flies. Father said the Iowa outfitters assured him that the oxen were both abolitionists. Well, I can tell you from viewing their hind sides for nearly a month, when we traveled from Iowa City to Plymouth, no two creatures on God's Earth are more oblivious to time and its duration than these two. But in all fairness, they are dependable and loyal, and as Father says, "They do not talk back."

The day we left it began to blow. The wind came out of the north and at times it almost tipped us over. The first night we stayed with a friend of Father's in a cabin in Clinton, maybe twenty miles west of Lawrence. The next night we found a boarding house in Wakarusa.

The third night, we stayed with Mr. Preston Plumb in his new settlement, Emporia, about halfway between Lawrence and Eldorado, and we had some fine "politicking" that night.

Adda and I didn't know that Father had done some surveying for him and Father didn't know about Mr. Plumb's barefoot visit to Plymouth last fall a year ago, so we had a nice time exchanging these mutual recollections, but things had changed. Mr. Plumb was much more serious, though no less concerned with local and national politics than before. But as I tested the situation, thinking to tease him about his barefoot rendezvous with Jim Redpath's southbound train in Plymouth and his visit with us that night, I could never quite find the right time for that humor and I never brought it up.

Mr. Plumb had printing experience as a youth and he told us he intended to have a newspaper. He and Father also spent some time discussing just where to locate a hotel he planned to build. I must say, I was impressed by all the things he had accomplished for such a young man. I think he is just barely twenty-one.

Well, the next three nights, November 5th, 6th, and 7th, we camped on the prairie—not by choice. We were well beyond the frontier demarcation, without its hospitality: hotels and boarding houses. Nor was the prairie very hospitable. The wind that came up the day we left Lawrence seemed to get worse the closer we got to Eldorado.

I can tell you it wasn't like camping out with the Van Curens and the Strongs in those balmy July days in western Iowa. By November 6th the wind had developed into a blizzard. We had blizzards in Michigan but they were pygmies compared to a Kansas blizzard. The prairie, being so flat, offers no obstruction to the wind. And any woods that might act as a windbreak are usually down in the valleys and streambeds, below the general level of the prairie.

November 8: Well, it was still blowing and snowing today but we managed somehow to stay on the trail. Thank God for those indelible ruts of the Old Santa Fe Trail. It was getting dark when we arrived at the site of Eldorado. It reminded me of Plymouth, no houses, no streets, a few tents and prairie. Where Plymouth had the Nemaha River, Eldorado had the Walnut , which looked much larger. We pitched a tent—in the dark—and how we managed to pound the stakes into the frozen ground, with the wind howling like a banshee, baffles me to this day. Father had the top-maul for his stakes, but in the dark I couldn't find our large hammer. I did find our large cast-iron skillet, so I used that, but I worried about the cold crystallizing the metal of that old skillet such that, if I pounded the stakes too hard, I'd poke a hole in the bottom of it. But I got my stakes into the ground and when I was finished, the skillet was none the worse for wear. And I did all this with mittens on. Now that I think back on it, I see some humor in our groping around in the dark with the snow blowing while we were carrying our "stuff" from the wagon to the tent. But at the time, it wasn't funny. Finally, we got our table into the tent, but we couldn't find our coal oil lamp. We did find an old shoebox where we kept our candles (most of them just butts) and we lit four or five of them and tied them in a bundle. Father brought in the stove. Adda remembered where she had put some firewood in the wagon and in no time we had a fire going and the tent warmed up nicely.

From Lawrence to Eldorado is about 125 miles. It took us six days to make the trip. We made about twenty miles a day, which was our average speed crossing Iowa in July of last year. We didn't do as well after leaving Tabor, because from there on, we traveled in a company; we didn't get on the road as early nor did we stay on it as late as when we had traveled solo. Coming here to Eldorado I believe we could have made better time, if it hadn't been for the snow and wind of the last three days.

After we had the stove up, Adda and I began to prepare supper. We heard a commotion outside. Our first thought was that we had some visitors—Indians.

Well, it was a "neighbor," one of the early settlers. He had left his wagon outside and made some humor with Father about bringing his horse in.

The young man said he had set up a tent-store and belonged to the party that had come to Eldorado during the summer. (This was the party represented by the advance scout Father had told us about last June.) Father seemed particularly pleased to see this gentleman, who had brought with him an earthenware jug. He poured himself and Father a "libation." I asked what he had in the jug. He winked and said, "apple cider."

Well, after a few additional pleasantries, which included some more exaggerated humor about bringing the horse in, but keeping him in the parlor, our visitor stepped out of the tent and returned with a large, steaming cast-iron pot with a heavy lid. With some fanfare, he lifted off the lid and exposed a roasted turkey with all the "trimmings."

Just when we were feeling sorry for ourselves, this Good Samaritan had appeared at our doorstep with this bountiful supper. It was duly appreciated—and never forgotten, for it was so kind of him and came so opportunely, after traveling in the storm the night before and with the day's weariness added to our hard trip. That turkey, consumed in candlelight, much of it with our fingers because we had not located the box with the tableware, was as elegant a meal as I have ever had.

Our new friend was the local grocer, Erastus Howland, who had established the first store in Eldorado.

The next morning, we put up a second tent and were able to start keeping house. Later that day, Father said we would have company for supper. Aggie Rourke had given me some good flour before we left, so I said I'd bake some bread and it turned out fine.

As a welcoming present, someone from the July arrivals had given us some venison, a rather small rib of deer referred to as a "rack," which I roasted. One rib bone was badly shattered, no doubt from the bullet, but the meat was unscathed, and it was lean and not as red or pink as fresh beef. About 5 p.m., Father came back with our supper guest. It was almost dark. Our visitor was none other than Captain Joseph Cracklin, whom Adda and I knew from working at Mrs. Gates' house last winter, when he was in charge of the Stubbs Company.

We had a fine time renewing our acquaintance and recalling events associated with the Gates House. The Captain had a great appetite. I swear he ate almost half a loaf of my bread. I had kept it hot in our oven. We had plenty of butter for it from the neighbors. Both Father and the Captain said the venison was as good as any they'd get in the best Chicago hotel, which was most flattering, considering my stove and my kitchen-in-a-tent.

There was simply nothing between us and the elements but a layer of canvas, but we couldn't have had a better time if we'd been in the most sumptuous dining room of Chicago's finest hotel. I learned that night that you don't need a big, elegant house to be happy with old friends.

During supper, Captain Cracklin, who had been with Father last June in the party that "founded" Eldorado, told Adda and me that he was the one who had given the town its name. "The new name," he said, "is Spanish and is a contraction of 'el hombre dorado'—the gilded man. Dorado means 'golden' or 'gilded.'

"After Columbus discovered America, some of the Spanish explorers heard a story about a ritual in South America that involved gold. At a certain time of the year, a tribe would select a particularly well-built youth, remove his clothes except for a loincloth and cover his body with a paste of gold dust: He became 'el hombre dorado'.

"As part of the ritual, he would dive into a sacred pool.

"The Spaniards reasoned that any people that had enough gold to sacrifice it that way had to have plenty of it.

"The Spaniards did indeed find a tribe that practiced this ritual, locating the tribe in what is now Venezuela, but the rumor persisted that this ritual was also practiced in other parts of the Americas. The explorers, De Soto and Coronado even sought el hombre dorado in what is now Mexico and up here, in southwestern part of our country."

Captain Cracklin said that the surveying party, led by your father[63] came to Eldorado last June had gone west all the way to the big bend in the Arkansas River, looking for a town site. "Finding none that suited our fancy, we turned around and headed back east. We approached this area from the west, getting here on June 6th as the land was bathed in the glow of the late-afternoon sun, and was so golden, I exclaimed, 'Eldorado!'"

Captain Cracklin was from Massachusetts and had been part of Lane's Army in September of last year when General Lane's stepped up his recruitment to do battle with proslavery forces but the Captain avoided being captured and so avoided the prison at Lecompton.

---

[63] Also confirmed in history Butler County's Eighty Years, 1855-1935, p. 11.

The Captain spent the night with us, was up before me and had started a fire in the stove. While I was making coffee, I noticed he was handling some books from a box we used as a weight to hold the bottom of the tent flap down.

"Who's the big reader?"

"We all are, but most of those books are mine and Adda's. Father's books are still in the wagon."

As he leafed through one of them, he remarked with a chuckle that, "This one has a lot of blank pages."

"Yes, that's my journal, which I started when we left Michigan. I have lots of notes from our days in Plymouth that need to be rewritten as entries. They will fill up the blank pages, and more."

"Why didn't you make those entries at the time?"

"Some of them dealt with the whereabouts of General Lane and occasionally John Brown and those two gents at that time both had a price on their heads. By October, the Army had established a large camp near us across Pony Creek and they felt at liberty to search our wagons and cabins whenever they pleased." I laughed and mentioned, "One time they found a keg of powder under some flooring right in our cabin but they never found the cannon, though they suspected we had one. That day they also found three more barrels of powder."

I hesitated to discuss the proposal from Captain Henry. I saw no point in this information getting back to Frank Swift. Nor did I tell him that Adda and I had good reason to believe that Plymouth was a "stop" in the underground railroad.

Captain Cracklin said he knew both General Lane and John Brown and it was probably wise to have hidden those notes.

The Captain asked me what I proposed to do with the Journal. The question took me by such surprise I was, I suppose, slow to answer. Finally, recalling how impressed I was with Sara Robinson, the Governor's wife, that she'd written a book about the troubles here in the Territory, I replied, "I hope some day to publish this in a proper book, like Sara Robinson. Mine will be more personal, less political." The Captain agreed that Sara Robinson was an impressive lady, adding his opinion that she discredits the importance of General Lane and the militia, he almost single handedly organized. "And," he said, "She's simply wrong about John Brown." I so wanted to continue this discussion but we were distracted by Adda and Father getting up. I want to ask him if he had her book. I guess I wanted to brag a little, that I had a copy.

A fine sunny day is this November 21st. The wind has died down, but there are patches of snow here and there and we are still living in our tents. Adda and I were outdoors, hanging some laundry, when we saw a wagon coming down the grade on the other side of the creek. We both wondered if it was "the boys," meaning Frank Robinson and Jacob Chase. Ever since our arrival, we more or less have been expecting to see them. That is, they led us to believe that they intended to come out.

After the wagon crossed the creek, one of the men started up towards the tent on foot. "I wonder if that's Frank Robinson," said Adda.

"Stop that, they'll see you."

We stayed out in front of the tent and chatted. I could see that there were three others in the wagon. Noticing my curiosity, Frank laughed and said, "Your friend Chase is in the wagon, with two more carpenters who came down with us from Rulo, Mr. Benton and Mr. Buchanan." All four of them had come to Eldorado to take up claims and help build our town.

Though it was midmorning we invited them to tea and supper, if as Adda joked with Frank, "You shoot a couple turkeys to earn the invitation, as you did last year at the Strongs' place over in Archer.

Of course, with game so abundant, we had a turkey in the oven by mid afternoon. Well, we had a rousing good supper, supplied by Frank Robinson on special request by my rather "forward" sister.

It's hard to believe that a year has gone by since Mr. Chase and I saw each other.

When he came into the tent for supper, he bowed rather formally and we shook hands. There seemed to be a great distance between us. He was so changed in appearance and demeanor that I had difficulty recognizing him. That is, I had trouble reconciling the person now in our tent with my romantic memories of him as my dancing partner.

The Jacob Chase I remembered from our social days up in Archer, during the "season" that started with the big autumn ball at Miller's Hotel, didn't square with the Jacob Chase with us this evening. That was the ball that was announced by the mysterious invitations, which gave Adda and me and our fellow detective, Mrs. Strong, so much fun in unraveling. Though I've been busy since then, I have on many occasions recalled those halcyon days and wondered if I'd ever again see days as pleasant and carefree, though Lord knows Mrs. Strong kept us busy with all her boarders. Down deep, I'm so flattered that he's come all this distance.

One day, later in the fall, sometime in November or December. Father, Frank Robinson, Mr. Chase and others had gone off to survey their claims, leaving Adda and me alone. About midmorning, three Indians came to the tent. I assumed that they were Osage since that tribe has a government-provided claim some distance east and south of us. They wanted to come in.

It was a chilly day—I know because my inkwell froze during the night. After Father left, we had laced the tent flap closed. Adda peeked through the tent flap and told them to go away. Those tents only had one entrance and you were obliged to stoop to get in. I was doing the morning dishes and Adda was writing in her journal. Oh yes, we both have journals now, so you can imagine what an entry this will make!

The Indians kept fiddling with the small rope that held the tent flap closed. They managed to get it open enough to put one head, sometimes two heads in. Well, seeing those dirty grinning heads, with all the hair shaved off except for a brush like strip that runs from front to back, frightened us almost out of a year's growth (as they say) and I suppose the Indians knew it.

Adda seemed less upset than me. She quickly marched over to those Red Skins and began pushing their heads back out of the tent flap. It became quite a contest. Adda would push the head of the Indian who was on top and it would disappear, then the Indian below, taking advantage of the extra space would force his head in further and try to get his shoulders in. "If you're cold, go to Howland's store," she told them. None of the Indians spoke. They just continued their attempt to gain access. I said, "Adda, those Red Skins don't understand a word you're saying."

The big one kept on fumbling with the flap laces and Adda continued pushing their heads out of the opening each time one of them came through. Occasionally, she used their ears as handles. Adda was soon kneeling on the dirt floor tugging on both ends of the laces. I thought she was going to choke the little fellow on the bottom. The first thing I knew was this big fellow had pulled the laces away from Adda and was coming into our tent on his hands and knees. On the way in, he just pushed Adda to one side. He didn't hit her. In fact, once he had made it into the tent, he ignored her.

"There's not enough room in here for three Indians and the two of us," I said. "Adda, just let them come in. When they get in, we will go out." We both got outside. Adda stayed near the tent. I was bareheaded and my sleeves were up above my elbows from washing dishes. In fact, I remember my hands being wet, and the wind whistling through my hair. I glanced back. The Indians had followed us out of the tent, I guess to see what I was going to do. I suppose they thought I was going to the wagon to fetch one of our Sharps rifles, with which I had become reasonably proficient. We kept at least one of our Sharps rifles stored either in the tent or in the wagon, loaded and "half-cocked". Instead, I walked swiftly until I got beyond a bend in the creek ,then I ran to the blacksmith's shop. To my great relief, I found our old friend, Tom Cordis. Though he said he was not feeling well, he didn't hesitate to come running back with me. We knew Adda could put up a good fight—but we weren't sure she could handle all three Indians.

When we returned, the Indians and Adda were all inside the tent. They were handling our things, not with malice or intent to steal, but with curiosity; mostly they were "milling about" the stove, making gestures indicating that they were cold. Upon seeing us, Adda's attitude turned very indignant towards them.

Tom Cordis is a big man and, as he moved around in the tent, his head touched the roof in several places. He said if they were cold, they should go up to the store and warm up. Mr. Cordis added that he would not stand for their barging into tents when women were alone. They smiled at him and I must say, now that the danger had passed, that they were not hostile, just curious, and I suppose they were cold, but with all the talk about Indians, the persistence of the three Osage getting into our tent had been very unsettling.

After things calmed down a bit, I realized these fellows were very young, maybe Adda's age. They weren't by any measure old enough to be considered "braves" or "warriors." They were simply Indian boys out on a lark, curious about the White settlers.

After some time, all of a sudden one of them spoke up and with the King's English, if you please. He said he was their interpreter. Adda walked right up to this bird and, with enviable indignation, said, "Why didn't you say something when I was trying to keep your heads out of our tent?"

Adda continued scolding the Indians, telling them that their behavior wasn't proper and that they might get shot one of these days by someone less patient than us.

"What's your name?" she demanded.

"Paul."

"What's your name in Osage?"

"Ee Win Ee Say."

"What's it mean?"

"He who smells like a White Man."

"But that wasn't your original name, was it?"

"True, but that's my name now."

Calming down a bit and lowering her voice she asked, "Well, Paul, where did you learn your English?"

"East of here in the Neosho Valley. It's where I attended two Christian missions. First, I went to a school on the Osage Reservation. Then later, I went to the Quaker mission school after the Government and the Quakers moved us a little farther west. We weren't on the reservation anymore but on our own land."

"What are you doing way out here?"

"We are on a buffalo hunt."

"Why aren't you out hunting? Why were you hanging around our tent, scaring us to death? I don't understand why, when I was pushing at your heads and yelling for the three of you to go away, you couldn't have just said something in English, like 'I'm cold' or 'I'm hungry.'"

Paul paused and looked at Adda. They were about the same age and about the same size. "I don't think you will understand."

he said. "I mustn't talk too much." Then, pointing to the big Indian, he added, "His name is Mas-Mas-Nas-Conu. He is the son of our chief, Mint-Sho-Shin-Ka. He knows when I speak to you that I'm not speaking in Osage tongue. He knows when I speak English in the presence of my people, some of the powers of my manhood will escape in my breath and I can never, ever recover them."

"Who told you such nonsense?"

"Our medicine man. He says if I keep talking the White Man's talk, finally after enough talk, I will become a ghost and join the wind."

"Nonsense, utter nonsense! Paul, do you know the word nonsense?"

"Yes, but this omen is true. Each White Man sound I make reduces my spirit and my body. I am already shunned by the older braves. Today they are out hunting buffalo but I was left behind. They say because I speak like the White Man, I smell like the White Man and the buffalo can smell me. My smell would spoil the hunt. When I become a ghost, I will cease to smell."

"I've never heard such drivel in my life!"

That night we related the whole episode to Father. Before it got dark, Father took the small wagon and drove two or three miles south of us to their camp. They had left their own reservation east of us seventy or so miles and had come this far west to hunt buffalo, Father later reported. Paul was there and acted as the interpreter. Father said he told them they were not to come round when he wasn't there and that their visit and their manner of pushing their way into our tent had been frightening and he wouldn't tolerate it.

I suspect that his trip was wasted. We don't scare the Indians. In fact, man for man, their bravery exceeds ours because theirs is so deeply ingrained and cultural.

Eventually, we became accustomed to the Osage. They would visit us occasionally and irregularly but always at mealtime and if there weren't too many of them, and if Father (or a neighbor) had just killed some game, we would feed them.

Christmas day, we moved from our tents into the house that Father has built with the help of several neighbors, using logs that he had accumulated since last summer. After hand-hewing flat two sides of each of the logs, and we only have three adzes in our settlement, the neighbors all vowed to be investors with Father in a sawmill!

The house has no floor; that is, it has a dirt floor like the one up in Plymouth, (which I imagine to this day still has no floor.) But we had walls that withstood the wind. Father had plastered chinks between the logs. He first located a source of limestone and devised an oven to "bake" it; then, with some pounding, he converted it to a yellowish white powder, which became plaster. We complimented him on this invention. Father replied that the Egyptians had used plaster for the tomb walls of their pyramids, and the Romans certainly knew how to fire limestone, so it was hardly a new invention. Nevertheless, Adda and I were still impressed with his resourcefulness.

We had an interesting Christmas Day. I wouldn't say it was exactly a celebration of abundance in material things. Oh, the food was plentiful. But gifts, store bought, were not. Howland, Frank Robinson, Adda and I made three or four kinds of Christmas candy. It included the meat of black walnuts, which Frank broke open on Father's old anvil. And we had a supply of local hazel nuts, some of which we roasted and then stirred in a pan of melted sugar until we had a thin hard-caramelized shell built on each nut, a trick we'd learned from Mrs. Strong.

Our best Christmas present is our one and one half story house, though it's far from finished. The log walls are up and we have a roof over our heads but we've had no recent rain, so we don't know if it leaks. A canvas flap serves as the door, though Father and Mr. Chase are working on a proper wood door, metal hinges, etc. We have space for three windows, each facing a different direction except south, but they aren't in yet. The door is on the south side to avoid the incessant, down river, north wind.

Jacob Chase and Frank Robinson stayed over with us this Christmas Night. Erastus Howland came back for supper and we had some fine singing, including all the old Christmas Carols.

Father, Mr. Chase and myself had a long talk about the need for a sawmill in the area. Of course, Father sees himself as an expert, since he comes from a long line of sawmill builders, owners, and operators. His last mill was the one he sold in Gibraltar on Lake Erie in preparation for our coming out to the Territory. I'm well aware that the money from the sale of the mill and store gave us a degree of independence not possessed by most other west bound travelers.

"Some months ago," said Father, "I sent some specifications to a factory in Providence, Rhode Island for three circular saw blades, ranging from sixty to seventy-two inches in diameter." He looked at Mr. Chase. "They will be the largest blades this side of St. Louis."

Father added that the main shaft—an axle four inches in diameter made in Brooklyn, New York—together with two big bearing boxes, one for each side of the axle, were that very day waiting in Lawrence to be picked up. This news came as a pleasant surprise to me. I knew Father had dispatched the order, but wasn't aware that those parts were already in the Territory.

Facing Mr. Chase, Father said, "There are two journeyman carpenters coming out our way. Plus you, that makes three available builders for new houses, barns and commercial buildings. The journeymen told me that they have already built over fifty houses in the Chicago area. They said that they are using the new stud wall process. With better and cheaper nails, the old method of joining wood with mortises and tendons is going to disappear, but more importantly, all wood construction within a hundred miles of a mill, will be done with timber pre cut into dimensions 2" by 6" and so on. These two fellows told me that they have patterns to make roof trusses out of pre cut timbers, which they can use to create ceiling spans twelve to fifteen feet. These two journeymen plus you should be our town's main builders and you'll have access to wood from our mill."

Years ago, he said, his father had developed all the drawings and specifications necessary for building sawmills. "I've kept them, and I brought them here in the big steamer trunk that we carried out from Michigan." He added rather philosophically that since timber sizes don't change all that much, there was no need to change sawmill designs much.

"Obviously" he said, "I'd prefer to have a head of water power to propel the saw as my father did in upstate New York, but since that's not possible with the Walnut, we'll use the river's water by converting it to steam, burning local wood as fuel." Father said that our new steam boiler would be here soon, adding that he had ordered it from the same factory in Philadelphia, where the boiler for our mill in Gibraltar came from. "I've been using their catalogues for years. It's the same company that supplied my father. He bought several from them over the years to power the various mills he built as a contractor.

"Your grandfather discovered that one of his early boilers, purchased to power a sawmill, made so much surplus steam it was a sin to waste it, so he raised more working capital from several of his friends, most of whom were already in on the first mill, and they built a flour mill close by. They planned to use the surplus steam from the boiler to run the flourmill. The sawmill corporation was already profitable, and the boiler had already been paid for. So when the flour mill got up and running, all of the profits were distributed to the sawmill shareholders—and that was mostly us, 'cause the Stewarts were the biggest shareholders."

Father continued this story of Grandfather's acumen and success. "With all that surplus steam he could charge about ten percent less to grind a hundred pounds of grain than any other mill in Onondaga County. We couldn't handle all the business. You see, one of the major expenses of running a steam flourmill is the cost of the power to drive the mill. Since the boiler was right there, we could have dropped our prices another two or three percent and still made money." Father added that the profits from those two mills had made his family one of the most comfortable in that part of upstate New York.

"The lesson I learned there, Augusta, is that when you buy a boiler, always get one with more capacity than you need for the first job. Then, when the first mill gets up and running and is profitable, you can begin planning the use of the surplus steam for other ventures, like a gristmill.

"So first, Augusta, we've got to get that sawmill up and running. I've ordered one hundred bags of pure cement from Chicago, which a freighter will be bringing out in the next few weeks. When the weather warms up a bit and the ice on the river breaks up, I'll hire two men to wash gravel and sand from that sandbar that sticks out on the river north of the town site. I'll use that gravel and sand for the foundations for our sawmill. It will take two pilasters twelve inches thick to support those shaft bearings and it will be tricky to build, 'cause I'll need a clean-out pit under the saw blade deep enough for a man to get under there to bucket up the bark chips and sawdust. And, Augusta, do you know what? We will use those chips as fuel in the boiler, yes, siree!"

It amazes me that Father can't simply say, "yes or no." It is always "Yes, siree" or "All righty" or "Yes, indeedy" or "No, siree". Occasionally, with his cronies, it was "No siree, Bob" or "Nope" or "Well, of course not." I impute these peculiarities to Grandmother Gates.

It was midmorning of January 29. Adda came in with the smell of smoke about her clothes and body. She and Jerry Jordan had been cleaning up brush and burning it in a big bonfire at his claim Adda was all excited about a conversation she'd had with Mr. and Mrs. Carey, who had stopped by Jerry's claim to report that they had just returned from Chelsea, where an itinerant preacher had preached four sermons in two days. The Careys were so invigorated by the traveling preacher that they invited him to come down to Eldorado. He didn't know that there was a settlement west of Chelsea until the Careys invited him down with a promise of a big turnout. He has been working his way west. The Careys stopped at Jerry's long enough to invite him and Adda to a meeting they plan to hold at their place tomorrow night.

Adda says Mrs. Carey was so stimulated by this preacher that she gave them a detailed report on his religious beliefs and handed them a little folded notice stating the preacher's doctrine. According to the folder, he advocates ignoring all religious authority except Jesus Christ and The Scriptures. He thinks the Pope's authority should be questioned or ignored, and that goes as well for the imputed authority of the archbishop of Canterbury, the head of the Church of England. He's also against the Calvinists' preoccupation with damnation and original sin, creeds he thinks we've imported from the Old Country. He questions the doctrine of hell's everlasting eternity and the existence of the Devil being as corporeal as God. And claims he can't find anything in the Scriptures that justifies all this worry about hell and damnation.

Reading from the little folder, Adda said, "He believes in the doctrine of baptism with total immersion." I interrupted to ask if he was a Baptist.

"Well, I doubt it."

"Why?"

"Well the Baptists have worked so hard to endorse the separation of church and state that it has driven the Baptists, especially the Southern Baptists, closer to the position of the slaveholders than the position we take. I can't imagine a Southern Baptist coming out here."

"By the way," she added, "Mrs. Carey reported that several souls came forward for salvation in Chelsea."

"Do you suppose that included baptism? If he thinks he's going to baptize with total immersion down here that might be a little nippy with the river frozen over. Oh, I suppose in a fever of high piety we could find a volunteer sinner or two to go out and break the ice." Adda was so serious she didn't catch my humor, or she ignored it.

Adda continued with Mrs. Carey's report, "Mrs. Carey said that he devoted one entire sermon to modern literature and the decadent influence it's having on our culture. He's against literature that springs from the imagination because he says that the characters in novels are seldom made to suffer the consequences of their acts. He thinks writers shouldn't be the ones to determine what is acceptable behavior. According to him, the Old Testament teaches that those things should be left to the clergy.

"Apparently he's paid by his church, which enjoys generous contributions from Eastern abolitionist groups. So, I assume he's definitely an abolitionist.

"He was assigned by a central agency in Ohio to come out and preach in the territory and has been here since summer.

And—oh yes—he told the Carey's that he expects supper, fodder for his horse, a night's lodging, and breakfast before he leaves."

"Are you going?" I asked her.

"You betcha, wouldn't miss it." She added, "You know this is going to be the first formal religious meeting in Eldorado, so you ought to note it in your journal." And I have.

Father is away in Lawrence, serving as a Legislator. Too bad. I think he would enjoy going to the meeting. I hope the weather holds up. "Let's get word to Jacob Chase and Mr. Howland," I suggested.

Added replied, "They already know about it. The Careys haven't missed a single person in the valley."

Father returned from Lawrence last night (January 30.) He was cold from his long trip but after he had warmed up, he gave us a report on the Legislature. "It looks like we Free State men, will be able to take control of the Territorial Legislature. There's much confusion about who will do what but it looks like we've finally got a majority. Now we must use it wisely, and the first step is for us to press on with a convention to write a Free State Constitution, so we can have a document forbidding slavery that can be ratified by the people out here."

Later in the afternoon Father and Jerry went off to do some survey work in Arizonia, one of the town sites established by the exploring party of last June.

It was so nice to see Father, but he says he must return to Lawrence within a week to continue his work in the Legislature and to work on the new constitution. I'm a little put out that he must go back so soon.

The next day, February 2, Mr. Chase was here again, but didn't speak to me at all. He had some questions for Father about where to setup the syrup mill when it arrives. Mr. Chase and I don't seem to be very good friends lately. What I think this community needs is a good lively dance, the likes of which we had a year ago up in Archer. But, of course, we can't have a dance—we lack musicians.

After packing up yesterday, Father left again this morning (February 5) for Lawrence. Though Father is rather quiet about his plans, he did say that he would be attending a meeting to organize a Free State Constitutional Convention and to nominate and elect delegates.

Without a big discussion about the dangers, Adda and I know that these organizing sessions are deemed illegal by the establishment, which is the territorial government.

In the afternoon, Mr. Howland came by. I fixed the two of us some hot tea. He had brought some little hard cookies from a bakery in Chicago with which he does business.

Mr. Howland said he really would have chosen to have his store farther east—Lawrence was his choice—but couldn't afford to have his inventory ruined as happened with the Free State Hotel,[64] which was destroyed by Sheriff Jones "General" Persifer Smith over in Leavenworth could have controlled that mob," he said. "And if his proslavery sentiments prevented him from enforcing the law, he should have asked his subordinates to do it. He has excellent lieutenants with plenty of military experience, such as Colonel Cooke."

I recounted my meeting with the colonel up in Plymouth in what seems ages ago, yet it was only a year or so.

Mr. Howland continued, saying that the federal government's refusal to perform the most fundamental responsibility of a government, namely, to protect its citizens, has worked a cruel hoax on the immigrants that are abolitionists.

---

[64] The Eldridge House in Lawrence was also known as the Free State Hotel.

"The government has converted a rosy, hopeful prospect into a painful illusion. Our federal government has failed us."

"The first three or four lines of our Constitution," he pointed out, "lays out the basic obligations of our government: 'to establish justice, insure domestic tranquility, provide for the common defense.' It doesn't say the 'defense of proslavery'—it says the 'common defense' and the Preamble goes on to say that the government has an obligation to 'promote the general welfare. Well, if what happened to Lawrence is promoting the general welfare, I don't want to be there when the federal government gets ugly!"

Mr. Howland added that the government had financial limits and couldn't afford to provide us with complete safety, but it must do more than it's doing, especially for the abolitionists.

"There are plenty of soldiers to defend us." He explained that ninety percent of the U. S. Army's 7,000 men are posted out here on the frontier. "The Army has set up almost eighty forts west of the Mississippi. So I have to believe that the problem isn't a lack of manpower, but lies with Army's senior officer," he said. "Most served in the Mexican War under President Polk. Almost all of his generals were Southern Democrats and were proslavery."

Mr. Howland said he wasn't at all sure we should even be here. "We've only owned this area for fifty years. For heaven's sake, there's plenty of farmland east of the Missouri or the Mississippi."

Mr. Howland said that when Jefferson bought this land from Napoleon in 1803, he had planned to set it aside as a sanctuary for the Indians. "What's more, he actually prepared an amendment to the U. S. Constitution prohibiting us from using this territory. And twenty or so years later, when the Congress authorized Zebulon Pike to explore it, Pike wrote a report recommending the same thing."

Mr. Howland added that the government didn't just have benevolent reasons for wanting to keep this land for the Indians. "When John Calhoun was Secretary of War thirty years ago, he gave a speech, in which he said that all this territory out here was a good place for the Indians because he the land was useless for agriculture, but with the buffalo and other abundant game, it could still provide for the Indians. He didn't consider the land worth settling.

"Some people used to call this area 'The Great American Desert.'

"But in the last few years, things have changed quickly, in large part because of the gold strike in California. In 1849 alone, 100,000 people trekked to California. During the next three years, 150,000 more went west. Many of them used the 'river system' as well as the trails that pass through here including the Santa Fe and the California. Some of the Southerners came up through here on the Cherokee Trail. Now that all those people have actually seen the territory, they know it's not a desert. And we know it, too, from settling here and growing our first crops last summer. You think there's any chance the government will now just turn this land back over to the Indians?"

Mr. Howland dropped by for a "little tea" this afternoon, February 7th, and told me that an old friend of ours was up at the store.

"Why didn't you bring him along?"

"First he had to go see Tom Cordis and Jerry Jordan about their parole papers from Lecompton, and he also wanted to lookup A. D. Searle." I wondered, "Who this could be?"

Mr. Howland and I planned a grand supper party. "I'll bring a pot of roasted prairie hens together with your friend," he volunteered. If we may, we will be here at five o'clock." I agreed and began wondering what else we could have for supper.

I had made a large pan of corn bread the day before. We could use that. Then I thought, "If I can locate Mr. Chase, he would enjoy the dinner and the company. And it would also give me an opportunity to extend a little more friendliness to him, which maybe he will reciprocate." Well, I found Jacob Chase and Mr. Searle both at the Cordises' claim and invited them all.

At five o'clock, all the guests arrived in Howland's wagon and who should come in first but our "mystery" guest, Frank Swift! It was such a pleasure to see him again. Since I knew he had been serving as an officer of the Stubbs Company, guarding Lawrence. I wanted to ask him how he got relieved of that duty, but the evening was so full, I never had the chance. Since we moved to Eldorado, Frank and I have been carrying on a correspondence—well, as much of a correspondence, as our unreliable Southern-controlled federal postal system will allow.

As Frank was taking off his coat, his eyes seemed to search the room. Without addressing anyone in particular, he asked, "Where's your father?"

"Father returned to Lawrence day before yesterday. He'd be disappointed that he missed you," Adda said, adding "I bet you two passed each other on the Santa Fe."

"Well, I'm really sorry he's not here. I have some legal papers for him."

"Dealing with what?" questioned Adda.

"Last October, while we were all in Lecompton prison, Judge Cato singled out several of us: your father; Mr. A. C. Soley from the old Lexington Company; John Lawrie; that fellow over there, (pointing to Jerry Jordan); about twenty all tolled, including me. The old rascal had sentenced us to five years in the penitentiary. The conviction was recently rescinded, nulled, by a judge in Washington who has legal authority over the territories in these matters, and I have some parole papers and legal releases we all need to sign. And here's an envelope with various printed notes, dealing mostly with the Territorial Legislature, a scheduled meeting January 8th, a set of minutes he's supposed to read and sign and finally there's an invitation to the governor's supper on February 13 at the Morrow House in Lawrence."

Frank asked Adda, "Do you know the Morrow House? I wonder why the governor isn't having the affair in Eldridge's Free State hotel or the Cincinnati House? By the way your father is now a council member representing one of these outpost districts. That notice is also in this pack."

Adda asked Frank how he knew the contents of the big envelope. He laughed and said, "Well the trip out here takes five days—and I needed something to read. Anyway I'm the official courier for this stuff, and I wanted to read the notices that Cato's penitentiary sentences have been nulled. Your father and I are both on that list. I will be here a few days and if he doesn't get back in time, I'll have to carry them back with me."

Jerry spoke up, "Well, Frank, why don't you let me have my papers. I'll read them and sign them. Since the old sentence was nulled and we've been paroled all these months, I don't see what the urgency is.

"It's not a matter of urgency," said Frank, "old Judge Cato has resigned but they can't get rid of LeCompte, the chief territorial judge, and he is hopping mad about being overruled. He's particularly irked about the paroles and so are other proslavery officials, and I wouldn't put it past him to find some legal or technical reason to harass us if these formalities aren't taken care of. I certainly want my signature on record."

While Frank was answering Adda's question, Mr. Howland went out to his wagon to fetch the main course of our supper. He plunked down his famous big black cast-iron pot that has made this cabin a joyful place on several other occasions. Its very presence seems to create the atmosphere of an impending banquet, and when the lid comes off and the room fills with the aroma of what's been cooking in that reliable old pot, there is no doubt— we are about to have a feast; thanks again to Erastus Howland, . . . the grocer. The pot was still too hot to touch, but Adda and I gingerly lifted off the lid, which exposed four or five deliciously brown prairie hens steaming in the pot and the same number of baked Irish potatoes. One hen will feed two people, so we had more than enough, thanks again to our generous neighbor.

The meal was excellent. And although it was a delight to discuss the events at Mrs. Gates' house and the Cincinnati House with Frank Swift, who told us he was planning to settle in Eldorado (he is not married), as nice as it was to see him, the highlight of the evening was listening to the astonishing and funny adventures recounted by A.D. Searle, who is a great storyteller and is a member of the Eldorado Town Company. He reminded Adda and me that he was with Shalor Eldridge in Tabor two summers ago, helping to bring in our party of 500 or so settlers.

One of the stories he told us concerned Governor Reeder's escape two years ago, at the time the proslavery roughnecks had issued a subpoena for the governor and a company of them were intent on arresting and jailing him for treason. Mr. Searle said he became involved in hiding the governor in Shalor Eldridge's hotel in Lawrence. And so, since he was soon being hunted down along with the governor, it was decided that Mr. Eldridge and his wife would continue to hide the governor until a riverboat arrived in Lawrence, whose captain would be friendly to the abolitionists' cause and would agree to take the governor on board. And if that failed (which it did), Mr. Searle said, they would disguise the governor as an itinerant Irish man and take him to the Missouri River, where he could make his escape, which is the way it worked out.

A. D. told us that story as well.

But in the meantime, he said he had also become a "wanted man." Some armed men from the Missouri militia insisted on searching all of the rooms for him. A.D. said he ducked down a hall into a the room where his sister was staying and hid in the bed, sliding in between the mattress and the bed's lumpy feather comforter. His sister quickly got into her night clothes and pretended to be gravely ill. Presently the search party knocked on her door. A.D. said his sister moaned a little and in a weak voice said she hoped her sickness was not contagious but invited the gentlemen to search, which they did, but their sense of Southern chivalry, and their desire not to catch what was ailing his sister, caused them to fail to find A.D. in among his sister's bedding.

That night he escaped, leaving Lawrence with Morton Gaylord, a deeply religious, but it would be revealed, featherbrained acquaintance. They headed east, but got lost in a large stand of timber north of the river. A day later they made their way out of the woods, coming out onto the prairie near the Quaker mission, then fell immediately into the hands of another company of armed Missouri militia, who had been drinking. Several of the captors proposed hanging them immediately. A.D. claimed he had, just the previous evening, been at McGee's, a well-known proslavery tavern. That seemed to give him some credibility among the Missouri men, who didn't know his true identity.

A.D. said he was worried because he was carrying some very incriminating papers that he didn't have time to dispose of because they had been captured by such surprise. In his coat he was also carrying a bottle of whiskey that he had "spirited" away from the Free State Hotel in Lawrence. A.D. offered the whiskey to the captors, pretending to be sociable. The Southerners drank his whiskey, but didn't rule out their option to hang them. But as night fell, the whiskey acted as A.D. had intended: a postponing distraction—the captors agreed that the hanging could wait 'til morning.

Before dawn, the leader of the Missourians awakened Mr. Searle and his traveling companion and said, "I believe you are gentlemen. I don't think you are 'stinking abolitionists.' But my men might feel cranky when they wake up and they are apt to be in a sour and hanging mood," and so he released A.D. and his companion.

After they were well on their way, A.D. said Mr. Gaylord prayed and thanked the Almighty that he had delivered them from evil. Between prayers, Mr. Gaylord began to nag and admonish A.D. about his unchristian behavior, his excessive use of profanity, and all the lies he had told the evening before, made believable by the whiskey. This pious harangue went on and on. Finally, A.D. said he interrupted his sanctimonious friend and told him, "Yes, I lied repeatedly. I swore repeatedly and I drank whiskey and I encouraged others to do likewise." A.D. paused dramatically, then resumed his story, "And I said to Mr. Gaylord 'all that saved our bacon. We're out here in the woods, aren't we? Aren't we free of those roughnecks? Those Missouri pukes surely wanted to hang the both of us. So doesn't that square things? What's the matter with you, Gaylord? Wouldn't you rather be a live sinner, with time to seek forgiveness, than be a dead man, who was unwilling to use the wits God gave him and put them to self-preservation?' Mr. Gaylord said he wasn't sure. "Well," A. D. said, "You can be sure I've spent very little time with Mr. Gaylord since then."

February 8, a day after our big supper party and I want to jot down some notes about Frank Swift, since he has been involved in so many episodes that have touched our family.

Adda and I asked him to explain what had happened to the wagon train that had bypassed Plymouth two Octobers ago in order to avoid the government soldiers. I "primed the pump" by telling them how rudely Colonel Cooke's soldiers searched the wagons that came into Plymouth in the rain, throwing some of the settler's clothing in the mud. Frank Swift replied, "Well, Augusta, the other wagon train fared better, at least at first. Then two days later, as it approached the road between Lecompton and Topeka, the wagon train was intercepted by a small company of U. S. Troops. The soldiers searched the wagons and all the arms and sabers, were discovered and confiscated, and they forced the wagon train to disperse."

Frank went on to say that the arms were taken to Lecompton. "Shalor Eldridge had gone to a great deal of trouble to get the weapons, particularly the rifles. So he passed the word that we should organize a large party to recover them. That was a few days before Christmas of last year. Captain Cracklin and I were involved, and so were several other officers. We rounded up a party of about sixty men. We sent a delegation ahead of us to meet with new Governor Denver in Lecompton. The delegation went there to request that the arms be returned to our party, and the rest of us arrived in Lecompton on the morning of December 23rd to lend moral support.

"The word had gotten to Shalor Eldridge that we had organized the party and had headed for Lecompton. By December 23rd he was there already. Being older than most of us, and very experienced in business and politics, and a first rate negotiator, he did all the talking. And it didn't hurt that the Governor also knew that he had access to the White House. As the two of them negotiated, we milled around outside, appearing to be a large, friendly force, but not so friendly that we didn't make a show of displaying the weapons we had brought with us. The negotiation seemed to go on and on, but finally Mr. Eldridge came out and said that our guns, ammunition, and sabers would to be released to us, though the Governor had some apprehension about releasing the guns to us, since he had been appointed by an administration, which was mostly proslavery. His assistants showed their displeasure with the Governor's decision by carelessly tossing our rifles on a pile. Colonel Eldridge stepped forward and warned them not to damage our property."

Adda asked if he remembered how many guns they got back.

"About 250 and that's just the rifles. Shalor Eldridge had also purchased some of the new revolving-type pistols and we got those back, too. We distributed all the rifles and pistols to several of the companies that are guarding Lawrence."

Well, it was interesting to hear the complete story of what happened to the other wagon train.

INDEX

A

Abolitionists, xvi, 13, 15, 24, 27, 51
Boston abolitionists, 24
Adams, Sarah (Boston), 269
Akron, OH, 95
Alabama, xiv
Allen, Norman, 241
Antislavery convictions, 213
Archer, NE, 71, 74, 175
Arizona, 241, 298
Argyle, Archibald H., 50, 61, 63
　Officer: Ross Township
　　Arkansas, xiv
Statehood in 1836, xiv, 272
Arkansas-California Trail, 242, 245
American Revolution, xiv, 4, 108
　Minute Men:
　　Lt. John Stewart, 3
　　Private Charles Stewart, 3
Antislavery speakers, 12
Archives of the Vatican, 32
Atchison, Senator, 99, 119

August 8, 1886 (arrival Nebraska by Stewarts, 74
August 9, 1886 (arrival Plymouth, K.T. by Stewarts), 75
Austria, xiv

B

Bankruptcy, 38
Barrel of gunpowder, xi, 148
"bleeding" in Kansas, viii
Beecher, Reverend, 82
　"Beecher's Bibles", 58
　boxes labeled "Books", 254
　Kansas Bible, 58
Begole, Gov. Josiah W., 3
Beicher, 51, (ferry operator)
Bemis Family, 245
Benton Family, 286
Bickerton, Thomas, 121
Big Nemaha (River), 74
Blizzard, 280
　Nov. 6th, 1857 on way to Eldorado, 280
Blockade Missouri River, 65, 99

309

Bowie knives, 95
Bowles, William, 189
Boyce, Mr. (Plymouth
  Company), 109, 110, 152
"Breaking Plows", 243.
Brown, John, 53, 58, 76-78, 95,
  96, 99
"Old Osawatomie Brown", 78,
  142
John Brown's sons, 93, 97, 112
  George & John, Jr., 194
  John Brown, Jr., 93
  John Brown's retaliation, 96
    "Massacre" at
      Pottawattamie, 97
Brownsville, K.T., 97
Brownsville Road, 76
Buchanan, Mr., 286
Buffalo, K.T., 242
Buford, Colonel Jefferson, 93
Butler County, 242

C

California, xv
California (State: admitted in
  1850), 272
"California or Bust" (migration),
  272
California Gold Rush, 32, 94,
  270

California newspapers, 272
Camp Sackett, 134
Cantaloupes (Iowa), 43
  "Heart-of-Gold"
Cary, (Mr. and Mrs.), 296
Cato, Judge, 92, 130, 302
Central Committee, 13
  (Free State Advocates)
Chase, Jacob Eastman, x, 85,
  117, 118, 125, 126, 130, 180,
  247, 286
Cherokee Trail, 301
Chestnut, Mary Boykin, 26
Chelsea, K.T., 296
  Itinerant preacher, 296
Chicago, IL 15, 16, 18, 19
  "chik kaga"
Chicago-Rock Island Rail Road,
  17, 28
Chippewa Indians, 2
Christian Mission for Indians,
  209
Cincinnati House, 233, 237
Civil Bend, 36, 63
Civil War, xiii, xvi
Colonel Cooke, 134, 136, 137,
  195
Colonel Harvey (abolitionist),
  103, 109, 110, 120, 121
  Mounted Rifles, 122
Colonel Sumner, 93, 94
Colt Repeater, 195

Connelly, Jason, 244
Corcoran, Riggs and Paine, (Mortgage Bankers), 60
Cordis, Thomas, 240, 289
Council Bluffs, IA 37, 65, 70
Cracklin, Captain, 203, 218, 238, 285
Crawford, Alonzo, 74, 89, 130, 189, 212
Crimble, William, 241

D

Dame, John, 241
Davenport, Iowa, 20, 22
Davis, Jefferson, xvi, 94
Dearborn House, Chicago, IL, 17
   Spitting & cigars, 18
     Chewing tobacco
Dietzler, George W, 131, 193, 203, 205, 212, 254
Deserta or Deseretta or Zion, 39-40
Detroit, 10
Detroit River, 5
Dodge, Mrs. Sally (nurse in Archer), 187
Donaldson, the U. S. Marshall, 24, 93
Dred Scott Decision, xv
Dunning, Mr. (from Lexington), 87

E

Eastern Newspapers, 184
Boston Traveler, 184
Tribune, 184
Eastport, K.T., 36
Eastport Ferry, 62, 65
Eldorado, K. T., viii, 64, 279m
   El hombre dorado (the gilded man), 284
   Christmas Day (occupy new house), 292
Eldridge, Colonel Shalor, 13, 47, 80, 103, 153, 157
Eldridge Hotel, Lawrence, K.T., 237
Elliot, Mr.____, newspaper, 241
Herald of Freedom
Emancipation, xv
Emerson, 97
"Emma Harmon" ship, 254
Captain J. M. Wing, 254
   England, xiv
   British Fleet, xiv
   British Army, 108
English, xiii, 3
   King, George III, xiii, xvi, 107, 108
   Massachusetts, 107
     Red Coats, 108
   Subjects, xiii

F

Federal Government, xv
Ferry, 20, 22
  Steam-powered, 22, 63
  Fifleld, Donnali, xvii
  Forbes Publications, xvii
Filles du Roi (Daughters of the King), 220
  Old Quebec, 222
  Finley, Mr., 236
Fireflies, 27
Florida, xiv
Fort Plymouth, 134
Fort Riley, 68, 154
Fort Leavenworth, 60, 68, 73
Fort Titus, 118
France xiii
Frances and Loutrel, xi
Franklin County, 96
  Franklin 118
Free Kansas Committee, 64
Free State, 48
Free State Advocates, 13, 42
  Central Committee
Free State Constitution, 92, 272
Free State Rendezvous, 59
Free State Legislature (Topeka), 93
Free Staters, 99
Freedom For All, xvi
Fremont, Mr. (Republican), 116
French Revolution, xiii, 3
Friends of Freedom, 48
Frontier, (a definition of) 38
Fugitive slave law, 161

G

Galileo, 44
Gaston (later Percival) 65
Gates, Alphesus, 130, 212, 231
  9th of March (released from P.O.W. camp), 231
    House, 215
    Mrs. Gates, 215
    "Boarding contract" - Stubbs Company, 217
Gates, Hannah, 2
Gates, Fanny (Small Pox), 248, 251
  Variola & varrroloid, 248
    Epidemics, Small Pox, in Europe, 251
George Washington, 108
Georgia, xiv
Genesee, Genesee County, Michigan, 3, 4
  Upton Cemetery, 5
Gibraltar on Lake Erie, 5
Goss, Sarah, 258
Governor Geary, 119, 120, 132, 211
Governor Woodson, 108, 195
Great Economic Depression, xv
Great Flood, 45

Grimes, Governor Iowa, 79

H

Halbert, John, (Indian fighter), 108
Hampton, Levi (guard at P.O.W. camp) 214
Hapsburgs, xiv
Harris, E. P., 237
Health books, 249
    Gunn's Book of Medicine... or *New Guide to Health*
Henderson, Lt, U. S. Army (quartermaster), 144
Herald of Freedom, 93
Hiawatha, K.T., 77
Hickory Point, 109, 111, 117, 119. 120
Hildebrand, Mr., 243
Hinton, Richard (English reporter), 62, 63, 78, 79
Richard Hinton's article, 211
    Holton, K. T., 77 208
Howland, Erastus, 283
Huguenots (French Protestants), 220
Hunter County, 242

I

Indian Bureau, 209
Indian Trust Land, 91
    Sacs and Fox tribe, 91
Indianola, Iowa, 36
Indians in Iowa, 33, 67, 287
Pottawattamie in Iowa, 33
    Sioux (Western Iowa), 67
Comanches, K. T., 67
Sacs and Foxes tribes K. T. 75
Osage, 289
Paul, the Osage, 290
"In God We Trust", 193
Iowa City, 15, 22, 27-29, 31, 34, 35, 38
Iowa Point, K. T. 90, 103, 109
Iowa State, 272
Iowa State Central Committee, 35, 36
    Free Kansas, 35
    Overland Route, 35
Irish Immigrants, xii
Iron balls (fixed to leg-shackles), 131

J

Jay Hawkers, 111
Jackson, K. T., 209
Jefferson, Thomas, xiii, 1, 13
Jenkins, Galus (Free State leader), 193
Jones, Sheriff (proslavery) from Missouri, 80, 118, 131, 172, 213, 275
Jordan, Jeremiah, 131, 212, 240, 243
Journal of Lewis and Clark, 1
Journal writing, 105

K

Kansas Central Committee, 38, 47, 48
Kansas City, MO, 25
Kansas-Nebraska Act of 1854, viii, 12, 13
Kansas Regulars, 99
Kansas River, 24, 210
Steamer docks, 254
   Kansas Territory, xvi, 37, 38, 47, 65, 70
Kaw River, 109
Knoxville, IA 35, 36, 41, 42, 209
Kerr, Mr., (Plymouth), 188

L

Lake Erie, 8
Lake Huron, 8
Lake St. Clair, 8
Land-purchase laws, K. T., 19
   Township, 19
   Homestead claim, 19
   Residential lots, 19
   Eighty million acres, 23
   Five million acres (set aside for Indians), 59, 60
   Section, 206
   Town lots, 206
   Land Costs, 20
   File claims, 20
   Quarter of a section, 20
Land sales, 185
Lane, General Jim, 13, 35, 36, 42, 47, 48, 63-66, 76, 81, 87, 88, 90, 92, 113
   Ex congressman from Indiana, 13
   Gen. Lane's Company, 71
   Lane's Army of the North, 80
      Some still in prison. 212
   Indiana, 13
   Lane's Trail, 36, 199
"Lane's Chimneys", 75
   Laudando praecipere or laudando perdocere, 7
Lawrence, Amos, 235

Lawrence, Kansas, 13, 48, 60, 92, 94, 96
Lawrence, Miss Sara T. D., 271, See Illustration
LeCompte, Judge, the Chief Justice of the Territory, 25, 93, 208, 303
Lecompton, 208
Lecompton Prison, 127
   P.O.W. Camp, 130, 210
      "Vermin", 214
      Lecompton (proslavery choice for territorial capital), 92
Lecompton Constitution, xvi
Leavenworth, 99
Leaving Michigan, 1
Lexington (near Plymouth, K. T.), 77
Company, 107, 125
   Lincoln, Abraham xv, xvi
   Candidate 1859 xv, xvi
   Congressman, 48
   President 1860
Littlefield, (Plymouth citizen, K.T.) 152
Logs, float of, 8
London, xiv
   Downtown, xiv
Louisiana, 272
Louisiana Purchase, xiv, 1, 13
"Great American Desert", 301

Lowe, Captain H. A., 121
Lund, James L., x, xvii

M

Mack, John (Cincinnati House owner), 217, 233
McGee's (tavern), 305
Maine, (as a colony, Revolutionary War), 108
Major F. J. Porter, (finds kegs of powder at Plymouth, K.T.), 150
Manypenny, Territorial Commissioner of Indian Affairs, 60, 274
Marriage Proposal (Augusta's first), 152
Captain Henry, (U. S. Army), 153, 159, 167-169
Brass uniform button, 159
   Martin, Henry (Mr. and Mrs. From England), 245
Massachusetts, 52
Massachusetts Immigrant Aid Society, 60, 61, 64, 69
"Memories of Addie Stewart Graton", 142
Mexican Land Grant, 270
Mexico, xiv
Mexican War, 12, 30, 59, 66, 67, 92

Migration by river, 37
Miller, George, 177
Miller's hotel, 177, 180
    Mills
    Gristmills, 2, 3, 20
    Sawmills, 20, 293
    Steam and water-powered, 2, 3
    Boiler, 294
    Cement from Chicago, 295
    Sorghum, (first in Eldorado area 20
    Flourmill, 294
Mississippi, xiv
Statehood in 1817
Missouri Militiamen, 52, 74
"Missouri Pukes", 219
    "Kentucky Pukes", 219
Missouri River, 17, 27, 36, 38, 48, 52, 57, 65, 69, 90
    Ferry to Iowa, 17
    River Crossing 69
Missouri Roughnecks, 62, 63, 70
    "border ruffians", 75, 86, 97
    "Kickapoo Rangers" 86
    "Bushwhackers", 219
Missouri (State), 272
Monroe, James, xiv
Montague, D.H. (new Commissary officer - Veteran of Mexican War), 214

Moore, Reverend (rescued by John Brown), 82, 98
Mormons, 34, 35
Mule salesmen, 39
Murder in the First Degree, 130
89 P.O.W.s charged by Judge Cato (from Hickory Point Battle)
Muzzleloaders, 59, 106

N

Napoleon, xiii, ix, 1, 39, 40
Nebraska City (in Nebraska Territory), 65
Nebraska Territory, 72
Nelson, Admiral, xiv
Negro, 165
New England Immigrant Aid Society, 13, 60, 81, 82
New Georgia, 118
New Orleans, xiv
Newhall, Charles Granville, 125
Nichols, Sam (ferry operator) 62, 63
Nishnabotney Ferry, 49
North Carolina, xv

O

October 10, 1856, 136

"Old Sacramento", (cannon), 121, 148
Olds, George, 152
Omaha, 37
Onondaga County, NY, 2
Open insurrection and rebellion, 109
Oregon Trail, 82
Osawatomie, 118
Osceola, IA, 35, 36, 43
Otterson, J.P.S., 240, 241
Outfitters, Iowa City, IA, 28
   Wife, 30
Ox teams, 28, 39

P

Parker, Artemus, 208
Partridge, William, 241
Pate, H. Clay (proslavery captain), 97
Paten, Captain (Walnut Creek), 90
Penmanship, xi
Peters, Mr. (a southerner) 177
Phrenology, 234
Pierce, Alfred, 114, 115
Plumb, Preston B., (founder of Emporia, K.T.), 36, 114-116
   Leader of supply train, 114-116
Plumb's Route, 36

Plymouth, K. T., 64, 71. 74, 76, 81, 86, 99, 109
Plymouth Company, 99, 107
Pomeroy, General, 35, 157, 277
Pony Creek, 77, 87, 162
Popular Sovereignty, xv, xvi, 25, 92, 277
Port Huron, Michigan, 8
Pottawattamie Rifles, 95
Pottawattamie, K.T., 77
Powers, Ramon, ix, xvii
Prairie Hens, 301
Prairie Ruts, 32
   Wheel spacing, 32, 33
   Roman specifications, 33
   Wheel distances, 33
Prentis, S. B., 241
President Pierce, 13, 25, 92, 188, 212
   Pardons Sam, 212
   President Polk, xii, 13, 94
   War with Mexico, xii
Preston, William J. (U.S. Marshall), 148, 195
Pro Slavery, (K. T. shifts from) xvi
Proslavery marauders, 34
Pyle, Amy, 113

Q

Quaker Mission, 210

Quakers, 164
Quincy, IA, 38, 48
On abolitionist route map, 35
    As the frontier, 48

R

Rackcliffe, Mr. & Mrs. Sumner (early settlers), 241
Redpath, James, 113
Redpath Boys, 114
Reeder, Governor Andrew H., 35, 42, 47, 83. 267.
Reeder, James (nominated U. S. senator), 92
Republican Party, xv
Rhode Island Street, Lawrence, K.T., viii
Richards, Mr., 133
River steamer, 52
Robinson, Mrs. Alfred, 235
Robinson, Frank O., 117, 118, 126, 130, 180, 183, 265, 286
Robinson, Governor Charles, 92, 95, 96, 112, 193, 233
    Wife Sara, 96, 233 See illustration
Roberts, Governor
Robertson, Captain John, 121, 125
Rock Island, IL, 21
Rourke, Aggie, 216. 233

Russell, William, 60
Russia, xiv

S

Saginaw Bay, 8
Samuels, Miss Catherine (teacher Archer, Nebraska territory), 187
Santa Fe Trail, 96, 215
Searle, A. D., 64. 237, 301, 304
Senator Douglas (Illinois), xvi, xvi
    (resists Topeka constitution) 192
Sharps rifles, xi, 58, 67, 68, 73, 88, 106, 195
Christian Sharps, 58
    Cartridges, 59
    Connecticut 106
Shea brother, 176
Sherrod, William, 213
Sidney, Iowa, 35, 36, 65
Sigourney, Iowa, 35
Slaveholders, 24, 43
Slaves, 27
Slave State, 25
Small cannon (not discovered on Oct. 10th, 1856 search), xi
Small Pox, Lawrence, K. T., 247
Fanny Gates is sick, 248.

    Quarantine the Cincinnati House? 250
    Augusta appointed Nurse to three cases, 250
    Epidemics in Europe (60% of those exposed to small pox get it), 251
    Augusta studies symptoms, 252
    Augusta's patients recover, 253
    Augusta becomes sick, 255
Smith, General Persifer, Chief of the U.S. Army of the West, 37, 73, 94, 172
Snow, John, 241
Soley, Mr. A. C. (Worcester, MA), 73
Southern Congressmen, xv
Southern Declaration of Independence, xiii
Southern Democrats, 13
Southern Nebraska Territory, 38
Southern Pukes, 110
Squatters Rights, 173
Stewart
Addison Stewart, 5
  Adelaide (Adda) Henrietta Stewart, 84
  Charles (grandfather), 4,107
  Charles Samuel Stewart, viii, 117, 130
  Representative District 17, viii, 54. 238, 273
    Commissary Officer of the P.O.W. camp, 142
    Territorial Legislature, 273, 298
    Colrain, Massachusetts family origins, 2
  Laura Augusta Stewart 83
  Hepatitis, 257
  Dr. Lamb, 258
  Golden Seal, 258
  "feverfew", 258
  Cascara, 259
  ginseng root (extract - as medicine), 260
  Private and public schools, 2, 6
Cornelia Stewart 2
Ransom Stewart, 5
Clara Ella Stewart, 11
Stowe, Harriet Beecher, 82
"Uncle Tom's Cabin", 82
Stowell, Martin, (conductor: Massachusetts), 64, 76, 78
Strongs, 48, 49, 55, 58. 65, 90, 171, 178
Dutch Oven, 49
  Fruit Cobbler, 49
Stubbs Rifles, 219
Oread Company

"Jayhawkers" or "Jim Lane's Jayhawkers", 219
Studebaker, 15, 28, 175
Metal hoops, 15, 29
  Prairie Schooners, 15, 31
  Canvas products (tents, etc.) 28
  Wagon becomes a sled, 29
Stowe, Harriet Beecher, 26
Sullivan, Mr., 136
Surveying, 12, 25
Sutter's mill, Calif., 270
Swift, Francis, 130, 189, 218

T

Tabor, Iowa, 15, 36, 38, 49, 57
Taffy (candy) Dance, 186
Talleyrand and the Louisiana Purchase, xiv
Tappan, Samuel, 114
Taylor, Jane 5. 3
Texas, xiv, 12
  Statehood in 1844, 272
  Slave State, 12
Thoreau, 97
Topeka, KS (Capital of Territory), 35, 92
Topeka Constitution, 192, 193
  Town Company, 103, 108
Towne, Mr., (new corner to Plymouth) 132
Truxton, NY, 4

Two-wheel handcart (Mormons), 39

U

Underground Railroad, 98, 272
Upham, David, 240
Upton Cemetery, (Flint, Michigan), 5
U. S. Army patrols, 66, 74, 111, 117, 300
  Brownsville Road, 76
  Muzzleloaders, 106
  Cannons, 154
U. S. Army Regulars, 124
  Second Dragoons, 137, 147
VanCurens, 48, 49, 55, 58, 90, 95, 202

W

Wagon train, 38
  Oxen, 41
    "Tempus" and "Fugit", 279
  Blacksmith, 41
  July grass, 43
Wakefield, John A. (ex-territorial judge, was in party to found Eldorado), 240
Walnut Creek, 77
Walnut River, K.T., viii, 240
Walnut Valley Times, xii
Watts. R. A., 241

Wesson, James
   9th Regiment, 108
West Pointer, 32, 140
Col. Cooke, U.S. Army
Westerfield, 74
Westport Landing, K.T., 24
Whig Party, 108, 116
Whitman, E. B., 64, 241
Whitney, Eli, 166
Whitney, T. L., 241
Whitney House, Lawrence, K.T., 237
Widener, Miss Rebecca F.
  Miss R.E.W., Augusta's and
    Adda's teacher), 6, 9
  Latin & Roman Life 7
  Mrs. Chase's Boarding School, 10
  Capital School (private), 10
  Marries Sam Stewart on
    March 3, 1854
Wild Turkey, 72
Willmarth (local bookseller in
   Lawrence, K.T.), 234, 275
Winterset, IA, 35
Wisconsin Germans, 42
Wood, Capt. T. J., 37, 124, 140
Worcester ("Wooster")(Western
   Massachusetts), 72
World War II, xv

Z

Zimmerman, E. R., (early settler, Eldorado, K.T.), 241

Printed in the United States
125123LV00004BA/18/P